Imaginative Geographies of Algerian Violence

Stanford Studies in Middle Eastern and Islamic Societies and Cultures

Imaginative Geographies
of Algerian Violence

CONFLICT SCIENCE, CONFLICT MANAGEMENT, ANTIPOLITICS

Jacob Mundy

Stanford University Press
Stanford, California

Stanford University Press
Stanford, California

Printed in the United States of America on acid-free, archival-quality paper

Library of Congress Cataloging-in-Publication Data

Mundy, Jacob, author.
 Imaginative geographies of Algerian violence : conflict science, conflict management, antipolitics / Jacob Mundy.
     pages cm--(Stanford studies in Middle Eastern and Islamic societies and cultures)
 Includes bibliographical references and index.
 ISBN 978-0-8047-8849-6 (cloth : alk. paper)--ISBN 978-0-8047-9582-1 (pbk. : alk. paper)
 1. Algeria--History--Civil War, 1992-2006. 2. Algeria--Politics and government--1990-
3. Conflict management--Algeria. 4. Conflict management. 5. Policy sciences. 6. World
politics--1989- I. Title. II. Series: Stanford studies in Middle Eastern and Islamic societies and
cultures.
 DB86.M86 2015
 965.05'4--dc23
                           2015019435

ISBN 978-0-8047-9583-8 (electronic)

Typeset by Bruce Lundquist in 10/14 Minion

To Alethea

CONTENTS

ABBREVIATIONS

AIS	Armée Islamique du Salut (Islamic Salvation Army)
CNCPPDH	La Commission Nationale Consultative de Promotion et de Protection des Droits de l'Homme (National Consultative Commission for the Promotion and Protection of Human Rights)
DRS	Département du Renseignement et de la Sécurité (Department of Intelligence and Security, formerly the SM)
FFS	Front des Forces Socialistes (Socialist Forces Front)
FIS	Front Islamique du Salut (Islamic Salvation Front)
FLN	Front de Libération Nationale (National Liberation Front)
GIA	Groupe Islamique Armé (Armed Islamic Group)
GSPC	Groupe Salafiste pour la Prédication et le Combat (Salafist or Salafi Group for Preaching and Combat)
HCE	Haut Comité d'État (High State Council)
HCS	Haut Conseil de Sécurité (High Security Council)
MIA/MAIA	Mouvement (Algérien) Islamique Armé ([Algerian] Armed Islamic Movement)
ONDH	Observatoire National des Droits de l'Homme (National Human Rights Observatory)
R2P	Responsibility to Protect
RCD	Rassemblement pour la Culture et la Démocratie (Rally for Culture and Democracy)
SM	Sécurité Militaire (Military Security, now DRS)
TRC	Truth and Reconciliation Commission, South Africa

Imaginative Geographies of Algerian Violence

An official civilian militia member examines the scene of an April 1997 massacre in the Blida province in which thirty-one people were "slain" (*égorgé*) by unidentified assailants. Photo by Souhil Baghdadi. Courtesy of the *El Watan* archive, Algiers.

PROLOGUE
The Horror

ON AUGUST 29, 1997, various international news agencies began issuing reports of a massacre less than thirty kilometers from central Algiers. The massacre at Raïs (or Sidi Raïs), a small farming village in the Sidi Moussa district of Algiers, was not the first massacre of the war but, with a reported death toll of more than one hundred, it seemed to be the largest yet. An early dispatch indicated that two to three hundred people had been shot, butchered, dismembered, disemboweled, or burned to death.[1] Survivors, emergency workers, and hospital personnel floated even higher figures.[2] The Algerian government quickly provided an official death toll of ninety-eight, plus more than a hundred wounded. Attempting to account for such discrepancies, an Algerian paper wrote that, in the case of severely burned corpses, several bodies were being allotted to one coffin.[3] An early outside witness to the scene, a photographer from Agence France-Presse, described seeing dozens of bodies covered with blankets.[4] A schoolteacher who survived the massacre claimed it had started at around ten in the evening on August 28 and lasted four to five hours. Others said the killing had started early in the morning and lasted from one to six. The number of attackers, according to various reports, ranged from dozens to three hundred. The Associated Press quoted a survivor, "Amar," who said, "They took their time to cut throats and to burn the bodies."[5] A resident who survived by barricading himself in his house had to listen to his neighbors die by fire. "Burn them like rats," he claimed an attacker said. The killers then lobbed Molotov cocktails into homes.[6] Another survivor reported seeing one of the attackers slit his neighbors' throats, thirteen in all. One report described a house that appeared to have been in the middle of a wedding party when the door was blown

1

off and the attendees were all slaughtered.[7] Another said that a family had been celebrating a circumcision when they were attacked.[8] After some of the villagers were decapitated, their heads were placed in front of the doors of their homes, according to witnesses.[9] One survivor described the following scene:

> My baby son Mohamed was five and they cut his throat and threw him out of the upper window[...]. Then they cut the throat of my eldest son Rabeh and then my brother's throat because he saw they were kidnapping his wife and tried to stop them. They took some of the other girls. [...] They cut my throat and I felt the knife in my neck but I tried to shield myself and the man sliced me on the arm. My wife was so brave. She tried to help, to fight them, to save me. So they dragged her to the door where I was lying and slit her throat in front of me.[10]

A representative of the Algerian Medical Union later told a reporter, "Even the fetuses have been taken from their disemboweled mothers to be mutilated and massacred."[11] One witness claimed that a child of two had been baked in an oven.[12] Another survivor recalled several weeks later, "I could hear a young woman begging to be shot in the courtyard below my house. [...] She began screaming but the noise suddenly stopped. Yet, there was no sound of a shot."[13] The perpetrators, according to other testimonies, had also abducted some of Raïs's young women, taking with them as many as one hundred. Two days before the Raïs massacre, sixty-four people had met a similar fate in the mountain town of Beni Ali. The night after the events in Raïs, a massacre of three- to four-dozen occurred in Djelfa province, three hundred kilometers south of Algiers. An editorial that appeared in the *New York Times* five days after the massacre declared the previous week "the most violent in Algeria's nearly six-year civil war."[14] More was to come.

Roughly a week after Raïs, there were two consecutive nights of massacres in Béni Messous, a district of Algiers.[15] Early wire reports on September 6 indicated that between sixty and ninety people had perished the previous evening. Two leading opposition parties in Algeria—one secular, one Islamist—asserted that more than one hundred had died in the "shantytown" massacre of Sidi Youcef. The killers, reportedly numbering fifty and "howling like jackals," used axes, other sharp objects, and guns during the killings. Reports from hospitals indicated that many victims had been mutilated, primarily by throat cutting. One survivor recounted seeing a nursing mother's breast cut off after her child was decapitated in front of her.[16] Another, who had escaped into a nearby forest, told a reporter, "They kicked the door in, took the men, forced them outside, slit their throats. [. . .] They came back, took out my aunt and slit her throat, after slashing open her stomach."[17] Though the attackers apparently fled when security sources arrived after several hours of killing, the very next night, September 6–7, a massacre in the same area claimed forty-five lives.[18] After the two massacres of Béni Messous, Algeria experienced what one international press agency called two weeks of "relative calm."[19] The death count in each of the three massacres recorded during those fifteen days was less than two dozen.

This relative calm broke in late September with reports of new massacres in the Mitidja, the agricultural plain just outside Algiers. A mass slaughter in Beni Slimane (Médéa province) on September 20, in which nearly fifty people were killed, was followed three days later by an unprecedented killing spree mere miles away. The site of the latter was the Bentalha quarter of Algiers' Baraki commune, specifically the neighborhoods of Boudoumi and Haï Djilali (or Djillali). According to early reports on September 23, twelve dozen graves had already been filled in the nearby Sidi Rezine cemetery, and more coffins were still arriving.[20] The Algerian government backed a figure of eighty-five dead. Survivors, medical personnel, and relief workers insisted that at least two hundred had died.[21] During the killing, which lasted for several hours, victims' throats were slit, they were burned alive, or they were shot. Several children were reportedly thrown to their death from rooftops, and pregnant women were disemboweled; perpetrators allegedly made bets on the gender of unborn fetuses before cutting them out of their mothers.[22] Homes were bombed with Molotov cocktails while others were ransacked or looted. Describing the massacre to foreign journalists, a survivor pointed to the spot in his kitchen where his wife had been shot, his daughter hacked to death with an axe, and his son stabbed to death with knives. In all, forty-one people—including neighbors to whom he had promised shelter—died in his house.[23] Another resident recalled, "I stood here at the window and I could hear those poor people screaming and crying. When I looked out of my window, I could see them axing the women on the roof."[24] The attackers allegedly burned alive a mentally impaired man.[25] Said one survivor, "It's an unimaginable butchery."[26] A second "relative calm" followed.[27]

On Christmas Eve 1997, the Algerian government announced that more massacres had taken place. This time most of the killing was far west of the capital, in several villages on the border between the Tiaret and Tissemsilt provinces. Among the twenty-seven victims in Zouabria, one report claimed, was a decapitated twelve-day-old baby, found still clutching his slain mother. By the end of the ten days preceding Ramadan, more than three hundred deaths had been reported, including the Tiaret-Tissemsilt massacres. Then, on the first day of Ramadan, reports of several massacres in the western Ouarsenis mountains began to circulate. Algerian state radio claimed that villages in the province of Relizane had been targeted on the night of December 30–31, resulting in seventy-eight dead.[28] Subsequent reports in the independent Algerian press offered figures three to five times higher. The Algerian daily *Liberté* interviewed survivors who reported witnessing bodies being dismembered and decapitated, as well as infants smashed against walls. For the most part, the killers had used rudimentary weapons: knives, hoes, shovels, hatchets. The village of Kherarba (or Khourba) was purportedly decimated; one report indicated that, of the 200 families living there, 176 had been killed; another suggested that, out of 260 residents, only two had survived. One survivor claimed that he had helped remove eighty bodies from two houses. "I leave you to imagine the extent of the catastrophe in four hamlets," he said.[29] Another resident of the area recounted the death of his wife and three children, whose throats had been slashed. A young woman described surviving an axe blow to the stomach; several other women were seen being abducted by the attackers.[30] The killing had started shortly after sunset and ended the following dawn. Two police officers interviewed by an Algerian daily, *L'Authentique,* claimed that they had collected nearly two hundred bodies from two different villages.[31]

A week into Ramadan, a new wave of massacres was reported. One of the first accounts claimed that more than one hundred people had been murdered in the village of Meknessa and that a village near Had Chekala had been "razed" during the weekend of January 3–4, 1998.[32] Subsequent reports offered figures ranging between 150 and 500 killed. "The village is completely destroyed, burned to the ground and all its residents shot dead, slaughtered or burnt alive," recalled one witness from a neighboring area. He added, "Bodies of men, women and children still litter the area."[33] A witness from Meknessa said, "The bodies were mutilated, and many disfigured by axes."[34] Others spoke of seeing people burned alive, pregnant women eviscerated, and a baby killed with a hatchet. A donkey's head was allegedly placed on the body of a decapitated villager.[35] Official state radio reported three additional massacres in the same area, adding sixty-two deaths.[36]

Attention quickly returned to the outskirts of Algiers with the slaughter at Sidi Hamed on January 11–12. Sidi Hamed was not the last massacre of the war but it was the last to carry a reported death toll of more than one hundred.

Initial news reports claimed that "dozens of families" had perished, including children, women, and the elderly.[37] The killing began in the evening after the residents had broken their fast. The Algerian government circulated an official death toll of 103 (along with seventy wounded).[38] Other domestic press outlets put forward figures ranging from 256 (*La Tribune*) to 400 (*Liberté* and *El Watan*).[39] Visiting the site of the killing, a foreign correspondent wrote, "In one corner of the village, a crowd suddenly parted as four men emerged from one torched home, carrying the grisly blackened remains of yet another victim." He added, "Nearby, one pale villager scraped a gory mixture of flesh and bone off the side of a hut." A survivor told the reporter, "Look, on the other side of the road, you can see where they shot people and cut their throats." Another said, "My cousin also managed to keep them back, but only until his ammunition ran out. Then they killed him and cut off his hands."[40] Two Algerian papers published a photo showing the body of a child, apparently burned alive, with its skin charred away to a bare skull.[41] During the first fortnight of Ramadan, the death toll in Algeria had reached more than one thousand.

A new kind of war? In an undated photo (courtesy of the *El Watan* archive, Algiers), a local militia poses for the camera with weapons and family. By the end of the 1990s, official and informal militias (state sponsored and self-forming) were possibly the largest armed fighting force in Algeria at half a million strong; such estimates suggest that their numbers exceeded the combined strength of Algeria's military and security forces. Even lower estimates of 150,000–200,000 civilian militia members suggest that these groups were at least five times larger than the highest estimate of the Islamist insurgency's strength of 25,000.

INTRODUCTION

Conflict Science, Conflict Management, Antipolitics

A NEW KIND OF WAR emerged in the 1990s. It emerged not in the battlefields of the new world order but in the scientific practices and interventionary strategies of those who were seeking to understand and so manage conflict at the turn of the millennium. Little did these researchers and practitioners realize that they had played a role in making war anew.

At the end of the Cold War, there was much speculation about the newness of war and its new sources, and there were just as many policy debates about how to prevent or interrupt these new wars. Some saw the emergence of conflicts out of fundamental notions of human identity that had been suppressed during the Cold War. Others saw wayward rebellions that had become little more than criminal enterprises wrapped in political rhetoric. Still others saw transnational networks instrumentalizing communal grievances for larger ambitions. The primary tools of war had become terror, mass atrocities, ethnic cleansing, and genocide. The terrain of struggle was bodies, not boundaries; resources, not ideology. There were also those who insisted that war had not evolved at all and that what needed to change was our *understanding* of wars past, present, and future. These various and often competing visions of war all shared one conviction: even if war had not fundamentally changed in the 1990s, the effort to systematically explain and effectively engage mass violence was now free of the political and ideational constraints that had inhibited conflict management and science during the Cold War. Apolitical frameworks of management could now be based on apolitical frameworks of understanding.

These new scientific and managerial frameworks of late warfare often bore an ambivalent relationship to the mass violence that has tormented Algeria since the early 1990s. In some ways, these frameworks captured unseen elements of the conflict, but they also ignored, effaced, or invented other aspects. International efforts to transform the conflict in Algeria likewise had mixed results. What worked and why often stood in contrast to prevailing accounts of the conflict's inception, escalation, and termination. Put more concretely, international diplomatic efforts to end the conflict were as ineffectual as early economic interventions. The international community's inability to penetrate Algeria's violence through diplomatic and financial interventions has matched an epistemic incapacity to grasp the ways in which Algeria's violence could not be subordinated to new understandings of civil war. Yet these new understandings presented Algeria as an exemplary case study of just that—a model civil war. Meanwhile, increasing governmental and financial stability in Algeria coincided with the worst of the violence between 1996 and 1998, a period that saw repeated collective civilian massacres ravage villages, towns, and neighborhoods. The international response to these horrors revealed the conceptual and practical shortcomings of the humanitarian intervention paradigm that would later become the Responsibility to Protect (R2P) project. Launched in 2001, the R2P project forgot that in 1997 and 1998 Algeria's violence had become increasingly framed as an international humanitarian dilemma, a dilemma that proved to be far less understandable and manageable than almost any other instance of mass atrocities in the 1990s.

The new understandings of terrorism that emerged late in the Cold War and, more important, after September 11, 2001 (9/11) have treated Algeria far differently than the R2P project. Algeria's *décennie noire* (dark or black decade) of the 1990s has become central to the new sciences of terrorism and the related managerial strategies of counterterrorism. Terrorism research and counterterrorism practice will never forget Algeria's massacres because they have since become central to unlocking the enigma of civilian-directed violence in an Islamic context. Post-9/11 understandings of "Jihadism" and Islamic radicalization eagerly repurposed Algeria's violence—by negating the ways in which state and nonstate terror in Algeria were co-constitutive—so as to inform new doctrines of global counterterrorism. The way in which the Algerian polity actually chose to bring its violence to an end—through policies of national reconciliation premised on compensation, forgiving, and forgetting—were openly derided by the self-appointed technoscientific managers of the late postconflict environment. Their evangelical faith in the ameliorative efficacy of truth commissions was rooted in the recent evolution of the contemporary morality play now known as *transitional justice*. They suggested that "postconflict" Algeria's potential recidivism into mass violence depended on the performative elaboration of a particular kind of history of the 1990s. This faith in such narrative acts of contrition should have been treated with deep skepticism, particularly when concerned with a polity whose relationship to its own contested histories of violence has been intensely fraught. More important, this faith in the dramaturgy of truth commissions belied the antipolitics behind it.

Indeed, the pattern witnessed in these efforts to understand and affect Algeria's violence is constellated by the antipolitics of contemporary conflict science and management. At the most basic level, this antipolitics manifests in the core concepts that organize various understandings of warfare today. These concepts exhibit a relationship to forms of management in which questions of geography, history, and power are highly circumscribed or absent. Civil war, terrorism, and genocide, particularly in their most recent formulations, have been increasingly theorized and studied in depoliticized ways that flatten late warfare's historical, geographical, and ideational contours. The result is not simply problematic understandings of mass violence. The larger issue is the relationship between these depoliticized understandings and the strategies of conflict management that these understandings license. Some of today's most prevalent forms of international conflict management—the economic prevention and regulation of civil wars, global preemptive counterterrorism doctrine, the use of military force to interrupt mass atrocities, and the rectification of war-torn societies through truth commissions and other forms of transitional justice—arise out of depoliticized understandings of late warfare. At the same time, the warrant for such depoliticized understandings is rooted in a managerial logic that is similarly antagonistic toward questions of power. It is not just that the increasingly apoliticial sciences of conflict are creating apolitical frameworks for conflict management. These sciences in fact reflect the managerial logic that has come to dominate the ways in which the international community understands and regulates mass violence today. The danger of managerialism is not just that it misunderstands reality by evading questions of power, geography, and history. The danger of managerialism is that it is desperately attempting to fashion into existence its apolitical understanding of the world—a world of peculiar histories and credulous notions of power's spatial distribution.[1] Given managerialism's poor epistemological purchase on the varieties, ambiguities, and indeterminacies of human and nonhuman realities, its putative successes often arise out of catastrophes that it haphazardly helped to create.[2]

The antipolitics of managerialism—its ability to create and destroy, both imaginatively and materially, an ability that it is not particularly good at accounting for—was first recognized in the field of development studies. The persistent failure of development schemes in the postcolonial world owes as much to the inability of these schemes to understand the terrains in which they worked as to their inability to see how they have actually transformed relations of power.[3] The ostensibly neutral and objective science of economics is particularly guilty here. It often manufactures such experiments in development so as to confirm the validity of its theories. Yet its theories historically emerged from normative assumptions about how economies *should* work rather than about how they *actually* work. Economic science and its field experiments in development mostly serve to reproduce the ideational and material conditions of its possibility, but at the expense of delivering on its loftier promises.[4] It is thus a Janus-faced antipolitics: presenting itself as scientifically and managerially apolitical while failing to recognize either the extent of its effects or the regimes of power that give it momentum and legitimacy.

A similar lack of recognition haunts the ensemble of disciplines and interventionary practices of conflict science and management today. Scientifically, contemporary understandings of mass violence are often premised on ideas and imaginative geographies that are intelligible and compelling for reasons that have little to do with their ability to map and explain the empirical world. The legitimacy of these accounts is tethered to particular problematizations of conflict and postconflict environments in which the solutions of conflict management actually help make the problem that conflict science claims to find.[5] Such patterns have been explored in the strange relationship between terrorism and counterterrorism, a relationship in which the ostensible object of analysis and management—terrorism—would not be what it is today if not for the epistemological intervention of terrorism studies and the militarized intervention of counterterrorism. The result is a world in which terrorism seems like an apolitical phenomenon because the study of mainstream terrorism conceptualizes it as such. Meanwhile, there is very little debate about the North Atlantic world's maintenance of a global preemptive counterterrorism doctrine because terrorism is now understood as an apolitical and ahistorical form of violence practiced by implacable and irredeemable humans.[6]

Similar operations of knowledge and power can be witnessed in the relationship between how the mass violence in 1990s Algeria was understood and the forms of conflict management either applied to it or derived from it. Normally this relationship is theorized in a linear way: conflicts produce scientific studies that produce recommendations that then produce strategies of management. This approach is the initial problem with contemporary conflict management and science. These three elements—conflict, science, and management—should instead be treated as dialectically interactive and ultimately coconstitutive. As much as today's neoliberal systems of global governance would like to create strategies of conflict management based on facts, the emergent historiography of 1990s Algeria suggests otherwise. Today's strategies of conflict management play a role in the production of the very understandings they claim to follow. The frameworks of understanding and the doctrines of conflict management applied to, and derived from, 1990s Algeria allow us to see these processes unfold in a number of old, new, and related domains of conflict management and science: identity, terrorism, and counterterrorism; civil war, natural resources, and development; mass atrocities, the R2P project, and transitional justice.

THE ANTIPOLITICS OF CONFLICT SCIENCE

The wars that emerged in the imagination and practices of conflict management and science in the 1990s were the result of a number of conditions. The end of the Cold War unleashed a wave of new understandings of late warfare and the (post)conflict environment. With the putative end of global political struggle, intellectual and governmental energies could turn to regional and local struggles. Internal conflicts could receive the attention they deserved, for it was soon realized that they had actually been the most prevalent and deadly form of armed violence since the end of World War II.[7] The civil war, the failed state, the ethnic conflict, and other forms of interpolity violence became the security challenge of the post–Cold War world. What made these conflicts new was not that they were unprecedented, but rather the tendency to see them in new ways, to reproblematize them, and to suggest different forms of intervention to prevent or stop them. Central to this tendency was their de-internationalization and endogenization. The conflicts of the Cold War, whether wars of decolonization or civil wars, had been seen, in one way or another, as extensions or effects of larger historical and political processes.[8] After the Cold War, internal conflicts became just that—internal. Though they were an international problem, their causation was hypothesized in ways that limited or excluded the role of outside forces *a priori*.[9] External factors were forces that could amplify or terminate a civil conflict; they were not, however, important contributors to its preformation or initiation. Such assumptions about the endogenous character of civil war etiology also began to affect historical understandings of conflicts throughout the Cold War. Colonial wars and proxy wars had all along been no different than the civil wars of the 1990s.[10] The true nature of civil wars, from the Peloponnesian War to the present, was only now becoming clear.[11]

This change in how late warfare came to be understood speaks to another condition behind these recent trends in conflict management and science. Because armed conflicts were increasingly treated as internal, global security expertise on the causes of warfare was no longer dominated by the discipline of international relations. Seizing the opportunity, economists—and political scientists trained in economic methods—began to fill the void. The dominance of economic thought in the scientific debates about warfare in the 1990s and early 2000s was an extension of the hegemony that economics had achieved in the social sciences in general. Though the dominance of economics owes much to its role as the scientific foundation of neoliberal thought and action, its rise also owes much to the shifting terrains of geopolitics. With the end of European imperialism after World War II, an international system of states was created, one in which the discipline of economics could imaginatively and practically elaborate the national economy in its own vision. This had been otherwise difficult in a geopolitical environment wherein the various boundaries of so many European economies were indeterminate, spanning several continents.[12] Like the end of imperialism, the end of the Cold War—the putative end of geopolitics and ideology—laid the groundwork for a new understanding of warfare as neatly contained within the state as the most basic, primary, and ultimate unit of analysis. Quantitative and comparative political science and, more important, economics were better positioned to investigate this phenomenon. What they produced was discrete, internalized civil conflicts stripped of any global character. Development, not diplomacy, was the key to preventing contemporary war.[13] Peacebuilding and conflict prevention were increasingly premised on new models of civil war derived from these sciences—models, it should be noted, that could not even predict the very civil wars contained in the datasets used to construct the models in the first place.[14]

The endogenization of late warfare was also born out of a reaction to those who viewed it as the opposite. Some of the first and most popular theories of post–Cold War conflict saw it instead as an effect of transnational forces or warfare in the age of globalization. One of the most influential statements on the new global terrain of mass violence immediately after the Cold War framed civil wars as manifestations of larger, and essentially implacable, inter- and intracivilizational disputes.[15] Another equally influential assessment likewise saw transnational forces hiding behind seemingly localized manifestations of intercommunal fighting. These were the forces of a global Malthusian catastrophe born out of natural scarcity, rapacious human demand, and environmental degradation.[16] Contrary to such top-down accounts, others proposed that late warfare represented a perversion of neoliberal globalization in which local armed actors exploited the visible and invisible flows of peoples, goods, and ideas—legal, illegal, and extralegal—for their own political, criminal, or ethnoreligious agendas.[17]

The ways in which transnational circulations of ideas and things could actually be initiating, sustaining, and terminating armed conflicts since the end of the Cold War were largely ignored or poorly theorized in the economic approaches that came to dominate the study of civil wars. Some of this neglect had to do with the fact that the prevailing "technologies of truth" used in economic approaches—datasets and statistical analysis—placed methodological limits on what could be analyzed.[18] When notoriously irreducible and contextual ideas such as ethnicity, religion, and politics were quantified, they were rendered in terms of levels of national diversity or a spectrum of regime types, not in terms of the actual content of local, national, or regional claims to identity and polity. These epistemological maneuvers allowed the new sciences of conflict to focus on the structural conditions for civil wars and eschew the need for any kind of ethnographic understanding of the claims being made by participants and survivors. As leading researchers with the World Bank's project on civil wars insisted, "Grievance can be the constitutive grammar of conflict or simply its discourse, with no more explanatory power as to the determinants of observing violence than either perception or opportunity."[19]

Warfare after the Cold War was not only excessively endogenized, it was also depoliticized. The extent to which agency mattered was only in relation to how the putative structural causes of the conflict could constitute a motive for rebellion. The idea that state repression might play a role, or that regimes too might choose civil war over other alternatives, was likewise analytically off the table. Not only were states stripped of agency in the generation of late warfare, rebels were construed as criminal organizations owing to the ways in which a particular understanding of human psychology—rational choice theory—dictated that short-term profit making was likely behind most conflicts. The depoliticization and internalization of contemporary warfare should have stood in sharp contrast to a key finding of the new civil war research: the correlation between primary commodity exports and civil war onset. But this finding was interpreted as evidence of apolitical criminal rebels simply seeking a piece of the trade, rather than as evidence of corrupt states and complicit international actors.[20] From these antipolitical interpretations of late warfare sprung social movements, international mechanisms, and development policies seeking to regulate the circulation of "conflict resources" away from black markets, bad rebels, and impoverished populations, and toward good governments, multinational corporations, and ethical consumers.[21]

The violence in 1990s Algeria was subjected to scientific understandings and managerial strategies that problematized the warfare as internal and apolitical. In order for the warfare in Algeria to be useful to the new economic understandings of conflict, it had first to be rendered into an intelligible object for comparative analysis. That is, Algeria's mass violence had to be made into a civil war, which was possible only if two important sources of data were ignored: Algerians, very few of whom thought that the term *civil war* was applicable to their political situation; and the emerging historiography of the Algerian conflict, which has tended to see very little analytical value in understanding the violence as a civil war. But the greatest challenge to imagining that the Algerian conflict was a civil war was the violence itself. Despite the uncertainty and indeterminacy of even the most basic facts and figures attributed to Algeria's *décennie noire* (the 1990s), the new sciences of civil war have been largely indifferent to, if not simply ignorant of, these challenges. It is clear in the effort to frame Algeria's violence as a civil war that the world outside this frame—what the violence ostensibly is not—is playing a far larger role in producing what the violence ostensibly is—a civil war. No other words besides *civil war* were powerful enough to package the horrific violence of 1990s Algeria in a single term, save *terrorism* and *genocide*, which were problematic descriptors as well (see discussion later in this section). Similarly, Algeria was scientifically produced as a civil war because of the framework applied by the new economic understandings of conflict, which divided wars into three types *a priori*: wars between states, wars within states, and wars between states and nonstate actors abroad. It is this narrow trifurcated schema—wars as either international, internal, or extrasystemic—rather than the content of Algeria's violence, that renders that violence intelligible as a civil war in the new economic science of conflict.

Like efforts to *imagine* Algeria's violence as a self-contained phenomenon, efforts to *manage* it as such proved equally problematic. International efforts to address the violence were divided according to divergent interpretations of its origins and nature. Some interventionary strategies saw the core issue as political, defined narrowly in terms of how and who should govern the Algerian polity; other strategies assessed the Algerian conflict as economic, narrowly understood as the postcolonial mismangement of the country's oil wealth. Whereas political approaches to Algeria's violence tended to conflate proximate and underlying causation, economic approaches failed to appreciate the powerful, historically conditioned imaginative forces driving the violence. Moreover, political approaches to understanding and managing Algeria's violence were often grounded in simplifying and thereby addressing the concrete grievances of the participants, notably the denial of democracy (for the Islamists) versus saving the republic (for the regime). Yet the evolution of the violence on the ground raises questions about the efficacy of any account rooted in an analysis of the conflict's putative trigger events. It became clear that Algeria was in a protracted and serious armed conflict only one to two years after the allegedly fateful events of January 1992. What makes January 1992 Algeria's point of no return is not a sufficiently justified counterfactual argument but rather the partisan assertions of those participating in the violence, along with the liberal assumptions of those observing it. The repeated failure of international diplomatic interventions to have any effect on the violence is mirrored in economic interventions as well. Though there were compelling economic interpretations of the origins of Algeria's violence, the behavior of that violence was entirely disarticulated from the macrolevel economic picture of Algeria from the mid-1990s onward. Diplomatic and financial interventions had little effect on the violence; indeed, it only got worse. As the Algerian government began to return to democratic processes and the hydrocarbon sector rebounded, the country began to experience the widespread slaughter of civilians. These massacres, often claiming more than one hundred lives in a single episode, could not be accounted for by, and thus could not be addressed within, established frameworks of conflict science and management. International oil corporations and foreign governments were largely undeterred in their interests and operations in Algeria by the massive bloodletting of 1997 and 1998.

Though it was difficult for the new understandings of civil war to elaborate a compelling account of the worst of Algeria's violence, the massacres of 1997–1998 were easily incorporated into new understandings of terrorism, particularly as Islamic or *jihadi* violence. The antipolitical tendencies in terrorism research and management have taken the opposite approach to that taken in the research and management of civil wars. Whereas civil wars have been depoliticized through the excessive endogenization of their ontology and causation, terrorism has been depoliticized through its excessive transnationalization. Since 9/11, terrorism studies and counterterrorism doctrines have become less interested in the local specificities that give rise to putative terrorists and instead have come to view and confront terrorism as a manifestation of a transnational phenomenon.

Though terrorism was widely recognized as a global security challenge in the 1990s, its scientific analysis received far more attention in the final decades of the Cold War. Today's understandings of terrorism were first formulated in the 1970s. Though it was tempting to theorize such early "terrorism" as a set of insurgent tactics adapted to the global information age, in reality the force driving terrorism studies was the geopolitics of the Cold War. The Cold War's influence on the relationship between terrorism studies and its object of analysis became clear only after the end of the Soviet Union. Interest and funding in terrorism suddenly dried up in the early 1990s.[22] The 1990s were instead the decade of the ethnic conflict, the civil war, the failed state, and endless policy debates about military intervention, peacekeeping operations, state sovereignty, and humanitarian obligations. After the events of 9/11, the concerns of the 1990s were sidelined and a new international security order emerged, one centered on terrorism, which proved to be just as capable of maintaining and advancing preexisting geopolitical relations as the human security concerns of the 1990s had been, and in some cases old concerns were transformed by new ones. In the 1990s, Algeria seemed to manifest all of that decade's geopolitical anxieties: civil war, identity politics, and a failing state. Algeria's violence was even subjected to a debate about humanitarian intervention at the height of the killing in 1997 and 1998. After 9/11, Algeria became an index of the new international security order centered on terrorism—a site of Islamic radicalization, a cautionary tale about the democratic promises of Islamist parties, a pathway for *jihadi* circulations, and a testing ground for new techniques of horrific violence against civilians that connected directly to 9/11.

The antipolitical character of terrorism as a concept in the conflict sciences is well known. Terrorism, like genocide, is an intolerable form of violence. As such, it often produces antiscientific attitudes and irrationally reactionary policies. But the antipolitics of terrorism studies and counterterrorism doctrines goes further than that. First, the science and management of terrorism has largely failed to appreciate the political conditions of the origin of "terrorism" in the Cold War while, second, it has pretended to advance the objective and neutral study of an object that is essentially and incorrigibly political. That terrorism is thought of as irredeemable violence leads to increasingly exterminationist approaches in which there can be no political engagement or compromise. Whereas actors in asymmetric conflicts in the Cold War would have been described in Maoist terms as fish swimming in the sea of the general population, post-9/11 counterterrorism doctrine has increasingly described insurgent resistance in apolitical, and even ahistorical, terms. The wars in Iraq and Afghanistan were against an "accidental" guerrilla syndrome, one triggered by the exogenous shocks of terrorist infiltration into their societies and the counterterrorism presence that followed.[23]

The example of irredeemable violence that Algeria's conflict provides to terrorism studies is largely to be found in the massacres of 1997 and 1998, in which unspeakable acts of brutality were carried out. These acts became Islamic, and thus terrorism, through processes of making and unmaking in which the true agent of the violence was the violence itself. The Islamization of Algeria's violence, particularly the 1997–1998 massacres, was an effect of the horror of those killing episodes that, because of their extraordinary brutality, beckoned extraordinary explanations in an information environment defined by an astonishing paucity of basic facts. Imaginations began to make connections and Algerian violence began to be constellated within a global trend. Algeria's violence was then definitively transformed by the events of 9/11. The 9/11 attacks licensed new understandings of the Algerian conflict that reinscribed Algeria's violence as transnational *jihadi* terrorism. The horrors of Algeria's violence also helped to license new, aggressive global counterterrorism strategies based on the irredeemable nature of Islamic terrorism like that witnessed in Algeria in 1997 and 1998. The violence in Algeria and the violence linked to Algeria were ostensibly effects of identity's power in contemporary conflict. What they actually show is the power of violence to make identity. That these processes occur within, yet unbeknownst to, both terrorism studies (particularly those focused on Islamic violence) and counterterrorism practices are part of the antipolitics they have helped to constitute.

THE ANTIPOLITICS OF CONFLICT MANAGEMENT

These two competing visions of conflict after the Cold War—civil wars and terrorism—often saw different kinds of violence with different causal backgrounds. There was, however, an eventual convergence of thought in terms of how to manage both as problems of development—postconflict peacebuilding in the case of civil wars and counterinsurgency in the case of terrorism. In both cases, conflict management through development is an indicator of the anti-politics of how mass violence is internationally understood, confronted, and ameliorated today.

Conflict management is a term strongly associated with the world of business and finance. When it comes to issues of warfare, one is more likely to encounter notions of conflict *resolution*, though no practitioner or theorist of conflict resolution believes that conflicts are ever truly resolved. Though conflict resolution theorists and practitioners are often seen as liberals, a close reading of their analysis reveals a very realist sensibility in which individual selfishness, group irrationality, and inequities of power are baseline facts of political life.[24] Conflicts are never resolved; they are merely transformed. That is, they can only be managed. Actual conflict resolution requires much more than the substantive transformation of discrete conflicts. It requires substantive change in the terms of debate and the relations of power. Having never in the first place adopted this "maximalist," or "positive peace," agenda (that is, the agenda of developing scientific and government tools for addressing and eliminating the conditions that make war possible), contemporary conflict management and science are content to work within the global structures of thought and power that make seemingly "minimalist" advances possible, yet actual conflict resolution impossible. Meanwhile, warfare globally has been trending in the direction mapped out by the maximalist school of peace studies.[25] That is, there is less war and less intense warfare than ever before. This progress toward a more peaceful world has advanced despite any deliberate and coordinated effort. Moreover, no one in the conflict sciences is even sure why war is becoming extinct.[26] Such a failure of scientific imagination is not unheard of in the history of human efforts to understand and thus govern political life; indeed, such crises are central to the productive capacities of science and managerialism (see this book's Conclusion). More important, this failure exposes the extent to which the management and science of conflict today cannot be accounted for solely in terms of how conflict science and conflict management understand themselves and the world of war and peace around them.

The post–Cold War renaissance in conflict management is often considered one of the important reasons for the relative peace of the last two decades.[27] In just three years, from 1990 to 1993, the United Nations launched as many peacekeeping missions as it had in the previous four and a half decades of its existence. But the most contentious conflict management debate of the 1990s had little to do with the legitimate capacities of the United Nations. It instead revolved around the question of whether or not states could unilaterally or in coalitions take extraordinary measures to protect civilians from disasters and mass atrocities—to routinize what had been *ad hoc* in the early 1990s and impossible during the Cold War. The humanitarian intervention question was similar to questions about managing global conflict and postconflict environments through international law. The creation of international tribunals and hybrid domestic-international courts paved the way for the International Criminal Court (ICC), which sought to develop standardized procedures to advance the global application of humanitarian and human rights law vis-à-vis its most outrageous violations. The dream of the ICC was to take politics out of the application of these laws, to transform questions of will into questions of procedure. Though this antipolitical juridical vision has run headlong into the stubborn immediacy of geopolitics, these challenges have not stopped others from imagining a similar set of international technobureaucratic procedures for the application of military force to protect civilians from mass atrocities.

To advance this antipolitical vision of militarized humanitarianism, it was first necessary to frame the debate in terms of whether or not state sovereignty was still an inviolable guarantee against foreign interference in domestic affairs. This framing allowed the question of humanitarian intervention to pivot on an imagined impasse of procedure rather than an impasse of geopolitics. Proceduralization of humanitarian intervention evaded the real political heart of the matter and instead blamed the world's atrocities on postcolonial regimes that took advantage of sovereignty to commit massive, conscience-shocking crimes. As later embodied in the R2P project, the new humanitarianism of the 1990s would claim that thousands, if not millions, could have been spared horrific deaths in places like Rwanda and Bosnia if not for a simple rule change in the UN Security Council's attitude toward sovereignty.[28] Democratization of the Security Council—an actual rule change that might have a more substantial humanitarian effect on the world—was nowhere to be found in the mainstream of the humanitarian intervention debate of the 1990s. Rather than being seen as a curse, contemporary geopolitics and US hegemony were viewed as assets to those seeking to advance the cause of preventing future Rwandas and Srebrenicas.[29]

The antipolitics of the new humanitarianism of the 1990s, as a framework for understanding and managing mass violence, has several aspects. Its antipolitics first manifests in its efforts to make UN-authorized use of military power for civilian protection no longer subject to debate, or rather to make that debate procedural (driven by *how* questions) rather than political (driven by *why* questions). These efforts to automate humanitarian intervention also suggest that the determination of facts on the ground—whether acts of genocide, ethnic cleansing, or other forms of systematic mass atrocity were taking place—should be taken out of the hands of diplomats and politicians and instead determined by lawyers and human rights experts. The vision advanced by the new humanitarians conceptualized international intervention into mass violence as the securitization of human rights rather than as what it was: the militarization of humanitarianism.

The antipolitics of the new humanitarianism also manifests in how it conceptualizes the problem of humanitarian intervention and the history of that problem. Framing it as an issue of sovereignty's sacrosanct character is ahistorical, for two reasons. First, during the brief period in which most of the world was granted sovereignty via decolonization, the postcolonial world's tenuous sovereignty was regularly violated by former colonial masters and other global powers throughout the Cold War. Even among Western European states there was little respect for each other's sovereignty.[30] Second, the two most serious cases of "nonintervention" cited by the new humanitarians, the Rwandan and Bosnian massacres, were in fact cases of active and conscious UN withdrawal of international peacekeeping forces in the face of mass atrocities at the behest of a post-Mogadishu (post-"Blackhawk Down") Security Council. Despite these ahistorical roots, the new humanitarianism nonetheless invented for itself a justificatory history that imagined humanitarian intervention as a norm in international affairs prior to the creation of the United Nations.[31] That is, the new humanitarianism attempted to recode the racial and sectarian imperialism of the 1700s and 1800s as the first steps toward a more civil geopolitics underwritten by North Atlantic power. This recoding was not unlike how recent counterinsurgency doctrines have sought to manage conflict by first reimagining nineteenth- and twentieth-century colonial warfare as politically innocent prior illustrations of the situation that the United States faced in Iraq and Afghanistan in the first decade of the 2000s.[32]

Today the new humanitarianism is best known for the R2P project. The transformation of R2P from an intellectual proposal in 2001 to a putative global security doctrine in 2011 occurred during a decade in which most observers had written off the project as stillborn. The R2P project was initiated in the wake of the fierce international debate over NATO's humanitarian intervention in Kosovo in 1999, an intervention launched without Security Council authorization. When initially unveiled in late 2001, the R2P project fell on deaf ears; the international security environment had changed so radically on 9/11 that the humanitarian wars of the 1990s instantly became a quaint anachronism. Wars of naked national self-interest—but now in the name of eliminating terrorists, terrorist safe havens, and state sponsors of terrorism—had returned after 9/11. Not all was lost, though. Concerns about "ethnic" violence in Sudan's Darfur region seemed to breathe new life into the new humanitarianism, particularly when the label *genocide* was affixed to the violence by the US government in 2004. Darfur, a first test case for R2P, proved to be a kind of nonevent in the project's history. Overall, the UN response to Darfur was, to say the least, equivocal—neither heavy-handed intervention nor total international indifference.[33] The greatest challenge to the R2P project, it turned out, was not the atrocities in Darfur but rather the use of humanitarian justifications by Washington and London to support the 2003 invasion of Iraq *post hoc*.

Despite this lack of success in the field, and the appropriation of humanitarianism to justify the global war on terror, the R2P project strangely began to benefit from increasing levels of institutional legitimation. The 2005 World Summit recognized a shared international responsibility to prevent and interrupt mass atrocities. Offices were soon created within the United Nations to support the R2P project. Scholarship on its merits and deficiencies flourished, though there were no test cases to speak of, only regrets and missed opportunities. Intellectual architects of the doctrine (such as Samantha Power, Mary Ann Slaughter, and Gareth Evans) found themselves in positions of relative influence both inside and outside of government.

After a decade of imaginative and institutional elaboration, the R2P project was a solution in search of a problem, a theory in need of an experiment. Amid the regional turmoil of the Arab Spring in early 2011, the R2P project found its test case: the civil war in Libya. Mere weeks after the eruption of violence in Libya, the United Nations authorized NATO and the Arab League to uphold the international responsibility to protect by using military force to prevent the Gaddafi regime from carrying out a genocide. What was strange about this potential genocide was that there was no evidence for it; it existed only in the minds of the new humanitarians who demanded the intervention. By preventing this counterfactual genocide, the R2P project was vindicated. This "new politics of protection"[34] under the aegis of a field-tested R2P project was even explicitly stated in antipolitical language: the R2P project's triumph in Libya was the "end of the argument."[35] That is, there would no longer be any debate over the use of international military force to stop or prevent genocide. As an international norm or even a global doctrine, enforcing R2P would now become a problem of technocratic conflict management rather than of politics. The ghosts of the 1990s—from Mogadishu to Kigali, Srebrenica to Grozny—could now rest in peace.

The ghosts of Algeria's violence in the 1990s have been of little interest or use to the R2P project. The founding documents and supporting research of the R2P project have consistently avoided even the most superficial analysis of the international response to the mass atrocities in Algeria, particularly the mass killings of 1997 and 1998.[36] Given the extensive use of humanitarian and interventionary language at the time of those massacres, Algeria should represent at least a case of ambivalent nonintervention. Yet it is not represented at all in the vast research supporting the new humanitarianism and the R2P project. On the one hand, this lack of representation is attributable to the ways in which Algeria's violence was reimagined after 9/11, as a prologue to the war on terror. On the other hand, the R2P project was initially formulated before 9/11, when Algeria was still on the international radar, though it was certainly eclipsed by subsequent events, such as the interventions in Kosovo, East Timor, and Sierra Leone. Algeria's absence from the new humanitarianism is likewise difficult to attribute to there having been no intervention. The R2P project's ethical warrant issues from an extensive analysis of purported failures to intervene in, above all, Rwanda and Bosnia.[37]

What the international response to Algeria's atrocities shows is the strange processes through which conflicts are humanitarianized and dehumanitarianized. It shows that humanitarianization is driven not by a conflict's intrinsic characteristics but rather, largely, by forces outside of it. The humanitarianization of the Algerian conflict owed as much to the media representations of massive and horrific violence during the massacre crisis of 1997–1998 as to the fact that there was no way to explain the massacres; there were many theories of the violence but very few facts to confirm those theories. In this context, the international debate about intervention in Algeria became a debate about a kind of pre-intervention—a fact-finding mission—to determine whom to intervene against. But as with other efforts to come to grips with the atrocities in

Algeria and so address them, Algeria's violence was largely in the driver's seat. Humanitarian concern peaked as Algeria's violence peaked in January 1998, then dissipated as the levels of killing in Algeria retreated to internationally tolerable levels. Massacres of one or two dozen were normal; massacres of one or two hundred were extraordinary. The dehumanitarianization of Algeria's violence thus began with a decline in the massacre rate, not with the establishment of any facts on the ground. And because the international community was never able to establish any facts about Algeria, Algeria's violence could not be rendered in terms that made it intelligible and actionable for the new humanitarianism.

That said, Algeria's violence was, from its beginning, already at a disadvantage when it came to the frameworks of understanding and managing conflict advocated by the new humanitarianism of the 1990s. For the new humanitarianism, it is the quality of violence—asymmetric ethnic or interreligious atrocities, if not outright genocide—that matters most, not its quantity. The new humanitarianism considers all other forms of mass violence to be secondary. The Algerian massacres of 1997–1998, widely viewed as civil violence and *intra*-religious killing, if not Islamic terrorism, did not meet the standards of the new humanitarianism's genocide framework. Given the deeply contested and often undetermined nature of the killing in Algeria, the new humanitarianism determined—even predetermined—Algeria's violence to be unworthy of international humanitarian action to protect Algerian civilians from being slaughtered *en masse*. It was the new humanitarianism of the 1990s that contributed most to the dehumanitarianization of Algeria's violence.

The dehumanitarianization of Algeria's violence resulted in that violence becoming historiographically invisible to those who would elaborate the R2P project, even amid the ongoing massacres in Algeria at the turn of the century. In its own way, this historiographic invisibility helps to maintain the antipolitics of the new humanitarianism and the R2P project. At the heart of the new humanitarianism is already a depoliticized understanding of genocide in which the necessity of responding to it overwhelms the need to account for its politics. Indeed, it was the new humanitarianism of the 1990s that most often rooted genocide in notions of fundamental and irreconcilable ethnic and religious identities rather than notions of geography, history, and power. Genocide was therefore increasingly viewed as the inevitable outcome of implacable cultural forces. There could thus be only one response to genocide: to interrupt it. Given the power of the Holocaust in both the elaboration and maintenance of the post–World War II order, the new humanitarianism of the 1990s claimed to be making good on the age-old promise of "never again," a promise that the international community could neither keep during the Cold War nor uphold in Rwanda and Bosnia. In light of the international response to the Algerian massacres of 1997–1998, the centrality of genocide within the new humanitarianism suggests that the international capacity to understand and stop mass atrocities has been disabled rather than enhanced by the R2P project.

The invented traditions of global peacekeeping, like those of the new humanitarianism, are not unlike those found in global peacebuilding. Since the end of the Cold War, international capacity to affect postconflict environments has also grown by leaps and bounds. Today, various strategies ostensibly seek to understand and manage polities that are emerging from years, if not decades, of war or violent authoritarianism—statebuilding, reconstruction, refugee management, transitional justice, and national reconciliation, to name some of the most predominant. What these strategies have in common is a shared site of intervention: the postconflict environment. That these strategies of postconflict management play a significant role in the constitution of the very thing they claim to find and fix—the postconflict environment—is entirely absent from their understanding of the world and their role in it.[38] Just as the "new wars" of the post–Cold War era emerged largely within the sciences and management of those wars, so too did the new terrains of peacebuilding.

The ambiguities of Algeria's violence in the 1990s fed into an ambiguous postconflict situation. In the early 2000s, an international consensus that Algeria had turned a corner emerged and grew, but only because the violence simmered at levels far below what had been the case from 1994 to 1998. Part of this ambiguity issued from the Algerian regime's increasingly ambivalent attitude toward the insurgency—claiming to be at war with terrorism while enacting reconciliation measures with those very terrorists to end the bloodshed. Following initial efforts by President Zéroual to grant amnesty to insurgents, President Bouteflika, soon after being elected in 1999, continued these policies of reprieve and state subsidies for "repentant" insurgents. After his reelection in 2004, Bouteflika championed even more controversial policies to extend the amnesty to other insurgent groups, offering compensation to some victims of state terrorism, immunizing state agents against prosecution, and generally prohibiting domestic inquiries, whether academic, journalistic, or judicial, into the 1990s. Though these policies were not without their critics inside Algeria, they received strong support in national referenda.

Critics outside of Algeria alleged that the government had failed to meet international standards for transparency and equity in the context of national reconciliation. They frequently pointed to the 1996–1999 South African truth and reconciliation commission (TRC) and its purported role in that polity's transition away from decades of violent racial segregation as a model. As a peacebuilding strategy in the late postconflict environment, the truth and reconciliation commission is increasingly viewed not just as a tool to help such transitioning polities, but also as a necessity in any transition. Today's homogenized understanding of the truth commission emerged from a strange and awkward constellation of various forms of state and civil society initiatives to investigate abuses of governmental power. What constellated these initiatives was not the efforts themselves but the self-appointed international managers, both governmental and nongovernmental, of postconflict environments. Their faith in the power of the truth commission issued from its consistency with tacitly held liberal values rather than from evidence of any efficacy on the part of the commission itself. Algeria in 1999 was being advised to follow the South Africa model before any reasonable evaluation of the TRC's impact could have taken place.

The virtue of the truth commission is its alleged ability to reconcile polities in ways that neither punitive judicial proceedings nor simple immunity can. The "survivors' justice" of the truth and reconciliation commission is said to contrast with the "victors' justice" of the international criminal tribunal, from Nuremberg to the ICC. Whereas such tribunals can offer only morality plays that vindicate those staging the trial, a national reconciliation commission can truly restore a broken polity. But how national reconciliation commissions accomplish this is ironic. They do so by staging a morality play, one whose dramaturgy is also cleverly planned in order to validate and legitimize the postconflict environment in which a polity finds itself. From South Africa to Morocco to Rwanda, the national reconciliation commission has functioned largely to christen a political order that remains profoundly unjust.[39] In so doing, it has made clear the antipolitics of the truth commission as an important strategy in postconflict management.

What is unclear is how a truth commission could repair Algeria through the production of a state-authored or state-condoned history of the 1990s. The question is not so much about the extent of official oversight or interference in the process of history making, but rather about the strange relationship between Algeria's history and Algeria's violence. For many observers, Algeria's violence in the 1990s was directly linked to Algeria's history as a site of one of the bloodiest wars of decolonization and one of the most violent conquests in the history of nineteenth-century settler-colonialism. The paradox in criticisms of Algeria's national reconciliation policies was the double assertion that history was Algeria's tragedy but a particular staging of history could also redeem Algeria. Simultaneously, history could be both disease and cure. A close analysis of the invented traditions of transitional justice suggests that the form of history making, rather than the content of the history made, has become the true imperative. The technology of truth—the truth commission—is more important than the truth it produces. Humanitarian intervention and transitional justice have thus become technical innovations in conflict management that produce the conditions of their necessity, especially within the sciences that attend to them. As is often the case in the history of technology, invention has become the mother of necessity.[40]

IMAGINATIVE GEOGRAPHIES OF ALGERIAN VIOLENCE

It was once said that the warfare in 1990s Algeria was a problem of imagination—the violent, war-oriented imaginations of the country's insurgents and regime elites. This assessment was according to the only monograph to feature interviews conducted in the field with the conflict's participants during the early years of the fighting. This study suggested that failed institutions (political, economic, and social) alone could not explain Algeria's descent into mass killing. The only viable explanation was that the Algerian polity had succumbed to its own innate, if historically conditioned, *imaginaire de la guerre*.[41] The warfare of the 1990s was animated by a culture that valorized the profit-seeking rebel as the fundamental archetype of Algerian masculine being. The Islamist insurgents of the 1990s were the reincarnation of a linage stretching from the Ottoman corsairs to the guerrilla's of the Front de Libération Nationale. Though this *imaginaire de la guerre* thesis was refuted and dismissed due to its historical determinism and cultural essentialism,[42] the idea of an Algerian *imaginaire de la guerre* elucidated the extent to which the horrific violence in Algeria was dictating the terms of its representation. It was a violence so extreme that it could be understood only as erupting from primordial reservoirs of malice and greed.

In assessing the conflict that ravaged the Algerian polity for more than a decade—a conflict that has made political life there precarious in the years since—the powers of violence, history, and imagination have often been ap-preciated.[43] But the extensive focus on the ostensibly endogenous forces that drove the Algerian polity to extremes has come at the expense of ignoring the ways in which other histories, imaginations, and violences were complicit. To treat the problem of 1990s Algeria as simply an Algerian problem is an incom-plete and misleading assessment. The violence in 1990s Algeria was as much a problem produced by the shifting geopolitical orders over which it unfolded as Algeria was a problem that helped produce understandings of those orders: the end of the Cold War and the rise of ethnoreligious conflicts and new wars; new paradigms of human security, humanitarian peacekeeping, and transitional peacebuilding; and then the new doctrines of counterterrorism and counter-insurgency along with the new sciences of terrorism, radicalization, and *jihadi* violence that attended to these doctrines.[44] Within these new frameworks of understanding and strategies of conflict management various Algerias, or meta-Algerias, were elaborated.[45] These imaginative geographies of Algerian violence have made surprising contributions to the various regimes of inter-national security that emerged after the Cold War, as well as to the insecurity that these regimes claim to address. That is, Algeria's violence has been not only the passive object of scientific inquiry and managerial intervention, but also an active agent in the production of global conflict, conflict science, and conflict management. As Elaine Scarry reminds us, violence has the power to make and unmake worlds.[46]

Terrorism, civil war, humanitarian intervention, and transitional justice have their own maps. That these maps do not correspond to the natural fea-tures of the world is partially what makes them imaginative. That the truth of these maps issues from humans agreeing that they are true is also what makes them imaginative. What makes them even more so is their ability to find and make historical, cultural, economic, and political realities that others do not. The imaginative geographies of Algerian violence found in contemporary con-flict management and science thus consistently behave in ways that Edward Said would have predicted:

> But if we agree that all things in history, like history itself, are made by men, then we will appreciate how possible it is for many objects or places or times to be assigned roles and given meanings that acquire objective validity only after the assignments are made. This is especially true of relatively uncommon things, like foreigners, mutants and "abnormal" behavior.[47]

These imaginative geographies of Algerian violence are also constituted in such a way that cause and effect are frequently misidentified in the way Said describes. For Benedict Anderson, the relationship between imaginative geographies and mass violence is clear if counterintuitive at first: "World War II begets World War I; out of Sedan comes Austerlitz; the ancestor of the Warsaw Uprising is the state of Israel."[48] To appreciate the productive powers of mass violence is to rethink its geopolitical role. Violence itself has an agency to produce the facts, agents, and sciences that are said it be its masters. "'The doer' is merely a fiction added to the deed," Nietzsche argues. "The deed is everything."[49]

What these scientific and managerial imaginations tell us about Algeria is far less interesting than what they tell us about the geopolitical order that underwrites their intellectual legitimacy and practical efficacy. In the various renderings of Algeria's violence that emerged from within conflict management and science at the turn of the century, we consistently witness the antipolitical tendencies inherent to a world in which there is no significant countervailing political imagination. The purpose of this book is not to account for the entirety of the contemporary geopolitical moment but rather to appreciate how this moment's antipolitical vision is increasingly being accepted and applied to some of the most pressing human concerns of the previous quarter-century. The critique advanced herein attempts to understand how these antipolitical operations of power act on and through the science and management of conflict, as well as on the conflicts themselves. Much of what the book documents—the rise of particular frameworks for understanding and managing late warfare—takes place in a geopolitical moment that has been widely described as neoliberal.[50] Indeed, the imprimatur of neoliberal thought, practices, and institutions is often present in the forms of conflict management and science examined in these pages. At the same time, there is no reason to view the operations of power examined here as necessarily neoliberal. These operations of power, along with their antipolitical imaginations and effects, seem to be working within the globalizing sovereignty that Hardt and Negri call *empire*.[51] The driving force behind today's imperialism is exclusively neither state power nor economic power, neither US hegemony nor the totalization of capitalism. Today's regime of global rule is instead *biopolitical* insofar as it has gone beyond the modernist project of securing states to the postmodernist project of securing human welfare, if not life in general.[52] Though neoliberalism was an important component in the articulation of late biopolitics, there are indications—notably in the growth of the human security paradigm—that contemporary biopolitics is leaving neoliberalism behind. As Paul Amar has recently demonstrated, "securitization" has overtaken neoliberalism as "the hegemonic project of global governance and state administration."[53] Through analysis of contemporary conflict management and science we are also able to witness the formation of this global security regime through its antipolitical operations of power.

Terrorists or saviors of the republic? A civilian militia stands guard in front of a mosque. Photograph (anonymous) courtesy of the *El Watan* archive, Algiers.

1 CIVIL WAR

A Name for a War Without a Name

AFTER FOURTEEN MONTHS of intense fighting, the conflict in Syria became a civil war on June 12, 2012. A spate of large-scale civilian massacres had been reported in the international media. It was widely suggested that these massacres heralded a significant transformation in the conflict. Hervé Ladsous, the head of UN peacekeeping, admitted that, in light of these new mass atrocities, *civil war* had become the best term for what was going on in Syria. Some international reactions to Ladsous's admission treated it as an official UN declaration.[1] Others saw it as too little, too late. "If you can't call it a civil war, then there are no words to describe it," France's foreign minister, Laurent Fabius, contended.[2] Almost as interesting as the response to Ladsous's admission was the caution exercised vis-à-vis the term *civil war* in the weeks and months prior to his admission. Though thousands of Syrians died in the first year of the conflict, it was often—and inexplicably—a qualified civil war, as if the term contained powers that, once uttered, could not be contained.[3]

A curious feature of this debate was its insistence that there would be consequences if Syria were allowed to drift into civil war. These alleged consequences were contradictory and vague. Civil war either beckoned or warded off foreign intervention. The latter view tended to equate civil war with chaos, to see it as a war in which the scale, intensity, and incoherence of the violence would soon become unmanageable by the international community unless dealt with promptly.[4] Then there were those who held the opposite belief: that the more serious the Syrian conflict became, the more seriously it should be addressed.[5] The term *civil war* itself holds little currency in international law. Unlike genocide, there is no international convention that obliges outside states to act in the face of a civil war. International humanitarian law is largely indifferent to whether or not armed hostilities are called a war, civil or otherwise. Nor are civil wars necessarily illegal. A state is fully within its rights to use lawful military force to defend itself against an internal rebellion so long as it adheres to humanitarian and human rights norms. The international toolkit for managing Syria's violence, whether or not it is a civil war, would remain essentially the same: diplomacy, sanctions, threats of military intervention, and then intervention itself. That final option, UN authorized military force, pivots on whether or not the UN Security Council chooses to designate a situation a threat to international peace and security, as was done in Libya in 2011 out of fear of mass atrocities, if not "genocide." Civil war has nothing to do with it.

Or does it? It is difficult to deny that there is a politics of naming civil wars. As one prominent argument suggests, the terms *civil war* and *genocide* now operate in tandem. These terms obscure the reality of mass violence because of the political dispositions of central actors in the international community. Conflicts are assigned the monikers *genocide* and *civil war* because of global relations of power, not because of the actual facts on the ground. *Genocide* is used to simplify conflicts and so to morally justify intervention. *Civil war* is used to complicate our understanding of mass violence and so to delegitimize outside action. The challenge is therefore to derive new policies based on understandings of conflict that are free of the obfuscating influence of geopolitics.[6] Another argument sees a politics of naming civil wars in the simple denial of such wars. If internal and external actors refuse to recognize mass violence as a civil war, they are doing so for political reasons, not scientific ones. The task of the social scientist is to ignore such politicizations of civil war and explore its true nature.[7]

Algeria in the 1990s appears to validate much of this debate. The term *civil war* was used quickly and frequently by external observers to describe the violence. As one might expect, the international response to this violence exhibited a clear reticence to get involved. The moment at which intervention was seriously being discussed was also the moment when the violence was at its worst, drawing comparisons with other inventions and other situations labeled *genocide*. Domestically, there was a tendency, particularly among the regime, to deny the situation's status as a civil war. Other Algerians embraced the term. Social scientists were likewise divided. Whereas area and country specialists were reluctant to call the conflict a civil war, generalists saw 1990s Algeria as paradigmatic. But, as noted earlier, there was little consensus within post–Cold War social science as to the basic definition of a civil war. There were also strong assertions that the wars of today are radically different from the wars of yesterday.

Science cannot save civil war from politics because science is entirely complicit. The problem is indeed not just "a violence whose proper name goes astray."[8] No war is naturally a civil war. If something is made, it is likely made for a reason. As much as there is a politics of denying a civil war, there is also a politics of affirming it. This goes beyond the simple politics of problematizing calls for intervention by construing violence as a civil war. The deeper politics of naming civil wars is to be found not in the conflicts themselves but in the post–Cold War geopolitical context that framed a wide array of conflicts as civil wars. What is being produced is a strange construct whose functions include the advancement of a particular global vision of politics by depoliticizing civil wars.

This antipolitical reimagining of civil wars occurs in two steps. First, the object itself has to be made if it is to be understandable and manageable. Contrary to Cold War understandings of civil wars as always-already embedded within geopolitics (and managed as such), civil wars are now rendered as discrete and isolated. An examination of scientific and political treatments of Algeria's violence as a civil war—affirmation and denial, formalization and problematization—denaturalizes the concept in such a way as to elucidate the broader conditions of its possibility. The wars of today and yesterday are indeed different, but for reasons that have little to do with their intrinsic characteristics. The second step in the depoliticization of civil wars—analyzed in the following chapter—follows from the first. Increasingly subjected to the logic and tools of contemporary economic analysis, civil wars have become economic phenomena managed as problems of development rather than politics.

A WAR THAT REFUSES TO SPEAK ITS NAME?

Civil war talk permeated the Algerian conflict from the very start. President Chadli Bendjedid justified the military crackdown against the October 1988 protests as the only alternative to "chaos and, subsequently, civil war."[9] The general strike called for by the Front Islamique du Salut (FIS, or Islamic Salvation Front) in May 1991 was likewise seen as something that could lead to civil war.[10] "It appears that the powerful FIS is not willing—or perhaps ready—to accept responsibility for setting Algeria on the road to civil war," one reporter speculated at the end of the strike.[11] Following the termination of the electoral process in January 1992, fears of a civil war became more pronounced. A US radio report saw "the specter of civil war in Algeria looming ever larger."[12] Hocine Aït

Ahmed, a leader in the war against the French and head of the Front des Forces Socialistes (FFS, or Socialist Forces Front) party, quickly called on both the authorities and the FIS to "prevent civil war."[13] During this period, various views of what would cause a civil war in Algeria were expressed. "If the FIS came to power, there would be a civil war. [...] A civil war!" one government functionary told a British journalist.[14] Algerian lawyer and human rights campaigner Abdennour Ali-Yahia made a similar suggestion before President Bendjedid's resignation on January 11, 1992. If the FIS did not respect the 1989 constitution, Ali-Yahia warned, "it's civil war, the army will move in."[15] After Bendjedid's resignation, Ali-Yahia added, "All the ingredients of a civil war are there."[16] Algerian author Rachid Mimouni likewise saw the potential for danger, but still placed hope in his country's civil society and its commitment to nonviolence. "I think that civil war is not a real possibility."[17] Other voices were more panicked. "Algeria on the brink of civil war," warned the paper *L'Événement* the day after Bendjedid's resignation. It added, "When shall we witness the militias? Yugoslavia is at our door."[18]

Throughout the conflict, Algerian officials vehemently rejected the label *civil war*. Shortly after coming to power in 1992, Algeria's interim head of state Mohamed Boudiaf insisted that the military's actions had saved the country from "civil war" and "foreign intervention."[19] After Boudiaf's assassination on June 29 and despite escalating acts of violence (such as the Algiers airport bombing on August 26, 1992), Algeria's first president, Ahmed Ben Bella, still insisted that the public would not accept a civil war.[20] Even as the violence intensified in the following years, officials continued to reject the term. "There is no civil war in Algeria as some people claim," insisted Interior Minister Salim Saadi at the end of 1993. He instead favored the language of crisis.[21] In late 1994, Prime Minister Mokdad Sifi likewise spoke of "crisis" and "terrorism," insisting that "there is no civil war in our country."[22] Declaring victory over terrorism in early 1997, Prime Minister Ahmed Ouyahia chastised the foreign media for "calling terrorism in Algeria political violence and a violence by all sides, and from seeing terrorism in Algeria as a civil war."[23] Algeria's then ambassador to the United Nations, Abdallah Baali, likewise asserted, "We do not have a situation of civil war in Algeria," one that would warrant foreign intervention.[24] Algeria's ambassador to the United Kingdom, Ahmed Benyamina, borrowed a turn of phrase from French philosopher André Glucksmann: "there is not a civil war in Algeria but a war against civilians."[25] A change of tone seemingly occurred under President Bouteflika, who was elected in April 1999. Distancing himself from his predecessors, Bouteflika accused them of leading Algeria "to a civil war, and we are not afraid of using this expression, which led to the death of at least 100,000 Algerians. Every drop of blood adds to Algeria's strength."[26] Official Algerian documents, such as the 2005 Charte pour la Paix et la Réconciliation National, adopt the euphemism *national tragedy* instead.

As the violence escalated, Algerian civil society and opposition figures followed similar patterns in their use of the term *civil war*. "We fear a civil war is coming," a FIS supporter complained to a foreign reporter in early 1993.[27] For some, the violence could not be a civil war because of the steep asymmetry in the conflict. At the end of 1993, Saïd Sadi, a leading figure in the Kabylia-based secular opposition, asked, "Are we going to come to civil war? I hope not. All hypotheses are possible in Algeria today; nevertheless, we have not come to it. A civil war is when part of a society fights against another part of society. For the time being, one part is attacking a society which does not defend itself with arms."[28] In 1994, three years before his assassination, Abdelhak Benhamouda, secretary-general of the Union Générale des Travailleurs Algériens, Algeria's main trade union, argued that "the issue is not between Algerians, contrary to what is said by those who call for a civil war or predict civil war in Algeria, because when we say civil war this means that there is a group, social groups or social classes against other social classes, Algerian regions against other regions. This is the meaning of a civil war and we are not in a civil war."[29]

Around the same time, a letter from a young Algerian woman to friends in France began to attract attention in the French press. She expressed fears that the conflict "will soon be a full-scale Lebanese-style civil war."[30] A veteran of the Algerian war of independence expressed a similar fear to *Le Monde*: "The day is coming that will see the disintegration of the army. And at that moment, the true civil war will start. The real butchery."[31] The Rome or Sant'Egidio Platform, a framework for peace signed in January 1995 by several Algerian political parties, including the FLN and FIS, spoke of the need to avert a civil war, as if the intensity of violence or widespread participation in the fighting had not yet crossed that invisible threshold. Later that year, following a truck bombing in the Algiers suburb of Meftah, the Algerian daily *Le Matin d'Alger* ventured a comparison with Lebanon. A wire report claimed that this was the first time an Algerian paper had equated Algeria's violence with civil war.[32] Louisa Hanoune, head of Algeria's Parti des Travailleurs (Workers' Party), still rejected the term. Algeria was in not, "as they say, a civil war but a war of decomposition, disintegration of our country."[33] As the violence intensified in early 1997 in the lead-up to the April Bougara massacre, one exiled opposition leader with the FIS, Kamar Eddine Kherbane, was still hesitant to say that the situation was a civil war. "That's what I mean by being on the brink of civil war. The regime wants a civil war."[34]

The international press reflected and refracted the politics of naming Algeria's violence a civil war. Toward the end of 1993, the newspaper *Le Quotidien de Paris* expressed concern that the potential for civil war was "worsening" and so might spill over into France.[35] For the *New York Times*, there was little doubt what the situation constituted. An April 1994 editorial claimed that the events of January 1992 had "plunged [Algeria] into an abyss of terrorism and civil war with no end yet in sight."[36] Drawing direct comparisons with the 1954–1962 conflict, one of that paper's journalists saw the situation as Algeria's second civil war of the twentieth century.[37] A prominent British paper waited almost three more years to suggest that the violence had "assumed the character of a civil war."[38] It was not alone in cautiously assessing the violence as a civil war. Algeria was variously said to be "sliding toward civil war,"[39] in "the shadow of civil war,"[40] in an "undeclared civil war,"[41] near "the brink of all-out civil war,"[42] or on "the brink of open civil war."[43] The violence was "something like a civil war,"[44] "something approaching civil war,"[45] an "essentially civil war situation,"[46] a "climate of civil war,"[47] and a "civil war that does not speak its name."[48] It was a "low-grade,"[49] "de facto,"[50] "latent,"[51] and "virtual"[52] civil war. As the violence peaked in 1997, the qualifiers finally changed from cautious to denunciatory. The civil war was now "ruthless,"[53] "deadly,"[54] "raging,"[55] "brutal,"[56] "desperate,"[57] "barbarous," and "gruesome."[58] A civil war was "ravaging Algeria," "bloodying the Algerian land," and "tearing apart Algeria."[59]

Even with the noticeable increase of violence in 1993 and 1994, the opinions of foreign leaders and experts were still divided. Although the French Minister of Defense, François Léotard, spoke of the Algerian civil war as "ongoing" in December 1993,[60] President Mitterrand saw Algeria as only in "the beginnings of a civil war" in early 1994.[61] Six months later, the French president would state unambiguously that the conflict in Algeria had become a civil war.[62] A regional expert on the Clinton administration's National Security Council assessed Algeria in 1994 as "on the edge of civil war," "in the midst of a war that is civil in name only," and "hesitating between military rule and civil war," yet having undeniably suffered a "bleak degeneration into civil war."[63] Deputy Assistant Secretary of Defense Bruce Riedel cautioned the US congress in 1995 that Algeria could deteriorate into "full-scale civil war."[64] A 1996 report commissioned by the US army describes Algeria as in a state of both "virtual civil war" and "ongoing civil war."[65] Former White House official Peter Rodman described Algeria in 1995 as "on the precipice of civil war,"[66] and yet three years later, with the violence seemingly having spiraled out of control, another former US official, William Quandt, explicitly described it as a crisis, not a civil war.[67] The Clinton administration likewise never used the term during the worst of the massacres.[68] Other voices in the international community remained hesitant as well. Shortly after the violence peaked in early 1998, then UN under-secretary-general for the Department of Peacekeeping Operations, Bernard Miyet, would call the Algerian crisis only "a situation of quasi-civil war."[69]

The emerging historiography of 1990s Algeria likewise reflects the broader ambivalence about the applicability of the term *civil war*. Some studies use it with little hesitation and no argument.[70] One of the few instances of an argument being made for the applicability of the term *civil war* to Algeria's violence, Luis Martinez's *La guerre civile en Algérie* (*The Algerian Civil War*), is a telling example because of the debate it caused. Not only does this debate highlight different understandings of the conflict's most fundamental aspects, but it also points toward different understandings of the concept of civil war itself. According to this argument, the conflict in Algeria constituted a civil war for several important reasons: it was intraterritorial, the level of violence was intense (particularly by 1994), and most of all, armed actors were using violence to control territory. Hence the country's sovereignty was fractured into countless and fluctuating spaces of state and rebel control.[71] Other observers found this last premise unconvincing. Apart from the urban and semirural periphery of Algiers, where most research on the insurgency has been conducted,[72] questions were raised as to whether or not the various rebel groups ever really controlled territory in the same way the government did. The insurgency remained relatively small throughout the conflict, including its three main branches: the Mouvement (Algérien) Islamique Armé (MIA or MAIA, or the [Algerian] Armed Islamic Movement); the Groupement or Groupe Islamique Armé (GIA, or Armed Islamic Grouping or Group), which was sometimes called the Groupes Islamiques Armés (GIAs) given the lack of a clear structure, program, or leadership between the various units claiming to be the GIA; and the Armée Islamique du Salut (AIS, or Islamic Salvation Army), formed to support the FIS, largely in response to the GIA, given widespread suspicions among Islamists that the GIA had been infiltrated by Algerian military intelligence. The highest estimates of the combined strength of the Algerian insurgency suggested that there were no more than twenty-five thousand active fighters at its peak in the mid-1990s.[73] Though this figure represented a threat to Algeria's security, it nonetheless seemed to indicate a massive failure to rally popular support to the cause of re-bellion—most of all the support of the hundreds of thousands who voted for the FIS.[74] Blame for these small numbers focused on the insurgency's purported ideological and organizational incoherence, traits that led to, and reinforced, a tendency among insurgents to engage in internecine fighting.[75] For some schol-ars, these and other factors were thought to place Algeria's violence in a different category than civil war. The rebellion was a mess and it had little apparent pop-ular support.[76] And even if, to some scholars, Algeria's violence approximated a civil war, it was a qualified one—a "virtual" civil war.[77] It was also argued that, regardless of whether or not the facts on the ground warranted calling the con-flict a civil war, it was enough to know that the Algerian regime did not like or use the term. Doing so would only have hampered international efforts to end the violence through diplomacy by alienating Algiers.[78]

MAKING CIVIL WAR

This lack of consensus on Algeria's status as undergoing a civil war stands in sharp contrast to the way the conflict was treated by a particular group of ob-servers: mainly social scientists interested in civil wars as a general problem rather than in Algeria specifically. Not only was there widespread agreement among these social scientists—largely economists and political scientists—that Algeria had been in a state of civil war since 1992, but Algeria even featured as an exemplary test case.[79] The irony of this consensus was that this generalist literature lacked agreement on a formal definition of civil war. A metastudy of the civil war literature found that, depending on the criteria deployed in any given research project, the total number of civil wars ranged from fifty-eight to more than twice as many between 1960 and 1993.[80] As with the study of terror-ism,[81] this lack of consensus on a formal definition has been largely ignored in the new research on civil wars, though it has also been central to this literature's intellectual productivity since the end of the Cold War.

Though the case could be made that Algeria's violence was a strange kind of civil war, stranger still were the formal criteria used to define and measure civil wars. The baseline criteria for distinguishing civil wars from other types of mass organized violence drew heavily from a trifurcation developed dur-ing the Cold War.[82] Early efforts to create quantitative data on wars started with the assumption that they were either international, civil, or colonial, yet the boundary between colonial and civil wars was often unclear, and explicitly transgressed in some studies. Short of foreign military intervention, the other ways in which outside actors influenced civil wars was not considered a relevant correlate. Thus the illusion of civil wars' internality was maintained mostly at a conceptual level. Civil wars were distinguished from lesser forms of internal or regional armed conflict by counting the number of formal combatant deaths incurred in battle, though defining combat and combatant was easier said than done. Putting aside concern about the accuracy of casualty statistics, information on the context in which combatants actually died was typically inferred from their deaths rather than through an actual investigation of the circumstances. Combatant deaths made battles rather than vice versa. And as long as the ratio of losses between the warring parties was not too asymmetrical, it was safe to conclude that atrocities had not taken place. Civilian deaths were largely treated as inconsequential. The number of combatant deaths required to make a war had been fixed at one thousand per year of conflict, though some studies relaxed this to one thousand per conflict. Others lowered this threshold further still (as low as two hundred) or made exceptions on an *ad hoc* basis to include low-intensity civil wars that would otherwise fail to meet the baseline standards of lethality. Armed opposition groups were treated as politically coherent and militarily organized institutions simply by virtue of their ability to inflict losses on the government forces. The start and end of a civil war were often measured using a similar functional analysis based on combat deaths. The putative effects of civil war—casualties—were being used to determine its institutional characteristics. What a civil war does opens the black box of what a civil war is.[83]

How Algeria's conflict then becomes a civil war under these parameters is an even stranger process. There is little doubt that Algeria suffered more than a thousand deaths. But very little is known about the context of these deaths. Who killed whom and why? These would seem to be important facts for determining a conflict's status as a civil war; but as was just noted, most "facts" about civil wars are derived from brute fatality numbers rather than from an empirical investigation of the actual content of the violence or the stated politics of the participants. To adapt Algeria's inchoate violence to these models of civil war thus requires taking several problematic steps. Given the heavy focus on combatant losses in formalistic definitions of civil war, Algeria's conflict was not recorded as such until several years after the events of January 1992. From 1992 to 1994, Algeria was not listed in the most widely used catalogue of large-scale armed conflicts as having a civil war. It was only after the accumulation of a substantial enough number of deaths that the violence was "back coded" as a civil war starting in 1992, though other lists have pinpointed the start in the unrest of the summer of 1991.[84] An important effect of this back coding is the impact it has had on other studies. Once Algeria's violence was coded as a civil war with a start date of 1992, other studies then assumed that the conflict must have accumulated at least a thousand war-related deaths by the end of 1992.[85] That is to say, facts about the Algerian conflict were created by those who insisted on interpreting it through the civil war framework.

There are, needless to say, problems with these "facts" owing to the framework used to produce them. On the one hand, the framework largely assumes that the deaths recorded were government or rebel forces who perished in a context that could reasonably be considered combat. On the other hand, Algeria's cumulative death toll at the end of 1992 is, like most aspects of the violence, unclear. News reports and human rights groups suggest that a total of no more than six hundred, including civilians, died within the year after Bendjedid left office.[86] By mid-1993, some foreign news agencies were speculating that the violence in Algeria had garnered a thousand fatalities.[87] Other monitoring bodies concluded that Algeria had reached the magic threshold of one thousand deaths by 1994.[88] For the most part, these numbers were assumed to constitute battle or combat deaths, though basic distinctions between armed and unarmed actors, as well as the circumstances in which people were dying, were entirely absent from the data.

There is perhaps no clearer indication of the qualitative and quantitative imprecision of Algeria's fatality statistics than its most basic one—its cumulative death toll. A range of one hundred thousand to two hundred thousand is now commonly used in the media and academic literature, but with no disaggregation. Again, basic distinctions between combatant and civilian deaths, between government and opposition deaths, or among deaths within specific armed groups (AIS, GIA, and so on) and security forces (military, police, civilian militias, and so on) are absent. Table 1 illustrates the chronic imprecision and low resolution of the data used to frame Algeria's conflict as a civil war.[89] Several studies have since suggested an average of twelve hundred battle deaths per month by interpolating backward from the one hundred thousand total endorsed by Bouteflika in 1999.[90]

As the conflict intensified in the mid-1990s and became more inaccessible to outside observers, foreign monitors became less a source of primary information

Table 1. Estimates of Annual Fatalities in Algeria (1991–2001)

Year	UCDP-PRIO *Yearly Fatalities*		SIPRI Yearbook *Running Total Since 1992*	
	Low	*High*	*Low*	*High*
1991	100	100		
1992	600	600		
1993	2,400	6,000	1,700	3,000
1994	10,000	30,000	10,000	25,000
1995	6,000	12,000	25,000	45,000
1996	4,000	12,000	30,000	50,000
1997	6,000	12,000	40,000	80,000
1998	7,000	10,000	40,000	100,000
1999	3,000	3,000	40,000	100,000
2000	2,500	2,500	40,000	100,000
2001	1,650	1,650		
Total 1993–2001	**42,750**	**89,150**		

SOURCES: Lacina and Gleditsch, "Monitoring Trends in Global Combat"; SIPRI Yearbooks 1994–2001.

and more an echo chamber for speculation. As Human Rights Watch lamented four years into the conflict, "precise data was notoriously elusive on how many persons were killed, by whom and why they were targeted, owing to strict government censorship and the hazards of investigating the violence."[91] The rapid deterioration in the data can be seen in several sources. In its annual report, Human Rights Watch could only repeat government claims that it had lost two hundred members of the security forces between January and November 1992.[92] Amnesty International could add little clarity to the situation. It recorded 600 violence-related deaths during the first year of the state of emergency, including 270 government losses to the insurgency, 20 civilians killed by insurgents, and 300 civilians killed by the state.[93] The following year, Human Rights Watch tallied 100 civilian deaths, 100 security deaths, and 500 insurgent deaths from press accounts during the first nine months of 1993.[94] Citing "unofficial" sources, Amnesty International saw its aggregate fatality statistics balloon to 20,000—if not 30,000—over the course of 1994.[95] Previous efforts to disaggregate such numbers into basic victim classes fell to the wayside, as did efforts to count the dead independently of Algerian government figures. In 1996, the accepted range became 30,000 to 50,000. At the end of 1997 it was 70,000.[96] The 1997 figure can be sourced to the US State Department's annual report on human rights in Algeria, which claimed that "there were estimates" by other sources—unnamed—suggesting 70,000 deaths.[97] Since President Bouteflika endorsed the figure of 100,000 in his first term and then inexplicably doubled it in his second term, human rights monitors and the press have quickly become accustomed to using the 200,000 figure as an official and authoritative death toll for the conflict.[98]

An important effect of Bouteflika's willingness to endorse these figures was the end of the persistent foreign criticism that Algeria had been downplaying the violence of the 1990s.[99] Algerian government figures were indeed taken seriously only when they met or surpassed foreign estimates. That the government had rarely provided aggregate facts and figures at all had been part of the problem. In September 1994, for example, President Zéroual, responding to international pressure, put forward a figure of ten thousand deaths since February 1992.[100] Though this number was double the previous government figure of four thousand,[101] it was still half of what foreign human rights groups were saying. Months later, an alleged secret Algerian military report appeared in the French press. It reported 48,530 deaths over the first ten months of 1994 alone.[102] Later, an official statement from the Algerian government's human rights monitoring body, L'Observatoire National des Droits de l'Homme (ONDH, or the National Human Rights Observatory), contradicted the secret report's findings. Based on figures tallied from government statements carried in the press, ONDH gave a total of 5,029 insurgent and 1,400 civilian fatalities in 1994 and 1995.[103] Amnesty International criticized these Algerian government figures, noting that the Interior Minister had boasted of twenty thousand dead insurgents at the end of 1994.[104] As civilian massacre activity began to ramp up in late 1997, the Algerian government was facing significant pressure to account for the worsening violence and their apparent failure to control it. In this context, new official figures were provided in January 1998. Algerian authorities were now saying that a total of 26,536 civilians and security forces had been killed from 1992 through 1997. No new figure for insurgent deaths was provided.[105] Two efforts by Algerian dissidents to document the civilian massacres between 1993 and 2002 can account for only some 7,500 to 8,000 deaths.[106]

When President Bouteflika endorsed the widely circulated figure of 100,000 dead, he received praise internationally and criticism domestically.[107] International human rights NGOs had been using the 100,000 figure for several years, whereas previous official Algerian figures had been one-quarter[108] to one-third[109] as much. The outlawed opposition had been using a similar figure of 120,000,[110] though one of Algeria's independent human rights groups had already suggested

190,000 deaths by late 1996.[111] Bouteflika's endorsement, whether accurate or not, appeased many foreign actors but did little to end the politics of numbers inside Algeria. Early 2001 saw another alleged secret military report appear in the French press; it reported 9,006 losses in the year 2000 alone. This number included 1,025 insurgents, 603 government forces, and 117 civilian militia members. If true, these numbers would have made the year 2000—the first full year of Bouteflika's tenure and of his signature national reconciliation policies—one of the deadliest of the conflict. Such figures would then call into question the efficacy of Bouteflika's peacemaking initiatives, notably the insurgent amnesty programs enacted in the 1999 Concorde Civile.[112] If it seemed that elements of the regime were inflating perceptions of the violence in order to undermine Bouteflika's positions, others continued to downplay it. General Abderrazak Maïza, head of the country's primary military command, told an audience at an international conference on counterterrorism that only thirty-seven thousand lives had been lost to the violence between 1992 and 2000. Forty percent were insurgents.[113] Maïzia was pressed on the discrepancy between the president's figures and his. He replied, "100,000 dead, that's a political number. [. . .] As for me, I have the names."[114]

Algerian peace initiatives like the 1999 Concorde Civile and the 2005 Charte pour la Paix et la Réconciliation Nationale have done little to clarify these numbers. During the implementation phase of the latter in early 2006, the government's human rights body, La Commission Nationale Consultative de Promotion et de Protection des Droits de l'Homme (CNCPPDH, or National Consultative Commission for the Promotion and Protection of Human Rights), successor to the ONDH, raised the official death toll from 150,000 to 200,000.[115] The government later recognized its responsibility for 17,000 insurgent deaths[116] and 6,154 instances of civilians "disappeared" by state actors.[117] The latter figure was initially taken from dossiers submitted by domestic human rights groups, mainly the work of SOS Disparu(e)s, an association representing families of the "disappeared." But the figure 6,154 fell short of the figures circulated by international human rights groups, which suggested as many as 12,000 state-sponsored "disappearences."[118] The official number of state-sponsored disappearances later grew to 8,024 when additional petitions for compensation were allowed; as always, there appeared to be no actual investigation into these additional cases.[119]

Though the Algerian state had ostensibly been fighting a war on terror, the victims of nonstate terrorism ironically had a far more difficult time seeking recognition and compensation than the victims of state terrorism. Without official documentation of their victimization (such as police, municipal, or military reports), the direct and indirect victims of the insurgency faced an uphill battle against the state's Byzantine bureaucracy. By 2010, the government had received some fifty thousand applications for compensation from the victims of the rebel groups; half of these were recognized as legitimate under the laws of the 2005 Charte pour la Paix et la Réconciliation Nationale.[120] Families of insurgents killed by state agents were also allowed to seek compensation; some seventeen thousand deaths—a figure close to Maïza's 2002 claim—were recognized. What this assessment did not take into account was deaths from internecine fighting between and within insurgent groups. Just as in the 1954–1962 war, the number of deaths related to this kind of warfare is one of the most opaque aspects of Algeria's *décennie noire*. Whether or not the compensation was sufficient to overcome the stigma of having family members in the insurgency is unclear enough to suggest that these figures could be underreported as well. Though estimates suggest that an equal number of persons were "disappeared" by the insurgency (four to ten thousand), these cases apparently have been treated as ongoing and unsolved kidnappings.[121] How all of this adds up to the commonly cited 100,000, 150,000, or even 200,000 deaths has yet to be accounted for by either the Algerian government or the community of scholars who allegedly specialize in civil war violence.

THE USES OF CIVIL WAR

The end of the Cold War saw the emergence of a new kind of war. It emerged within a number of sciences trying to understand, and so manage, mass violence within a post-ideological framework. This understanding borrowed extensively from a well-established taxonomy that trifurcated wars into the categories *international, civil,* and *colonial.* But the scientific efforts of the 1990s and 2000s represented a new push to elaborate an intrinsic understanding of civil war's initial causes and sustaining dynamics. Internal armed conflicts were no longer understood in relation to the global politics of the Cold War, as proxy sites of the US-USSR contest. These new civil wars were understood within a neoliberal framework, as a problem of development. Civil wars as "development in reverse" problematized armed conflicts as domestic and economic issues.[122] Civil wars were not, as previously understood, inherently political and international phenomena. The major findings of this research agenda suggested that ethnic, religious, and ideological grievances were negligible. The more powerful forces were the ones conditioning the motive and opportunity for a rebellion to take shape, especially economic forces.[123] An analysis of the international political economy of civil wars—one that would question the utility of understanding these conflicts as internal—was entirely absent. By framing civil wars in this way, this research paradigm suggested that the kinds of technoscientific expertise needed to understand and manage civil wars would be found not in diplomacy and peacekeeping but in development economics.[124]

The conflict in 1990s Algeria becomes one of these civil wars because of what it is not, not because of what it is. What produces this conflict as a civil war, more than the violence itself, is the ternary schema of international, civil, and colonial wars that is still in use today. Coupled with the sheer volume of killing, this schema is what makes Algeria's violence a civil war. The essentials to understanding a civil war—the spaces of terror and safety; the identities and motives of those who killed, were killed, or survived; as well as the myriad forces acting on all of these elements—have simply been subordinated to the schema. These essentials, like the civil war object itself, are made by the schema. Understanding the conflict in Algeria as a civil war has allowed social scientists to determine the conflict's causation (see the following chapter) in much the same way as calling it a civil war has allowed others to render the "logics" of its violence (see Chapters 3 and 4).

Not only are the civil wars of today robbed of their politics by the illusion of internality, but the actual politics of their causes and evolving violence are negated and supplanted as well. The alleged antipolitics of naming a conflict a *civil war* is the capacity of that name to disable foreign intervention. But the politics of naming Algeria's violence *civil war* elucidates a different set of antipolitical features inherent to the new understandings of armed conflict that emerged after the Cold War. The most important feature is the tendency to understand and manage civil wars as discrete, isolated political objects in which questions of geopolitical power matter little, if at all. This is not to say that a more internationalized understanding of civil wars would produce a more coherent object of analysis and therefore a more politically manageable object. Nor is it to suggest that the main problem with today's highly internalized understandings of civil war is that they are insufficient understandings and therefore produce bad social science and even worse policy. Rather, it is to say that today's understandings of civil war—whether right or wrong—and today's major approaches to managing civil wars—whether helpful or not—are part of the imaginative and performative constitution of the antipolitics of contemporary conflict management and science.

Slimane El Ghoul and his group: veterans of the 1954–1962 war join a younger generation of *patriotes* in a self-defense militia. Crude weapons (swords and knives) from captured and killed "terrorists" are proudly displayed in front of the group. Photograph by Kader B. Courtesy of the *El Watan* archive, Algiers.

2 GREED AND GRIEVANCE

Political and Economic Agendas in Civil War—
Theirs and Ours

THE HISTORY OF MODERN WARFARE in Algeria has been useful to a variety of understandings and approaches to managing conflict. Early French suppression of Algerian resistance in the 1800s provided important case studies in the formation of small wars doctrine in late British imperialism and early US imperialism. The 1954–1962 French-Algerian war became an invaluable source of lessons guiding the geopolitics of confronting Communism.[1] These lessons have since fed into today's doctrines of counterinsurgency, deployed in Iraq (2007–2009) and then Afghanistan (2009 onward).[2] The purported lessons of 1990s Algeria quickly became a reliable source of information for global counterterrorism doctrines, especially after 9/11. The lessons of Algeria's *décennie noire* could also be found in academic and policy debates about how to understand and manage the Arab and Islamic worlds after the Cold War and then 9/11.[3]

The Arab Spring was no different. Algeria seemed to hold lessons for the 2011 overthrow of the Tunisian and Egyptian presidents; the civil wars in Libya and Syria; the significant protests in Western Sahara, Morocco, Yemen, and Bahrain; as well as the notable demonstrations in at least a half-dozen other Arab states.[4] Attention to what had happened in Algeria in the late 1980s was renewed, as were questions about the relationship between Algeria's October 1988 protests, the reforms instituted after those protests, the violence seemingly triggered by the regime's unwillingness to see an Islamist party take power in 1992 via those reforms, and the mass terror that followed. Central to this trope, yet unstated, was a politics of naming the causes of Algeria's violence: either the Algerian government had caused the violence of the 1990s by suspending the democratic transition, or the Islamist opposition had caused it by exploiting a democratic opening to advance a covertly antidemocratic agenda. The apparent parallels with Egypt in 2013, when the military ousted the democratically elected government of the Muslim Brotherhood, were too profound to ignore.[5] A politics of comparison likewise emerged: Algeria was Egypt's fate or Algeria was nothing like Egypt.[6]

But for there to be any lessons from Algeria would first mean producing or recirculating a narrative of the Algerian conflict, particularly a story about its causes. Just as there was a politics of naming Algeria's conflict a civil war, there was similarly a politics of naming its proximate, ultimate, permissive, underlying, necessary, and sufficient causes. Not only were there debates between those privileging political interpretations over economic interpretations of the violence (and vice versa), but there were also debates within these two camps over the moments or conditions, as well as the agencies and ideas, that mattered most and those that did not matter at all.

Political interpretations read the warfare of 1990s Algeria in Clausewitzian terms, that is, the resort to violence was understood as the continuation of politics by other means. In this sense, the violence in 1990s Algeria was read as an extension of the institutional nature of the two main participants, the regime and the Islamists. Political interpretations of Algeria's violence thus essentially held that where there is a will, there is a way. That is, to understand the violence of the 1990s, one had to understand the motives of the main actors behind it. The task of political interpretations of Algeria's violence was to elaborate a compelling story about the formation of those wills, motives, and grievances such that the story could then account for the bloodshed that followed. This is how the events of January 1992 became paramount in political interpretations of Algeria's violence: only the denial of democracy or the safeguarding of the republic could constitute both the scientific *casus belli* (cause of war) and the normative *jus ad bellum* (justification of war) behind the horrific violence that followed.

Economic interpretations of Algeria's violence were much less interested in the conflict's trigger event. They instead explored the warfare's Malthusian aspects: how the violence was created and conditioned by the scarcities and competitions produced by Algeria's hydrocarbon wealth; local, regional, and national struggles over resources and the instruments of resource distribution; and the inherent greed of armed actors, whether regime elites, the insurgents opposing them, or private actors taking advantage of the chaos. In one important way, economic interpretations inverted political ones: where there is a way, there is a will. The idea that the will to violence in Algeria had been produced by the conditions that allowed and even incentivized violence (such as financial decline, monetary turbulence, collapse of the welfare state, and even the post-independence baby boom) elicited cries of economic determinism, most often from defenders of political interpretations of the violence. But political understandings of the violence were likewise guided by deterministic think-ing: the solution to Algeria's woes—restoration of a multiparty constitutional democracy—had produced a simplistic understanding of the conflict's cause—the suspension of multiparty constitutional democracy. In other words, nor-mative assumptions about the proper form and function of government were driving interpretations of the violence's roots.

In many ways, this debate about the deep and superficial causes of Algeria's violence anticipated and embodied a major research agenda in the conflict sci-ences after the Cold War. This agenda emerged as more and more research on mass armed violence was subjected to statistically driven analysis of quantified data comparing dozens of civil wars since 1945. Widespread claims that the wars of the 1990s were new kinds of wars and, more important, were driven by erup-tions of ancient ethnoreligious hatreds, if not larger civilizational differences, that the Cold War had suppressed, subordinated, or otherwise repurposed, were the foil for this new civil war research agenda. Leading the charge against the identity thesis and claims of "new wars" were economists and like-minded polit-ical scientists. Their agenda began with framing civil war etiology as a question of agent-level motivations versus structural forces. Early studies in this agenda found little reason to believe that agent-level grievances articulated in terms of religion, ethnicity, or political ideology were important factors in a civil war's inception, whereas stronger correlations manifested as structural factors (such as primary export commodities, population size, or geography). For these cor-relations to have any causal plausibility, they nonetheless had to be interpreted in such a way as to explain agent-level action. The only agents that needed to be explained were a conflict's rebels, because in this research agenda the problem of civil war causation had been understood *a priori* to be a simple problem of rebellion. An even deeper assumption about the ultimately selfish nature of ra-tional human behavior allowed such greed-based interpretations of rebel moti-vation to gain currency. To understand the causes of civil war was to understand the resources that fed the selfish motives of those who rebelled against authority.

Like their political counterparts, economic accounts of civil war etiology are haunted by normative assumptions. Critics of neoclassical economics have long tracked the early neoliberal ideological agenda that both predates and continues to influence the now pervasive rational choice understanding of human behavior as inherently and irrevocably individualistic and selfish. That is to say, a particular vision of how humans ought to behave has become a widely accepted scientific assumption about actual human psychology. This assumption now underwrites a vast array of governmental policies, from economics to military strategy.[7] Causal accounts of rebel behavior in civil war are thus arrived at through structural correlations interpreted through ontological and political assumptions rather than through any kind of ethnographic appreciation of the actual people engaged in the fight. Even more pertinent is the problematization of civil wars as rebellions, which implicitly vindicates state power (and all of the violence associated with it) while treating rebels as the vector through which the disease of civil war plagues economic development. To view the problem of civil wars as a problem of rebellion unduly obscures the complicity of states in the generation of civil wars when in fact such agency is amply demonstrated by the Algerian regime in the crisis of 1992, from its escalation to its appalling aftermath.

Whether or not political and economic interpretations correctly diagnosed the Algerian polity's core ailment was put into question by the violence's stubborn resistance to outside political and economic interventions. International diplomatic and financial engagement had little apparent effect on the levels of killing in Algeria. The paradox of violence in 1990s Algeria was the increasing disarticulation of the localized warfare from the political and economic picture at the national level. The financial and governmental rehabilitation of the Algerian state from 1995 onward tracks with an intensification of the violence, which became more and more difficult for outside observers to interpret through established political and economic frameworks of understanding. The degradation of these frameworks' explanatory capacity is one of several conditions that allowed other understandings to assert themselves. It is also one of the conditions that simultaneously enabled the internationalization of the conflict while disabling the possibility of any meaningful humanitarian intervention stopping the atrocities and protecting civilians.

THE *JUS AD BELLUM* OF A *CASUS BELLI*

Political and economic interpretations of the violence in 1990s Algeria are often presented as mutually exclusive. Those favoring the former have leveled allegations of "economic determinism" against the latter.[8] A key moment in political framings of Algeria's violence is October 1988, when widespread protests brought the country to a standstill and were repressed by Algeria's security forces. These disturbances appeared to erupt on October 4, reportedly in response to new government austerity measures. Demonstrations continued for several days and spread from the capital throughout the country. Local and national police forces seemed incapable of managing the protests. So, on October 8, soldiers from the army fired on crowds in several major cities. Nearly a week later, the unofficial death toll was suspected to be two hundred and more than thirty-seven hundred had been detained. Reacting to the turmoil, President Bendjedid announced plans for reform and won a third term in December. A new constitution secured passage by popular referendum in February 1989. Nearly fifty political parties quickly formed. Among them was the FIS, which coalesced in March 1989 to unite several Islamist tendencies. Exiles returned, new media outlets were born, and civil society entered a stage of florescence. Social discontent continued to express itself, however, in reports of small-scale demonstrations, strikes, and riots across the country throughout the transitional years of 1989 to 1992.[9]

Not only have the October 1988 riots become a kind of year zero in the history of Algeria's *décennie noire*, but they can also be seen as a decisive moment in the contest between economic and political understandings of the crisis of the late 1980s and the mass violence that soon followed. The widely reported economic nature of the protests has been challenged on several grounds, notably the rhetoric of the protestors and their response to the kinds of concessions the government made. Analysis of the language used in October 1988 suggests a population whose anger is directed entirely at leaders in the government, particularly the president. It might seem natural for a population to articulate economic grievances in political language to a government such as Algeria's, which exerted overwhelming control over the economy via its socialization in the 1970s and its privatization in the 1980s. This anger was dramatically assuaged, it seems, when on October 10 the president announced sweeping political reforms, though no economic concessions were included.[10] But an important fact bears mention: the state's willingness to fire live ammunition into crowds of protestors, as was done in downtown Algiers just hours before Bendjedid made his announcement. By the end of the protests, which lasted from October 4 to October 10, the official death toll was put at 150; unofficial sources claimed as many as 500 deaths, most resulting from the army's indiscriminate firing at protesters.[11] The significance of October 1988 might lie in the violence itself— the symbolic violence of the population rising up *en masse* against the state, and the physical violence leveled against them by the security forces. More than any other moment in Algeria's history since 1962, this one demanded interpretation. What caused October 1988 was October 1988.

October 1988 is also significant because it ostensibly set in motion the chain of events that led to January 1992. Political understandings of Algeria's violence now widely treat the January 1992 "coup" as the proximate cause of the warfare that ensued. That is, the rest of the conflict followed from January 1992, but the importance of that month was not given at the time; rather, it was formulated by the violence's primary stakeholders in the crucible of the subsequent conflict. As the violence grew, so did the importance of January 1992. At the time, Bendjedid's resignation and the constitutional crisis it triggered was far from extraordinary given the already extraordinary times in which Algerians were living. In the months leading up to the January "coup," Algeria had already witnessed conflict between the regime, its supporters, and the opposition, particularly those who were supporting the FIS.

The road to Algeria's *décennie noire* has many contested inflection points from October 1988 onward.[12] One of those points, Algeria's first multiparty local elections, occurred on June 12, 1990. This vote saw a turnout of 60 percent, with the FIS grabbing more than half of the municipalities (853 of 1,535) and two thirds of the forty-eight provinces up for grabs. The Front de Libération Nationale (FLN, or National Liberation Front), which had governed Algeria since its independence began in 1962, came in second, winning 487 councils and fourteen provinces.[13] Elections for the national legislature were announced in April 1991 and scheduled for June 27. At the end of May, with no clear timetable for presidential elections and the promulgation of a new set of controversial election laws, the FIS called for a general strike. When confrontations with security forces resulted in the death of several protestors, the government postponed the legislative elections and instituted a state of emergency on June 5. After temporarily suspending the strike, the FIS supported new demonstrations, renewing its demands for timely legislative and presidential elections. Scores died in the June clashes and several hundred were detained, though the FIS and rights groups claimed several thousand among the latter. The government began cracking down on the FIS leadership when Abassi Madani, then leader of the party, reportedly articulated the need for a *jihad* during a speech that month.[14] The military quickly seized the party's headquarters and, on June 30, arrested Madani and his deputy, Ali Benhadj, followed soon by Mohammed Saïd, the FIS spokesperson. Madani and Benhadj received twelve-year prison sentences in July, and the French and Arabic newspapers of the FIS were shut down in August. Interim FIS head Abdelkader Hachani was detained in September, though he was released in October and Saïd was released the following month. Though the state of emergency was lifted in late September, government repression of the FIS continued: officials were arrested, publications were shut down, and offices were raided. At the end of October, Bendjedid announced a new date for the national legislative elections: December 26. Even with Madani and Benhadj still in jail, the FIS remained committed to participating. Supporters of the FIS were able to stage a rally of some one hundred thousand people in the run-up to the vote. A week after the vote, just as many Algerians marched on January 2, calling on their government to cancel the second round of elections.[15]

As they had in the 1990 municipal and provincial elections,[16] the FIS dominated the first round of the December 1991 national elections, winning 188 out of 430 seats. The Front des Forces Socialistes, a secular party with strong support in the Kabylia, and the FLN came in second and third, respectively. With official figures suggesting unenthusiastic voter turnout at roughly 60 percent, the FIS's victory had been achieved despite managing to garner support from only a quarter of the electorate. Reports of fraud and irregularities put upwards of 30 percent of those seats in question.[17] The runoff for the 199 undecided seats was scheduled for January 16. A sense of panic began to set in. Fears began to accumulate that the FIS would use its power to advance a conservative social agenda, if not rewrite the constitution to guarantee its control in perpetuity. Everything now depended on whether or not the secular opposition could rally its supporters in the second round of voting. Unwilling to leave the fate of the republic in the hands of democracy, the regime began to act. President Bendjedid dissolved the legislature on January 4, and then resigned on January 11. The dissolution of the parliament had the effect of disrupting the chain of succession laid out in the 1989 constitution. Last in line, Abdelmalek Benhabilès, head of the Constitutional Council, refused to assume the presidency.

Waiting to fill this vacuum were powerful members of Algeria's security apparatus. The army had already deployed throughout the country at least three days ahead of Bendjedid's resignation.[18] A six-member *ad hoc* body, the Haut Conseil de Sécurité (HCS, or High Security Council), took the reins of government on January 12.[19] Their first move was to cancel further elections, both legislative and presidential. The HCS became the Haut Comité d'État (HCE, or High State Council) on January 14. Algeria's Supreme Court approved these measures, providing its imprimatur two days later. That same day, the chair of the HCE—Mohamed Boudiaf—arrived. As one of the original founding leaders of the FLN, Boudiaf's revolutionary credentials were impeccable and untarnished by the postcolonial regime as he had lived in exile in Morocco for most of Algeria's independence. Boudiaf's term as chair of the Council was supposed to last until the end of Bendjedid's third mandate in December 1993.[20] Instead, Boudiaf died in a hail of gunfire less than six months after returning to his homeland.

Prior to Boudiaf's assassination, the remaining top FIS leadership, including Hachani and Rabah Kébir, were arrested in late January. Following violent demonstrations in early February, the HCE enacted a state of emergency that remained in place for nearly two decades. It essentially banned public gatherings and instituted a curfew. This transitional regime also created prison camps in the Saharan interior that housed FIS members and other detained Islamists; several thousand people, perhaps as many as twenty thousand, circulated through these camps in the early 1990s. In March and April 1992, the regime then outlawed the FIS and dissolved all of the localities that had been under its control since 1990. By the time Boudiaf was assassinated in June 1992, dozens of civilians, security forces, and armed opposition fighters had died in the escalating violence. A year later, hundreds of deaths were reported. The end of the decade would see the arbitrary figure of one hundred thousand dead receive widespread support, notably from President Bouteflika.

As that conflict evolved, so did the explanatory power afforded to the events of January 1992 in political framings of the violence. How January 1992 came to be seen as the conflict's most decisive period is difficult to understand. The violence in Algeria did not escalate for some time. Before January 1992, most acts of armed violence had been limited to confrontations—sometimes deadly— between protestors and security forces. This pattern continued during the first two months of 1992, with as many as 103 deaths reported in such incidents.[21] Significant acts of antiregime violence were relatively rare in 1992 when compared to the far bloodier years of 1993 and especially 1994. The two most infamous episodes in 1992 were a raid on the Port of Algiers (February 13, 1992), which allegedly signaled the birth of the insurgency, and a bombing at the Algiers airport (August 26, 1992), which indicated a willingness to attack so-called soft targets. Violent interactions between government forces and armed groups were otherwise sparse in 1992—on average, fewer than one per week. By the end of the year, estimates of the number of casualties ranged from 130 to 350.[22] Viewed as a rate of intentional homicide, even a total of 500 casualties in 1992 would not have put Algeria among the twenty most murderous countries worldwide. A state with Algeria's capacity, though arguably degraded at that time, should have been quite capable of managing the violence in 1992 as a simple policing matter. Casualty reports increased dramatically in 1993 and then skyrocketed in 1994. Foreign governments felt that the Algerian state was most threatened by the insurgency two to three years after the HCE took power.

The etiological role assigned to January 1992 is strange for another reason. Armed rebel groups did not appear *ex nihilo* after the installation of the HCE.[23] The HCE took power in a context of increasing insurgent activity. One group in particular—an Algerian version of al-Takfir wa al-Hijrah—drew its inspiration from a similarly named Egyptian organization. These militants had reportedly been advocating armed resistance against the FLN regime since the inception of their organization in the mid-1970s. In the late 1980s, it was often portrayed as the natural home for Algerians returning from the battlefields of Afghanistan in the recently concluded US proxy war against the Soviet occupation. This group was also seen as a key instigator of the small acts of violence—murders, property destruction, riots—that added much to the tension felt between 1988 and 1992. These acts were against the state, society, and fellow Islamists. Moreover, members of the ill-fated 1982–1987 Islamist rebellion of Mustapha Bouyali allegedly reconstituted the Mouvement (Algérien) Islamique Armé as early as January 1991.[24] In June 1991, the Algerian government claimed to have discovered arms caches in mosques around the country.[25] Several months later, in late November, an armed group attacked a military outpost, killing three soldiers, near Guemar in the eastern El-Oued province. In media reports, both the MIA and al-Takfir wa al-Hijrah were blamed for the incident. Khaled Nezzar, then Defense Minister, took the opportunity to link the incident to the FIS.[26] In retrospect, these insinuations were somewhat ironic. Subsequent disclosures, including some from Nezzar, revealed that Algeria's military, intelligence, and security forces had already developed a counterinsurgency strategy well before the events of January 1992. This strategy's goal was to sow confusion and discord among the Islamists' ranks so as to radicalize them. Undercover agents and "turned" militants were already embedded in the Islamist opposition's political and armed movements. A divided and radicalized opposition—one under close state surveillance from the inside—would be easier to manipulate and discredit.[27]

Political readings of the violence in 1990s Algeria imbued the events of January 1992 with paramount causal significance. This significance was not historically given because the events' counterfactual efficacy is contested and contestable on a number of grounds.[28] Given the low levels of violence recorded in 1992, the conflict was neither inevitable nor inexorable following the installation of the HCE or the outlawing of the FIS.[29] Only when the events of January 1992 are taken out of context and disarticulated from the chain of contingencies that produced and followed them do these developments seem paramount to those political actors who think they are and to those political accounts that take their cue from them. The only way to explain the potency of January 1992 is to understand the power of the normative assumptions driving political interpretations of the violence. These assumptions are based on a political imagination that can imagine only one form of good government—the liberal model of representative democracy.

HOGRA METRICS

An economic approach to understanding the conflict in Algeria, and so to managing it, was frequently said to yield more insights than an approach focused on the ostensible politics of the fighting. As one study argued, it was wrong to adopt "the view that the conflict is an Islamist-military war that was the mere consequence of the interruption of the 1991 election process to keep the Islamists from power." Instead, "the facts that the crisis is inherently economic and that the initial rise of Islamism, as well as the suspension of the political process, are themselves the result of economic collapse, has largely been ignored. This suggests that resolving Algeria's crisis effectively requires new thinking and a new approach."[30] Economic readings of Algeria's violence posit a far different year zero than the political ones. Economic year zero in Algeria's violence is the financial crisis of the 1980s, specifically the 1986 collapse of global hydrocarbon prices.[31] Following a peak in 1980, the price of oil began to decline. It hit a plateau of roughly thirty dollars per barrel (unadjusted) between 1983 and 1985. It then plummeted in 1986 to half the previous year's average price. The Algerian state had derived between half to two-thirds of its budget from petroleum exports since 1974. It thus faced an insurmountable shortfall in 1986. Coupled with a weakened US dollar, the oil price collapse saw an 80 percent decline in foreign exchange earnings for Algiers.[32] To help make up for the loss, the government reduced imports and increased taxes and foreign borrowing. The ratio of export earnings to debt payments more than doubled between 1985 and 1993. At its 1988 peak, the debt service ratio was 86 percent. As a whole, Algeria experienced negative or marginal economic growth between 1986 and 1994; some areas outside the hydrocarbon sector continued to experience significant contraction through 1997.[33]

Economic framings of the violence that followed Algeria's financial downturn in the late 1980s were a natural outgrowth of the ways in which many had come to understand the mechanics of power in Algeria. New research interest in the state as a unique institutional actor in the early 1980s contributed to new understandings of the international political economy of rule based on export dependency.[34]

This understanding saw the state's acquisition and distribution of rents, particularly hydrocarbon revenue, as key to understanding the paradox of plenty and the durability of authoritarianism in a variety of countries.[35] The simplest version of this thesis simply flips the liberal political contract on its head: because the state does not need to tax its citizenry to obtain revenue, the state does not need to be governed by representatives of its citizenry. Government spending then supplements coercion as the other tool through which social conflict is regulated. One of the appealing aspects of rentier theory was the way in which it could account for the alleged lack of democracy in North Africa and Southwest Asia without reference to culture or religion. A geographical curse—oil—was to blame.

Elegant accounts of Algeria's descent into mass violence easily flowed from such theories. The Algerian regime's ability to govern had rested on a capacity to appease the population through public spending on employment, services, and goods, among others. With the oil price collapse compounding an already troubled economic picture, these techniques of rule were no longer sustainable. Making matters worse, the initial response of Bendjedid's administration was to place further burdens on an already stressed population. Taxes increased and imports were restricted, resulting in inflation. Unpopular austerity policies were adopted. These largely targeted the masses with little to no income. By contrast, the top 10 percent of Algerians by wealth remained largely untouched by such austerity measures.[36] Not only had the FLN state lost much of its limited capacity to govern, but it was also losing what was left of its legitimacy.

Efforts to account for Algeria's violence within an economic framework subsumed politics in other ways as well. New economic understandings of civil conflict often consider such periods of weakened state capacity as conducive to the outbreak of warfare. There are both political and military aspects to this argument. Politically, states occupying the zone between dictatorship and democracy seem to be more susceptible to armed conflict than states at the authoritarian or democratic ends of the spectrum. Potential rebels see such periods as the most opportune times to strike: the state is at its weakest, as are electoral processes, which fail to regulate conflict within the polity nonviolently.[37] Algeria from 1988 to 1992 seemed to fit this story all too well by sending mixed signals. Civil, social, and cultural freedoms were at their zenith; there was an explosion of new political parties; but the state was also attempting to control, subvert, and suppress the opposition, particularly the FIS in 1991. These developments become effects of economic phenomena in that they are interpreted signs of a rentier state in financial disarray.[38]

Framing Algeria's violence in economic terms also required mapping the effects of this macro-level financial crisis onto the realities of life at the micro level. It was, as it were, an effort to put numbers to the thing Algerians call *hogra*—the attitude of contempt and policies of dispossession that the elite continually exercise against the masses.[39] Central to *hogra* was widespread unemployment. Employment, a central tool of government according to rentier theory, became difficult for the Algerian state to regulate, or even create, as the financial crisis deepened in the late 1980s. Unemployment nearly quadrupled between 1985 and 1993.[40] A third of the labor force found itself out of a job by 1991.[41] Throughout the 1990s and early 2000s, employment failed to reach the early 1980s' high-water mark of 16.2 percent. Across the board, wages decreased from the mid-1980s through the 1990s. The public sector, accounting for 64 percent of the formal workforce, saw decreases in salaries of sometimes more than 30 percent by 1996.[42] In 1992, 15 percent of the population was listed as having no source of income.[43] Adding to this stress, inflation skyrocketed beyond Depression-era rates, from 11 percent in 1986 to 30 percent in 1992.[44] Leading up to the October 1988 riots, food prices increased 40 percent from the beginning of that year.[45]

Economic accounts also reduced issues of security to a function of finance. In general, economic theories of civil violence often suggest that states with poor economies also have poor security capacities, creating further opportunity for armed rebellion. Despite the financial crisis, the Algerian security apparatus was, on paper at least, still formidable during the transitional period and first years of the violence. This formidability, though, depended on the comparison being made. The military's budget was relatively low in 1992, at 3 percent of GDP. Praetorian regimes like Syria and Iraq, by comparison, spent 10 to 20 percent of GDP on security. Southwest Asian rentier states like Saudi Arabia simply made Algeria look relatively poor. But in comparison to its Maghrib neighbors, Tunisia and Morocco, countries that seemed immune to mass armed conflict, Algeria was relatively prosperous, had better infrastructure, and could field one of the region's best militaries—again, on paper—at the beginning of the violence.[46] To make the theory work, questions then had to be raised as to whether it was a matter of military quality, not quantity. That is, Algeria had a large conventional army, but one ill-suited to the kind of irregular warfare necessary to fight both an urban and a rural insurgency.[47] It should also be noted that, as in most economic framings of civil conflict, causal agency is afforded entirely to the rebellion, with the state's forces playing a passive role in the genesis of violence.

Economic interpretations not only offered a passive account of the Algerian state's dysfunction, they also purported to explain the origins of rebel motivations and resources, if not the rebel bodies themselves. First, the economic production of rebel subjectivities draws from a potential pool of recruits produced by Algeria's post-independence economic boom. Between 1962 and 1982, Algerians nearly doubled their number to twenty million, driven by one of the world's highest birthrates in the 1970s. An effect of this increase was a disproportionately large youth segment. A census conducted the year before the 1988 riots found that more than two thirds of Algerians were under age thirty.[48] Within this group, nearly 90 percent were unemployed in 1992. Algeria also experienced an increase in household size as construction slowed, with an average of three Algerians per bedroom in 1992. At the height of the conflict, Algeria had one of the highest household densities in the world.[49] The gender balance of Algeria's youth bulge was tilted slightly toward males, who tended to favor younger spouses. The birthrate peaked in 1970; in 1988 an eighteen-year-old male was said to be facing a diminishing pool of younger potential mates. His chances of finding a job and housing—both often considered prerequisites for marriage—were significantly constrained by unemployment, inflation, and the lack of housing.[50]

Second, economic conditions allegedly provided the wherewithal to sustain rebellion. Informal, parallel, and illegal markets were treated as signs of corruption, of authoritarianism, or of a failed or failing socialist state. The Algerian state's haphazard effort to privatize its assets and markets in the 1980s followed various experiments in a centrally planned economy in the 1970s.[51] In this context, the unofficial economy had become a major source of funding for clandestine political interests and, later, insurgent activity. Before January 1992, 15 percent of the GDP could be sourced to the black market, and upwards of half of the country's cash was circulating within it.[52] Other figures suggested that the Algerian black market accounted for as much as 70 percent of GDP by the late 1980s.[53] Accounts of rebel groups manipulating the black market to fund their activities are not difficult to find.[54] Nor is it difficult to find insinuations that hybridized private-public "mafias" have played an equal, if not greater, role in the evolution of the shadow economy.[55] Though it is difficult to see how it could constitute an incentive for armed rebellion, black marketeering's participation in a "conflict-poverty trap," once catalyzed by armed fighting, was easily sketched out.[56]

Overall, economic accounts of Algeria's violence exhibited and enacted the antipolitics of neoliberal approaches to understanding and managing warfare after the Cold War. At one level, accusations of economic determinism were warranted, though for different reasons than usually suspected. Typically cited was an unhealthy bias toward economic factors over sociocultural, geographical, and political ones. Yet all science is reductionistic by nature, and economics tends to be more ruthless in its parsimony than history and politics. Economic theories of late warfare were deterministic at two levels: the paradoxical role assigned to motivation and the methodological reduction of war to a problem of rebellion.

Prevailing economic understandings of late warfare were paradoxically uninterested in the actual dynamic motives of rebels, yet these economic theories depended on a static understanding of human motivation as inherently selfish. They dismissed the ways in which rebels articulated their motives as mere rhetoric.[57] At another level, rebel motives in the abstract were critical to accounting for rebellion: to understand a rebellion is to understand that "no profitable opportunity for violence would go unused."[58] What rebels say is allegedly propaganda; what they do in reality is, apparently, to advance their petty self-interest through armed struggle. Economic understandings of late warfare attempted to reconstruct the social, economic, political, and geographical environments in which an omnipresent desire for selfish advancement could be actualized. If the "way" could be plausibly established, the "will" would follow. While real rebel motivations were rendered statistically insignificant, theoretical understandings of human motivation as inherently Machiavellian were central to making these understandings convincing.[59]

Another way in which understandings of warfare after the Cold War stripped away politics from armed conflict was to reduce the problem of war to a problem of rebellion. The dismissal of actual rebel discourse is matched by another key *a priori* assumption: states are assigned a secondary or reactionary role in the generation of late warfare. Reducing the problem of civil wars to a problem of rebellion further strips away the politics of the violence. It also implicitly takes sides in the politics of naming causation, insofar as states, such as Algeria, are vindicated and rebels, such as the FIS, are held responsible. After all, the Algerian officials who took control in January 1992 often insisted that the state faced an existential threat. As much was claimed by Nezzar during his testimony in a French court in 2002 in which he defended the actions of HCE, describing himself as a leading figure (see Chapter 6).[60] Nezzar's lawyer during that trial defended his client's actions in these terms: "It was that or Afghanistan. The Islamist savages put the republic in danger."[61] Former Prime Minister Sid Ahmed Ghozali, who served on the HCE, testified likewise in 2002: "To allow the Islamists to take power was to allow the fall of Algeria."[62] In May 1992, the then head of counterintelligence, Colonel Smaïn Lamari, reportedly told his deputies, "I am ready and determined to eliminate three million Algerians if necessary to maintain the order that the Islamists threaten."[63] Luis Martinez, in his study of the early insurgency, concluded, "The choice of civil war [was] made by the military leadership in January 1992."[64]

Even if we abandon January 1992 as the official start date of the conflict, it is worth considering whether or not the calls to jihad and small acts of terrorism attributed to Islamists throughout 1991 and 1992 provided the Algerian regime—then under threat from a multisided coalition demanding significant economic and political reform—with a "profitable opportunity for violence." The prolonged crisis of the 1990s and the gradual escalation of the violence allowed the regime to carry out otherwise difficult domestic reforms (such as privatization of state assets). It also helped a state that was receiving international financial and diplomatic support to stabilize a power structure that had been under serious threat of collapse between 1988 and 1992. The armed conflict also allowed the state to create a massive security and social assistance program in the form of civilian militias, reportedly numbering between 250,000 to half a million by 2000.[65] Economic understandings of mass violence embody the antipolitical tendencies of neoliberalism in so far as they understand late warfare as a problem of rebellion driven by primal human urges rather than as modern political agendas in which the role of the state is paramount.

MANAGING GREED AND GRIEVANCE

Political framings of Algeria's violence in the 1990s often confused the cure and the disease. October 1988 became year zero, and January 1992 was the conflict's trigger. This was true only insofar as the problem of violence in Algeria was understood mostly in relation to the steps that had to be taken to restore multiparty constitutional democracy. Such interpretations of Algeria's predicament should have collapsed vis-à-vis the realities of the violence in the years that followed. As the war dragged on, national-level politics became increasingly disarticulated from the violence at the regional and local levels. Whatever political character the violence had in relation to questions of democratic governance and party participation in early 1992, this character seemed to bear no relation to the killing that escalated from 1993 onward. Efforts to end the violence on the basis of political understandings of its causes failed to have any effect on the warfare. Indeed, the more regular and legitimate political processes became in Algeria, the more intense the violence became. Dialogue, power sharing, elections, and reconciliation initiatives between 1993 and 1995 coincided with the steep intensification of the warfare. The election of General Liamine Zéroual to the presidency in 1995, the adoption of a new constitution in 1996, and the holding of local and national elections in 1997 came amid the worst of the killing. The largest massacres occurred during the regime's secret negotiations with the FIS-AIS leadership that led to the AIS ceasefire of October 1997. The following months, particularly December 1997 and January 1998, would then see the worst massacres of the war. Bouteflika's 1999 amnesty measures, which formalized the 1997 ceasefire agreement between the AIS and the government, seemingly did little to hasten the agonizingly slow denouement of violence.

At the international level, public diplomacy and secret back-channel efforts to facilitate dialogue between the regime, political parties, and civil society also gained little traction. The 1995 Rome or Sant'Egidio Platform, signed by all major political parties, including the FIS, and widely supported internationally, largely fell on deaf ears in the Algerian regime, among elements of the insurgency, and in parts of Algeria's secular civil society.[66] Political understandings of Algeria's violence—framed as simply the regime versus Islamists—completely collapsed when confronted with the massacres of 1997 and 1998. In the face of these unspeakable and accumulating atrocities, the conflict met with strong calls for internationalization. Global leaders, particularly those in Paris and Washington, DC, did so, ironically, because they could no longer offer a basic account of the politics of the violence that was ravaging the Algerian countryside. Rote diplomatic prescriptions collapsed because no one could provide a coherent answer to the question of who was orchestrating the massacres and why.

Efforts to manage Algeria's crisis through economic interventions seemed to have little effect as well. Over the course of the 1990s, the economic picture improved, yet the warfare intensified. A 1989 International Monetary Fund (IMF) loan did little to reverse the country's financial crisis that soon led to more and more conflict and violence. With a credible, if questionably legitimate, presidential government in place, IMF loans signed in 1994 and 1995 provided Algeria with $1.8 billion in credit for the next three years—that is, during the apex of the violence. Algeria also rescheduled its bilateral debt with seventeen creditor nations in July 1995. It was afforded these benefits because its macroeconomic picture had actually improved between 1993 and 1996, the years that also saw the violence intensify. The European community—which between 1992 and 1994 had stalled disbursements of a significant loan to Algeria signed in late 1991[67]—eventually extended Algeria $156 million to help government reform and privatization efforts in late 1996, followed by $124 million to help Algeria with its debt burden. Amid the bloodiest periods then witnessed in the fighting—the violence during the month of Ramadan in early 1997—the Economist Intelligence Unit otherwise lauded "Algeria's spectacular macroeconomic performance," driven by increasing hydrocarbon prices.[68]

Even at the peak of the violence, foreign energy companies seemed just as undeterred. With Algeria boasting new oil and gas finds, British Petroleum signed a multibillion dollar agreement with Algiers in late 1995 to develop fields around In Salah. France's Total and Spain's Repsol signed a twenty-year $850 million contract with Algeria in January 1996 to develop gas fields in the deep southeast; engineering assistance would be provided by the US firm Brown and Root and by Japan's JGC. By 1997, perhaps the worst year of the violence, new investments were launched or announced by the US companies Atlantic Richfield and Anadarko, Spain's Compañía Española de Petróleos, and Italy's Azienda Generale Italiana Petroli. Governments in the United Kingdom, Canada, Belgium, the Netherlands, Italy, and Germany also took steps to help cover investments in Algeria, particularly in the hydrocarbon sector.[69]

That these diplomatic and financial interventions had little apparent effect on the violence—indeed, they coincided with its escalation—is of little consequence to the initiatives themselves or to the broader scientific and ideological imaginary underwriting them. As Naomi Klein has demonstrated, the only failure for neoliberalism in the face of a crisis it has co-engineered is not to take advantage of it. Even unintended and unmitigated disasters can be made politically and economically profitable if the governmental and financial capacities are available to do so.[70] In Algeria, what was largely accomplished through these interventions, whether intentional or not, was the political and economic rehabilitation of the very regime whose mismanagement of the Algerian economy and polity had helped generate the warfare in the first place. This rehabilitation—at the expense of the thousands more who would die in collective massacres, bombings, and other forms of intimate and impersonal violence in the final three years of the century—became more and more acceptable as the killing became more and more unintelligible to outside observers. The puzzle of Algeria's violence, particularly the identity and motive of the massacres' perpetrators in 1997 and 1998, would eventually find resolution in the aftermath of September 11, 2001. Questions surrounding the logics of violence in 1990s Algeria were largely dispelled that fateful morning in New York City and Washington, DC, and all political and economic efforts to rehabilitate the regime were thus rendered successful in retrospect.

August 1997: The corpse of a child killed in the Sidi Raïs massacre is displayed for identification prior to burial. Official figures claimed that 98 persons had been killed; a handwritten note on the back of this photo says "230 persons slain." Photograph by B. F. Zohra. Courtesy of the *El Watan* archive, Algiers.

3 IDENTITY, RELIGION, AND TERRORISM
The Islamization of Violence

SAMUEL P. HUNTINGTON put forward his "clash of civilizations" thesis at the end of the Cold War to account for the emerging post-ideological geopolitical order. No longer would a rivalry between political imaginations organize international state behavior. But neither would the totalizing vision of neoliberalism distend into and coordinate every aspect of life on Earth. Global politics would instead become an epiphenomenon and an instrument of deeper, more basic human identities than the ones that neoliberalism and socialism had tried to impose. In this new world order of multiple centers of power, the irreducible differences between nine fundamental cultural blocs, coupled with the irreconcilable forces of modernization and tradition, would produce intercivilizational and intracivilizational wars. According to this thesis, one major conflict between two civilizations was already well under way long before the fall of the Berlin Wall: the clash between Western and Islamic civilization.[1] This conflict between the Islamic and Western worlds was described earlier in Bernard Lewis's famous essay "The Roots of Muslim Rage." Lewis also saw core civilizational differences as the motor driving people to kill and protect at the behest of those identities.[2] That these two theses—Huntington's and Lewis's—prompted as much denunciatory criticism as productive debate goes without saying at this point.[3]

Irrespective of the theoretical coherence and empirical validity of the civilizational conflict thesis, it indicated a broader trend in the understanding and management of late warfare. This turn away from ideology and toward identity represented a noticeable shift in thinking about the fundamental sources of tension and mass violence after the Cold War. The turn was also an antipolitical reimagining of conflict's sources and solutions. Basic notions of power—its historical accumulation, its geographical distribution, and access to the means of its technological amplification—were marginalized or nonexistent. Marginal as well were suspicions that "civilization" and "identity" were part of the "cultural logic" of a nascent geopolitics that no one could explain without reproducing this logic's self-image.[4]

Instead, basic differences in religion and ethnicity were said to account for the killing fields of the new world order—from Srebrenica to Kigali, Grozny to Tel Aviv. Identity replaced ideology as the ultimate source of conflict after the Cold War. And like ideology, the putative contrasts between identities were viewed as sufficient conditions for generating mass violence. Peacemaking and peacebuilding strategies followed suit. The much-celebrated 1995 Dayton Accords, which ended the Bosnian war, were based on a wholesale acceptance of incompatible ethnoreligious identities as the conflict's core driver. The Solomonic logic of the Accords was to create a new map of Bosnia-Herzegovina in order to cantonize communities into separate spaces as much as possible.[5] Identity was inescapable. The antagonistic struggles to realize and resist neoliberal globalization were even recast in the 1990s *lingua franca* of identity conflict.[6] From Nobel Prize–winning economist Amartya Sen to critical theorist Stuart Hall, violence became a problem in which identity was central.[7] When the events of September 11, 2001, were said to confirm the clash-of-civilizations thesis and Islam's antimodern tendencies, prominent critics such as Edward Said and Mahmood Mamdani alleged that identity had merely been improperly conceptualized vis-à-vis the violence attributed to it, not that violence and identity bore no significant relationship to each other.[8]

Identity was also given a central role in accounts of the contemporaneous violence in 1990s Algeria. It was a decade of "ferocious identity politics";[9] a resurfacing of the "identity politics" seen in the war of independence;[10] a civil war driven by a violent imagination unique to Algerian national identity.[11] A mixture of identity questions were plaguing Algeria: What did it mean to be Algerian? What did it mean to be Muslim? What did it mean to be Arab (or Berber)? Most of all, Algeria had become an index of "Muslim rage" and a manifestation of the contradictory forces of modernity and tradition inherent in the clash of civilizations. Such understandings were brought to bear not only on the violence in general but particularly on the massacres of 1997 and 1998.

Yet there was something odd about this insistence on identity's profound yet abstract role in Algeria's violence. It was often difficult—and in some cases impossible—to identify the actual agents of the violence, let alone their concrete motives. This was particularly the case with the most horrific acts of Algeria's *décennie noire*, the 1997–1998 massacres. From the early days of the conflict, Algerians, as much as outside observers, expressed deep levels of uncertainly about the identities of the perpetrators behind the episodes of killing, both large and small. In Algeria, and later in the world outside Algeria, acts of violence frequently elicited the question *Qui tue?* (Who kills?) or *Qui tue qui?* (Who kills whom?). What these questions represented were a permanent state of incredulity toward official narratives coupled with a predisposition toward the conspiratorial, as if asking *Cui bono?* (Who benefits?) was the first step in answering the question *Qui tue?*[12]

From the very first days of the conflict, events such as the late 1991 attacks in Guemar, if not certain aspects of the 1988 riots, had engendered questions about those who initiated the violence, those who were killed, and those who benefited most from the mayhem. The June 29, 1992, assassination of Interim President Mohamed Boudiaf not only remains a source of contention in Algeria two decades later, but also seems to function as a kind of "original sin" in the *Qui tue?* discourse of 1990s Algeria. If they could kill Boudiaf, then no one was safe. But who were "they"? The bodyguard with Islamist political sympathies, as the government claimed? Or simply a patsy encouraged by elements of the regime, as many Algerians have suspected?[13] Subsequent high-level assassinations of political leaders, civil society figures, journalists, cultural icons, and foreigners have also been met with indelible skepticism, as have many acts of quotidian violence habitually attributed to individual Islamists or to the broader insurgency.[14] What changed with the massacres in 1997 and 1998 was the extent to which *Qui tue?* speculation became an international preoccupation. Prior to then, such speculation had been largely Algerian. At the height of the massacres in 1997, one of France's leading reporters on the conflict described the situation as so complex, so uncontrollable, and involving such a "multitude of actors" that it prohibited a coherent reading.[15] Reporters with Agence France-Presse, *60 Minutes*, and the *Irish Times* essentially agreed after visiting massacre sites[16] or speaking with Algerians fleeing the violence.[17] Algeria was suffering identity's wrath, yet the actual identities of the killers were often difficult to determine, if not deliberately subject to misdirection and obfuscation.

How then to account for the primacy of Islam and identity in explanations of the warfare in 1990s Algeria? In other words, how was Algeria's violence Islamized? It is difficult to answer this question without recognizing the continuing and pervasive power of Orientalism in the politics and science of contemporary conflict management's approach to the Arab and Islamic worlds.[18] With the onset of violence in Algeria in the early 1990s, the insurgency, largely by default, became responsible for much of it that otherwise lacked proper explanation. This default not only betrays the forces of Orientalism still operating in representations of violence in the Arab world, but also amplifies a fundamental contempt for rebellion that operates in prevailing understandings of civil war. The particularly "abnormal" violence of Algeria's massacres, which were even more difficult to explain, accelerated the process of Islamizing Algeria's violence. The mass slaughter of Algerian civilians was rendered all the more abnormal by press accounts in which unverified depictions of the sensational and the macabre were simultaneously used to illustrate the horror of the massacres and to mobilize international outrage. Stories of the insurgency's mobilization and abuse of women were used in a similar way. All of this speculation was possible in a discursive environment that was hostile toward domestic and foreign efforts to investigate the violence. Though this hostility was to some degree generated by the conflict itself, the Algerian regime used it to justify a series of policies that would quarantine the violence from rigorous local, national, or international documentation. That quarantine has lasted well beyond the worst days of the conflict and is now codified in Algerian law. As a result, constrained and distorted understandings of what happened in the 1990s, particularly the Mitidja and Ouarsenis massacres of 1997–1998, continue to shape important global security policies such as counterterrorism. Such policies have yet to realize that the Algerian massacres became a situation in which a putative effect of identity—horrific violence—was the actual agent driving accounts of Algeria's massacres.

AN ALGERIAN *RASHOMON*

Prior to the major massacres of 1997 and 1998, Algerians and foreign observers were already expressing widespread doubts about the authorship of much of the violence. An important aspect of these allegations was the suspected use of misdirection and "false flag" operations by armed actors. A particularly dreaded feature of life in 1990s Algeria was the *faux barrage* (false checkpoint), where insurgents would dress as security forces and stop unsuspecting vehicles to engage in robbery, extortion, murder, and sexual violence. The use of disguise, however, was not limited to the insurgency. In 1996, Louisa Hanoune, head of Algeria's Parti des Travailleurs (Worker's Party), complained, "We no longer know who kills who and why. You have false police, false Islamists, all kinds of armed groups, a GIA, several GIAs, militias, real armed Islamists, real checkpoints, false checkpoints."[19] Former President Ahmed Ben Bella described Algeria in late 1997 as "a situation in which no one knows who is a killer and who is not a killer."[20] Moustafa Bouchachi, a leading Algerian human rights lawyer, concurred that the violence had become inscrutable: "I really don't know much about what is happening. [...] It's a mystery even for me."[21] Foreign reporters expressed similar concerns. Roughly two years into the killing, Algeria's conflict was described in one foreign report as "Kafkaesque."[22] "Many people in Algiers," a reporter claimed in early 1997, "say they no longer know who is killing whom."[23] Several months later another reporter described Algeria's bombings and massacres as "mysterious atrocities that are difficult to ascribe to any one group."[24]

These were not just elite, opposition, or foreign opinions either. One Algerian swore that everyone disguised themselves when conducting killings.[25] An Algerian policewoman complained that she had no idea who had assassinated her husband, though she was told it had been Islamists: "The men who did this to him were dressed as policemen—and they killed him because he was a policeman. They kill without reason."[26] An Algerian solider complained to a British journalist, "Sometimes we fought an element who were definitely one type of GIA, sometimes we fought people who were another type of GIA. They all had different agendas and the only thing they usually shared was a brand of Islam and hatred for the Government. Sometimes we fought people of no particular definition at all. It was never concrete: neither their agenda nor ours."[27] In late 1996, Amnesty International expressed concern about civilian militias, both self- and state-armed, conducting counterinsurgency operations while dressed in official uniforms but operating independently of government control.[28] An Algerian who had fled the country told a French reporter, "That is what is unbearable: the doubt. If we knew that the military was attacking as terrorists, we would be reassured, but they leave us in doubt."[29] Witnesses to and survivors of several massacres said that some or all of the attackers wore security, military, or official militia uniforms.[30]

Part of the problem was an environment of incomplete, inconsistent, incoherent, and incorrect facts. Even before the massacre wave began in late 1996, rumors played a powerful role in the *Qui tue?* discourse. There were even rumors of events that seemingly never happened. A respected Algerian historian, Mohammed Harbi, and the controversial book, *La sale guerre* by Habib Souaïdia, have both accused the Algerian regime of massacring civilians as early as 1992 and 1993, respectively, though such reports have yet to be confirmed by other sources.[31] In August 1996, several international media outlets reported on a roadside massacre of sixty-three bus passengers somewhere between Batna and M'Sila, perhaps one of the largest massacres of the conflict. It is unclear, however, whether it actually took place. Rumor, confusion, and speculation seem to have played a role in the making of this "massacre."[32] A prominent French journalist, Jean-Pierre Tuquoi, suggested that these rumors were doing much more than simply sowing confusion. Algerian civilians were acting on them in the name of self-defense and vengeance.[33] "Terrified civilians," wrote journalist Lara Marlowe in early 1995, "whisper of special execution brigades, dressed in civilian clothes, that roam the country hunting down and murdering Islamists."[34]

As the intensity and frequency of the massacres increased in late 1996, so did international consternation about the killers' identities. The April 22, 1997, massacre at a collection of farms near Bougara, in the Blida province, was then the largest of the conflict, officially claiming ninety-three victims. In the wake of this unprecedented massacre, a French official admitted to the *New York Times*, "What's happening there is appalling, but there is no way to know for sure exactly who is doing what to whom."[35] Though the massacres abated somewhat in the summer of 1997, the Raïs massacre of August 29 revived foreign interest in Algeria's violence with its claim of two to four hundred slaughtered.[36] As always, blame naturally gravitated toward the insurgency on the basis of some survivor accounts and government vows to punish the perpetrators.[37] "The Government vowed that 'terrorists'—Algeria's term for Moslem fundamentalist rebels—would be eradicated."[38] But as several reports noted, there was no claim of responsibility for the massacre, as was the case for most of the violence in Algeria.[39] An Agence France-Presse report concluded, "The violence has been largely blamed on the extremists, although it is often difficult for the media to determine independently who is responsible or the casualty tolls."[40] Similar issues plagued the back-to-back massacres in Béni Messous, near central Algiers, on September 5 and 7: there was no claim of responsibility as witnesses provided contradictory accounts of the perpetrators' identity and the response of local security forces.[41]

The Bentalha massacre of September 23, thought to be similar in scale to the massacre at Raïs, could have been a watershed moment in the internationalization of the Algerian conflict. One massacre the size of Raïs was an anomaly; two might be a trend. But increased attention only increased the mystery. Initial reports on the Bentalha massacre, like the one carried in the *New York Times*, spoke of "casualty figures" that were "as murky as the identities of the killers." This murkiness was summarized in the following terms: "The splintering of Islamic movements in Algeria, the paucity of official information, the reluctance of authorities to grant visas to foreign journalists and fragmentary evidence that the army or groups linked to it have sometimes encouraged violence for their own ends have contributed to making the Algerian conflict one of the murkiest of wars."[42] "On the identity of the killers," *Le Monde*'s top North Africa expert wrote, "no reliable information is available."[43] An official from Human Rights Watch summed up the situation in these terms: "One of the problems is that we don't know. The army says it's the armed guerrilla groups, but the press can't cover the scenes of the massacres or speak to the survivors."[44]

A purported claim of responsibility for the massacres finally appeared in late September 1997. Communiqué 51 of the GIA, signed by its leader, Antar Zouabri, was dated two days before the Bentalha massacre, though it was frequently described in press accounts as a subsequent GIA admission of responsibility for Bentalha. Though the French Interior Ministry vetted the document as "seemingly authentic,"[45] questions were naturally raised about its true origins.[46] Such questions even led the London-based publisher of the GIA's *Al-Ansar* newsletter, Mustapha Kamel (a.k.a. Abu Hamza al-Masri), to distance himself from the GIA.[47] One of the GIA's primary concerns in the communiqué was the ceasefire announced by its rival, the AIS. The AIS ceasefire was motivated by two important factors beyond reconciliation with the government: to distance the FIS-AIS from the massacres and to expose the GIA for what many Algerian Islamists thought it truly was, a criminal organization manipulated by elements of the regime to discredit the insurgency and the FIS.[48]

Roughly a month later, and coinciding with local elections, the Algerian government provided foreign journalists with unprecedented access to the two major killing sites, Bentalha and Raïs, albeit under the watchful eye of plainclothes "minders" and uniformed military protection. Though the tendency to blame the insurgency for the massacres remained the default assumption in most reports, correspondents often came away with more questions than answers. "Accounts of the massacres remain contradictory," concluded the Associated Press, adding, "None of the residents of Bentalha or Rais questioned during a visit Friday could describe with any precision how the massacres unfolded."[49] Reporters with *Le Monde*, the *Guardian*, the *Independent*, and Agence France-Presse came to roughly the same conclusion.[50] Though the *Times* of London quoted survivors of Raïs who identified local insurgents as their attackers, survivors quoted in the *Sunday Times* were unequivocal that government forces had taken part.[51] *Libération* likewise interviewed witnesses to the Bentlaha massacre who suggested the complicity of Algerian security forces in the massacre.[52] An initial visit by the *New York Times* to Bentalha produced an ambivalent report; a subsequent visit by the same correspondent produced an account more friendly to the Algerian government narrative.[53] The Algerian government took other steps to control the narrative as well, such as allowing unprecedented coverage of an antiterrorism operation in nearby Oued Allel and holding press conferences with captured insurgents and their complicit relatives.[54]

The greatest challenge to the official Algerian government narrative began to appear at roughly the same time. A series of Algerian officials gave interviews in the French and British press. They claimed to be either former or serving members of the security, military, and intelligence agencies. They also claimed to have firsthand knowledge of direct and indirect state involvement in the massacres. Some of the massacres were allegedly perpetrated by special forces–type units, often disguised as Islamists,[55] whereas other massacres were perpetrated by insurgent groups with links to elements of the regime.[56] The international impact of these accounts was blunted, however, by the steep decline in massacre activity after Bentalha and the staging of successful local elections in late October. International attention drifted away from Algeria in November and December 1997 as the violence retreated to its normal, less spectacular levels. Though at least two-dozen massacres were independently reported during this period of "relative calm," almost all of them claimed fewer than fifty casualties. A major impediment to domestic and international reporting on such smaller-scale massacres was the government's refusal or inability even to acknowledge them.[57]

It took another wave of large-scale massacres, starting in the final week of 1997, to rekindle international interest in the Algerian conflict.[58] Over the next four weeks, Algeria would witness some of the bloodiest yet most obscure mass killings of the conflict. By the end of January 1998, official figures indicated that more than one thousand people had been killed in massacres, bombings, and other acts of armed violence.[59] It was reported that entire villages were razed and no life was spared.[60] These New Year's massacre sites—located in remote areas of the Ouarsenis mountains in the western provinces of Tiaret, Tissemsilt, and Relizane—were difficult even for Algerian journalists to visit.[61] In one case, an attacked village lacked phone lines and paved roads.[62] Unlike the Mitidja "triangle of death" massacres of August and September 1997 in the rural periphery of Algiers, the distant and isolated Ouarsenis massacre sites of December 1997 and January 1998 were never visited by foreign correspondents or international delegations. Reports on these massacres were thus even more vague and speculative than reports on other massacres. Responsibility for these new massacres again defaulted to the insurgency—"Islamic extremists"[63] or "terrorists."[64] An Agence France-Presse report simply deduced GIA culpability for these massacres from the widespread allegations of GIA authorship of the massacres at Bentalha and Raïs.[65] Some observers suspected that the Ouarsenis massacres were part of a war between AIS and GIA supporters;[66] others suggested more base motives—simple armed robbery.[67] Accusations of government complicity were still made, but like all other theses, they lacked empirical verification.[68] One reporter admitted that he could make sense of the situation only by concluding that none of it made sense: "as the terrorism has gained all the appearances of complete arbitrariness, losing any military or moral logic, it has appeared to serve only the causes of instability and murkiness."[69]

Not everyone bought into *Qui tue?* theorizing, least of all the Algerian regime and anti-Islamist voices in civil society. There was little doubt in their minds as to who was killing whom. Algerian officials often expressed dismay and anger toward such speculation, particularly when it came from other governments, journalists, or human rights groups.[70] Khalida Messaoudi, an Algerian feminist, chastised the international community for raising such questions at the height of the massacres in late 1997. "Who kills whom?" she asked rhetorically, addressing a Parisian rally in solidarity with Algeria. "I take the responsibility to say, on behalf of beheaded infants, on behalf of women whose throats were slit: it is the armed Islamic groups!"[71] Sectors of the Algerian polity thus responded to the events of 9/11 with expressions of sympathy and even a bit of smug satisfaction.[72]

Some foreign observers and mediators likewise insisted that it was clear who was killing whom. A US journalist blasted his colleagues for suggesting that anyone besides the insurgency had been involved in the killing. "The most likely explanation of what was going on did not seem to interest anyone," he complained.[73] Hélène Carrère d'Encausse, a EU representative who took part in an interparliamentary delegation visit to Algiers in early 1998, rejected the idea that anyone but the insurgents was involved in the massacres: "All interlocutors we met (that is to say all legal political parties, civil society associations), with one exception, say loudly that this is false. It is clear that the question 'qui tue qui' should never be asked. Everyone in Algeria knows who kills."[74]

The international community eventually stopped asking who kills whom, but this decline in curiosity had little to do with the facts of the matter ever being clearly established. As the violence subsided after January 1998, so too did foreign interest in potentially intervening. From early 1998 to 2002, Algeria's massacres became less frequent and less intense—one or two dozen killed in an episode rather than one or two hundred. Questions of perpetrator identity behind the massacres briefly resurfaced several times, such as in April 1998 at the United Nations and two years later in France with the publication of two sensational books, *Qui tué à Bentalha* in 2000 and *La sale guerre* in early 2001 (see Chapter 6). Though the taint of the 1990s continued to stain Algeria's reputation, no country tied its relations to Algiers with the question of who killed whom in the 1997–1998 massacres. For many, the truth of the Algerian massacres was established on 9/11.

THE FIRST VICTIM OF WAR

Reliable information on the violence in Algeria, and the massacres in particular, was difficult to obtain, for several reasons. As Algeria's conflict intensified from 1992 onward, the country became more and more isolated from the outside world. Algeria had never been an easy country for foreigners to visit in the first place. Successive post-independence governments shunned tourism, seeing it as a form of neocolonial cultural prostitution. Obtaining a visa to Algeria was frequently a complicated affair, and became even more difficult in the 1990s. As assassinations and bombings began to narrate daily life in Algeria in 1992 and 1993, foreigners were brought into this story. Diplomats, businesspeople, and quiet expatriates were subjected to threats and murder. Members of the domestic and international press were targeted as well. Nonessential personnel were moved out of the country; companies, embassies, and other foreign organizations operated with skeleton crews or left entirely. Not only did the quality of information suffer, but so did the quantity. Intergovernmental and human rights organizations were regularly refused access, as were journalists. The slow return of constitutional order, starting with the presidential election in 1995, did little to bring foreigners back to Algeria. The escalation of atrocious violence in late 1996, leading to the massacres of 1997 and early 1998, only reinforced Algeria's pariah status.

Press accounts were, and largely remain, the only source of daily information on the violence. During the 1990s and since, very few academic studies have attempted—or been allowed—to explore the realities of the armed conflict for those who lived and survived it.[75] Recent political histories of the conflict have relied almost exclusively on contemporary press accounts.[76] A handful of reports from civil society and dissident groups also attempted to relay firsthand accounts of the violence to the outside world.[77] More neutral organizations, such as international human rights groups, were denied access, and therefore often had to collect firsthand information remotely or from Algerians traveling abroad.

The challenges that faced the Algerian press and foreign journalists in the 1990s are difficult to understate, as are the effects that this environment of terror had on the quality of reporting. Algeria was widely recognized as one of the deadliest places in the world for journalists to operate. By 1998, seventy Algerian journalists had been assassinated, along with dozens of foreign citizens. In February 1996, a car bomb exploded in front of the offices housing several Algerian newspapers, the Maison de la Presse, killing three journalists and more than a dozen others.[78] Amnesty International reported in 1997 that not a single person had been held accountable for any targeted journalist. This impunity compounded the atmosphere of terror felt by media workers. Though rebels were widely blamed for these attacks, some Algerian journalists expressed fear of being killed or "disappeared" by state agents.[79] A 1997 Reporters Without Borders report likewise charged, "Many professional journalists admit in private that the government is behind certain assassinations, but all say they fear for their lives if they make their knowledge public."[80] The daily *Liberté* lost four journalists to the violence. One of them, Zeineddine Aliou-Salah, was more afraid of the government than he was of the Islamists who supposedly killed him.[81] Caught between the explicit terror of the insurgency and the implicit terror of the regime, Algerian journalism was severely compromised.

State control over the press was significant as well: individual editions were blocked or seized, publications were suspended, government ownership of all the printing presses and paper supplies was used as leverage, censors ("reading committees") vetted all editions prior to printing, and reporters and editors were fined and imprisoned.[82] A near monopoly of state control over domestic television and radio further constrained coverage of the violence. The government's refusal to acknowledge some violent events, notably massacres, often resulted in little or no coverage of them. When journalists were allowed to report on massacres and even to visit the sites, they were allegedly instructed by authorities to exaggerate or minimize the scale of killing depending on how officials wanted the event to be framed.[83]

Complementing this systemic bias, some independent outlets adopted explicitly pro-regime or anti-Islamist editorial lines, or a combination of the two. Staunchly secular journalists with *Le Matin d'Alger*, notably Hassane Zerrouky and Mina Kaci, often wrote for or had their stories picked up by a leading French postcommunist paper, *L'Humanité*. *Le Matin*'s hardline anti-Islamist or *éradicateur* (eradicator) stance was fueled by government sources that fed the paper insurgent documents and other information of questionable authenticity.[84] Then there is the simple problem of incompetent reporting, which affected domestic outlets as much as foreign ones. The London-based pan-Arab paper *Al-Hayat*, for example, published a number of dubious reports over the course of the conflict.[85]

The same forces that affected local journalists also conditioned international coverage of the violence in Algeria. Given the environment of fear and terror generated by the assassination of journalists and foreigners in the early years of the conflict, very few press agencies and major international outlets had a permanent presence in Algiers as the massacres were unfolding. Significant articles in *Le Monde* and the *New York Times,* for example, were written in Paris, culled from wire reports, Algerian papers on sale in France, and telephone interviews. Agence France-Presse, the Associated Press, Reuters, and Deutsche Presse-Agentur kept their Algiers bureaus open long after most other European press outlets had left. Some Arabic papers—notably *Al-Hayat* and *Al-Sharq al-Awsat*—also maintained a presence in Algeria. Reporters with Agence France-Presse and the Associated Press provided the bulk of international coverage of the conflict. But operating from Algiers required walking a fine line between the government's red lines and a foreign appetite that vacillated between indifference and voyeurism. Where that line stood at any given moment was often unclear, as evidenced in the controversy surrounding Agence France-Presse's award-winning "Madonna of Bentalha" photo and the retaliation from the Algerian government that it provoked.[86]

Foreign journalists making *ad hoc* visits to Algeria were ostensibly under less constraint, though they often reported on the challenges facing them. A "tour of the 'triangle of death' [that is, the Mitidja massacre sites]," wrote one, "requires movement in a bulletproof armored vehicle, in convoy with three others packed with rifle-toting soldiers."[87] Most on-the-ground international reports on the Algerian massacres took place in October 1997 in the lead-up to that month's local elections. Foreign journalists ostensibly covering the polls were granted access to several major massacre sites (including Bentalha and

Raïs). During these visits, members of Algeria's Interior Ministry and security services flanked foreign reporters as they recorded witnesses' testimonies. One journalist complained, "It is not easy reporting when surrounded by 20 armed guards."[88] The effects of these security precautions were noticeable. "In no other zone of conflict have I seen people so afraid to speak their minds to a foreigner. This fear is not eased by the constant presence of armed plainclothes 'minders' who shadow almost every move of foreign journalists," wrote a British journalist.[89] A dispatch from the Sidi Hamed massacre site claimed that locals began to criticize the role of the government when the guards and minders were not able to listen in on the conversation.[90] Veteran war correspondent Peter Stranberg complained to Human Rights Watch that people he had interviewed in Algeria were later interrogated by government officials.[91] By 1997, Amnesty International had already concluded that foreign journalists would be able to learn only what the Algerian government wanted them to learn.[92]

ANGRY AT GOD

The ambiguous violence of the massacres became Islamic terror in a discursive environment in which media coverage was highly constrained and impartial investigation was, and remains, impossible. Further adding to this process were efforts to irrationalize the violence in Algeria, particularly the massacres. Irrationalization and Islamization went hand in hand. Irrationalization of Algeria's worst violence often insisted that the mass slaughter of civilians held no strategic value; it fixated on the most macabre aspects of the killing and implied that a religious logic to the violence was not a logic at all. The most extreme accounts represented the massacres as sheer barbarism—a nihilistic orgy of blood, violence for the sake of violence. The irrationalization of Algerian violence often took cues from the regime's official narrative of the conflict. The Algerian government, which almost never identified groups like the MIA, GIA, or AIS by name, instead used the terms *terrorists* and *criminals* to name the perpetrators of violence.[93] A government statement carried on national radio after the Raïs massacre, for example, assured the citizenry, "The state will continue to fight mercilessly against the barbarian criminals until their eradication."[94] The Vatican's *L'Osservatore Romano* similarly decried the "blind and barbaric havoc wreaked by the Islamic extremists" following the Raïs massacre.[95] Following the Bougara massacre, a US spokesperson adopted a similar framing: "It is hard to remember a more vicious terrorist insurgency, a more cynical group than these Islamic terrorists."[96] A lengthy polemic in the *Atlantic Monthly* stated that the massacres represented a simple logic: kill them all, let God sort it out. Here was the author's reasoning: "The emirs and their drugged acolytes—drugged on evil brews of false religion and politics, and on every stimulant available, as autopsies of killed terrorists have repeatedly shown (I was told this by Algerian doctors assigned to hospital morgues)—had lost their bid to overthrow the Algerian state and were determined to bring down as many people with them as they could."[97] An article in *Libération* described the perpetrators of the massacres as "Islamists of the third kind," motivated by neither Islamic reform nor Islamic revolution but by simple, irrational bloodlust.[98]

Statements attributed to the insurgency, particularly to the GIA, often factored into this assessment. At the scene of a late 1996 massacre of thirty-one people in Sidi Kebir, a cardboard sign was left with "blood and destruction" scrawled across it in Arabic[99]—a "rare responsibility claim," noted a report on the massacre.[100] As the massacre crisis grew, so did references to *dam dam, hadim hadim* (blood blood, destruction destruction), an alleged slogan of the GIA.[101] The in-

A cardboard sign left at the scene of an attack on a family in Oued El Alleug (Blida province) on November 12, 1996. It reads:
   hadha hukum tarik al-salah [This is the punishment for those who abandon prayer]
   al-jama'ah al-islamiyah al-musallahah [Armed Islamic Group]
   dam dam, hadim hadim [blood blood, destruction destruction]
The photographer is anonymous. Courtesy of the *El Watan* archive, Algiers.

famous Communiqué 51 of the GIA, apparently written amid the worst of the Mitidja slaughters of August and September 1997, was purported to have confirmed the GIA's responsibility for the massacres. It also confirmed suspicions that the massacres were motivated by a horrific, Manichean impulse to cleanse Algeria of anyone who did not support the GIA: "The world must understand," the communiqué read, "that all the killings, the massacres, the burnings, the displacement of populations, the kidnappings of women, are an offering to God."[102] Such violence was justified, and would continue, the statement warned, because anyone supporting the regime, civilian or not, was an infidel.[103]

In some accounts, the bloodthirsty and nihilistic logic of the massacres was rooted in a rejection of Islam rather than in its realization. Reports of a splinter faction within the GIA—al-Ghadibun 'ala Allah, those "angry" or "revolting against Allah"—emerged in the days before the massacre at Raïs.[104] Not only was this declaration written across their headbands, but they were also said to have cut off their right index fingers as a sign of their rejection of Islam's most basic statement of faith, al-Shahadah (that is, there is no god but God, Muhammad is his prophet). The extreme radicalization of this group was said to have come about as a result of the popular embrace of the regime witnessed in the recent elections. These developments were interpreted as Allah forsaking the guerrillas, as well as the citizens who supported them, in favor of those in power, the Taghut (idolaters, false leaders, and tyrants).[105] The atrocities attributed to this band were equally shocking. Caricatured in news reports as howling like wolves during attacks, their eyelashes and eyebrows plucked out, these self-described dhabbahin (butchers) committed, among other horrendous acts, the incomprehensible practice of cutting fetuses from pregnant women's stomachs to stop more Muslims from being born.[106] As major massacre activity moved westward at the end of 1997, an elite group within the GIA, Katibah al-Ahwal (Horror Battalion), was said to be responsible for these new massacres in Ouarsenis.[107] An apocryphal yet unconfirmed story about a GIA dwarf executioner, Momo le nain (Mohamed the dwarf), who allegedly decapitated eighty-six people in the Bentalha massacre, continues to circulate globally, being frequently cited even in recent years as an illustration of Islamists' penchant for bloodthirst and beheadings.[108]

Some observers took a more historical approach to explaining the mass atrocities attributed to the Algerian Islamists in 1997 and 1998. There was some speculation that the GIA had become a neo-khawarij sect. In a Le Monde interview, Egyptian author Gamal Ghitany, for example, saw a genealogical connection between methods of the GIA and those from the early days of Islam. Ghitany suggested that the GIA was less akin to the Isma'ilis of Shi'ah Islam, as some supposed, and more like the *khawarij* movement of the seventh century, for the simple reason that "the Kharijites resorted to collective massacres."[109] Reporters looking for answers to the Algerian massacres in more recent history located the GIA within the political thought and movements associated with such figures as Sayyid Qutb or the Egyptian organization al-Takfir wa al-Hijrah.[110] For Shaykh Muhammad Sayyid Tantawy, Grand Imam of Al-Azhar in Egypt, there was nothing Islamic about the perpetrators of the massacres in Algeria. They were "not Muslims, they are not religious."[111]

The apparent coincidence of increased levels of violence in Algeria and the holy month of Ramadan did much to convince people to disagree with Tantawy's assessment. The "Bloody Ramadan"[112] trope was not limited to Algeria's violence but was applied to other conflicts in the Muslim world as well.[113] A central Algiers car bomb that detonated on January 30, 1995, killing forty, inspired the headline "Ramadan Perverted."[114] Another account from 1995 explained, "The month of Ramadan is seen by some as propitious for the 'jihad' or holy war and one fundamentalist group [AIS] has called on supporters to increase their activities."[115] While there was some significance to these claims, they also compensated for a lack of reliable knowledge about the agents and politics of violence in Algeria.[116]

As the "Bloody Ramadan" trope gained energy, the press began to expect violence in Algeria as the holy month approached.[117] Ramadan 1996–1997 and especially 1997–1998 did not disappoint this expectation. A spate of car bombs and massacres in early 1997 led one commentator to explain by insinuation, "Militants intent on [. . .] installing Islamic rule are suspected in a series of car bombings and massacres that began in mid-January with the start of Ramadan, the Muslim holy month."[118] The massacres of early 1998 were no exception. One radio program contextualized the height of the massacre crisis in these terms: "The Muslim world's just entered the month of Ramadan [. . .] which seems to exacerbate the situation [in Algeria]. There seems to be more zealotry around Ramadan."[119] "Every Ramadan is like this in Algeria," an Algerian scholar told the *Washington Post*. "For them, Ramadan is the month of jihad [. . .], because in the history of Islam all the conquests happened in Ramadan."[120] Following the Relizane massacres, a *New York Times* correspondent concluded that mass killing had become as much a part of the "ritual" of Ramadan in Algeria as Ramadan itself.[121] Though little was known about the Relizane massacres,[122] a Deutsche Presse-Agentur correspondent quickly concluded, "The terrorists came on the first night of the Moslem fasting month of Ramadan, posing a further escalation of the fanatical craze to murder by Algeria's militant fundamentalists during the fasting season."[123] Rumors circulated of a GIA leaflet that had been posted in western Algeria before the massacres there. Part of it read, "We shall come here soon; we breakfasted in Algiers, we shall sup in Oran."[124]

Violence against women and violent women also played important roles in the irrationalization of Algeria's violence. Figures and accounts vary as to the extent of violence against women perpetrated by the insurgency; by 1998, it was suggested that as many as eight thousand women had been abducted, raped, or murdered by the guerrillas.[125] International representations of the Algerian conflict, however, seemed less interested in these statistics than in the more bizarre and macabre acts of gendered violence attributed to the insurgency. Forced marriage with a guerrilla, a practice normally associated with Shi'ah Islam, was one such act. These war brides, or *zawaj al-mut'ah*, were held up as further indication of the GIA's inherently evil nature.[126] A survivor of the August 1997 Beni Ali massacre, for example, reportedly heard the attackers say, "Take the most beautiful girls and kill all the rest."[127] One British commentator described these "temporary marriages" as nothing short of sex slavery.[128] The Algerian government played a role in feeding the growing international appetite for such stories. At a press conference, survivors of the insurgency's depredations recounted being subjected to multiple rapes during their captivity. Women who became pregnant were killed or even "torn apart."[129] Algerian women as the core victims of the insurgents' massacres also features in the most globally iconic image of Algeria's *décennie noire*, the so-called Madonna of Bentalha photograph.[130] The irony that an Algerian woman had to be Christianized in order to be sympathetic was not lost on some observers.[131]

The Algerian government also used apprehended female supporters of the insurgency to demonstrate the evil that the rebellion had become. Following a large-scale counterterrorism initiative after Bentalha, a number of captured collaborators were paraded in front of the press. One of them, Zohra "Nacéra" Ould Hamrane, was allegedly a participant in the Bentalha massacre and the sister of a slain local leader (*amir*) of the insurgency. Her job during the massacre was to identify, with the help of her mother, those to be killed, and to loot houses and bodies.[132] Feeding into the Algerian government's insistence that the insurgent menace was being fed by forces from outside the country, Zohra claimed that a number of the other participants in the massacres had Moroccan, Tunisian, and Libyan accents.[133] One of the most important witnesses brought forward by the Algerian government was Nacera "Khadidja" Zouabri, the sister of Antar Zouabri, then the putative leader of the GIA. Khadidja also allegedly took part in the Bentalha massacre. In one of the more ghastly stories to emerge from the horrors of Algeria in late 1997, she and her fellow attackers were said to have wagered on the gender of unborn fetuses before cutting them out of their mothers.[134]

Contrary to this tendency to impose an irrational interpretation on an inchoate pattern of escalating violence, others attempted to infer a coherent logic to the massacres. Some suspected that the brutality of the killing was related to a defeated insurgency desperate for media attention[135] or one boldly attempting to create an internal refugee crisis that would flood Algiers and destabilize the regime.[136] To explain the massacres in the far west, hundreds of miles from Algiers, it was proposed that the GIA—dislodged from the Mitidja after Bentalha—had moved into the Ouarsenis, possibly on its way to the Moroccan border.[137] The desperation of the insurgency was related to its lack of military capacity and, more important, the routinization of electoral processes since 1995. Both the Bougara massacre of April 1997 and the subsequent massacres in the periphery of Algiers that August and September were thought to be related to June's national elections and October's local elections.[138] Additionally, it was noted that the massacres seemed to be taking place in areas that had been FIS electoral strongholds in the 1990 local and 1991 national elections.[139] Observers often found it incomprehensible that a political movement would massacre its support base.[140] For others, this was the precise logic of the massacres: to punish defecting supporters.[141] Supporter defection was also measured in terms of the growth of state-supported civilian militias, which ballooned in membership to well over one hundred thousand by the late 1990s.[142] Another sign of defection was said to come from the September 1997 AIS ceasefire, which had been negotiated in secret with the regime.[143] After the Béni Messous massacre, French Foreign Minister Hubert Védrine felt that this was the best explanation: "The resurgence of violence in Algeria appears to be the response of Islamists opposed to any compromise with the Algerian government. [...] We are not therefore talking about blind violence."[144] But were the massacres strategic punishment or spiteful revenge? The validity of either hypothesis pivoted on facts that were weak or nonexistent. Efforts to account for the massacres welded together their constellations of meaning from inconsistent, erroneous, and incomplete information as much as from suppositions, theoretical frameworks, and moral prejudices.

DEATH AND THE AUTHOR

The most important fact of the major massacres was the horror they presented to the international community. The killing between August 1997 and January 1998 was massive and incomprehensible—so much so that for a brief six-month period the violence in Algeria dared the international community to bear witness, if not to intervene and stop the killing. Though that challenge was taken up, foreign efforts to end the massacres did little more than broaden the participants in the *Qui tue?* debate. In late 1997, international efforts to manage the massacre crisis largely proposed forms of epistemic intervention that would establish the relationship between identity and the violence in Algeria—to provide an answer to the question *Qui tue?* Yet long after the images of the massacres were forgotten, the enigma of the massacres—if not the enigma of the violence in Algeria since 1992—remains.

Attempts to unravel their mystery of the Algerian massacres have often commenced with the presumption that somehow it was identity that produced or contributed to them. Yet we see how that relationship can work in the other direction. In the relationship between identity and violence, it is identity—an abstract, trans-subjective force—that is frequently given agency as the cause of violence. Violence is effect, a product of identity's power. But in Algeria, identity—the concrete agency of armed actors—was often difficult or impossible to establish. Sometimes the conditions of this difficulty or impossibility were intentional strategies of participants in the conflict; in other instances they were an effect of deeper problems in a discursive environment that few observers bothered even to problematize. A surplus of interpretation collided with a paucity of information.

One need only think of the cultural, scholarly, and political productiveness of World War II and the Holocaust to realize that violence, especially on a massive scale, has a power over our imaginations that is little understood, especially the power to demand understanding and intervention. The Algerian massacres also demanded interpretation and comprehensibility, which would eventually have to come in the form of agency, and so implicate identity. What was certain about the massacres (their brute, ghastly reality) called forth uncertain renderings of what was indeterminate about them (their agency, their subjectivities). The enigma of mass violence after the Cold War lies not in the dictates of the apolitical force of identity but in the dictates of the very thing that is said to be its effect—mass violence itself.

Survivors of the Relizane massacres. *Top*: a family flees the violence. *Bottom*: women and children in mourning. Photographs by B. F. Zohra, dated January 8, 1998. Courtesy of the *El Watan* archive, Algiers.

4 COUNTERTERRORISM

Out of Sedan Comes Austerlitz

WITHIN DAYS of the attacks on September 11, 2001, Algeria's recent and ongoing violence was used to give meaning to what had just happened in New York; Washington, DC; and the Pennsylvanian countryside. Elites in the Algerian regime were quick to make these connections,[1] but they were not the only ones. Philosopher André Glucksmann, who had left his own mark on the Algerian conflict three years prior, was one of the first to do so. He argued that it was Muslims, first and foremost, who needed to defend themselves against the *fascisme vert* (green fascism) behind 9/11: "the first victims of the Islamists are women and children, in Afghanistan as in Algeria."[2] Placing Algeria in sequence with Afghanistan was a powerful rhetorical move. After 9/11, there was no other regime in the world more despised in the West than that of the Taliban. *Le Figaro*'s Max Clos wanted to believe that Islam is a religion of peace, but he needed only three examples to remind him otherwise: Algeria, Afghanistan, and "the past week in New York and Washington."[3] The Algerian insurgency even surpassed the Taliban's barbarism in some accounts. Groups like the GIA were blamed for single-handedly authoring nearly one hundred thousand deaths in Algeria "in a nine-year struggle to create a theocracy."[4] Middle East and terrorism experts likewise contributed to these processes of constellating 9/11 with the recent and ongoing violence in Algeria. Scholar and commentator Walid Phares associated the insurgency and massacres in Algeria with the Al-Qaida network behind 9/11: "In Algeria, for instance, jihad forces linked to bin Laden perpetrated massacres against Muslims, killing whole families."[5] A terrorism expert likewise told the US Congress that rebels in Algeria shared Osama Bin Laden's unique "willingness [. . .] to kill a large number of civilians."[6] Marwan Bishara also situated Algeria's insurgency and Bin Laden in the same historical context, because both emerged out of the milieu of Arab fighters in the Soviet-Afghan war of the 1980s. This shared background, Bishara explained, produced 9/11 as much as it produced the political violence against civilians in the Arab world in the 1990s, particularly the Algerian massacres.[7] A year after 9/11, the US Assistant Secretary of State for Near East Affairs, William Burns, suggested during a visit to Algiers that "Washington has much to learn from Algeria on ways to fight terrorism."[8]

The putative lessons of 1990s Algeria often featured in the explosion of research on the new post-9/11 geopolitical reality. It was a reality in which understanding political Islam and its relationship to mass violence became the foremost challenge in the conflict sciences and the practice of international security. In this environment, 1990s Algeria functioned as an important case study. Algeria became an exemplar in the narrative of failed jihad against the "near enemy"—governments of the Middle East—and the resultant transnationalization of armed Islamist activity against the "far enemy" of the North Atlantic, primarily the United States.[9] In the 1990s, Algeria had seen the "most appalling example of violent Islamist activity";[10] it was a place where "emirs of differing extremist persuasions and various regions hunted and butchered one another and committed hideous massacres against civilians, government officials, and foreign nationals."[11] The meaning of the Algerian massacres and, more important, their lessons were now in plain sight for anyone to see. "The underlying justification for the [Algerian] massacres portended the later Al-Qaeda justification for 11 September and purposeful civilian targeting."[12] The lessons of Algeria even applied to Iraq after the 2003 Anglo-American invasion: "In Iraq— and earlier in Algeria—jihadists were primarily killing fellow Muslims, accusing them of collaboration with the 'infidels.'"[13] Several in-depth studies of Algeria's massacres likewise positioned them within the new histories and understandings of jihadism and jihadi violence being constructed to make sense of, and so manage, global security post-9/11. The *Qui tue?* debate surrounding the killing in Algeria—that is, questions about who was actually behind particular acts of violence and why—was simply dismissed or ignored. Post-9/11 analyses of Algeria's massacres instead focused on GIA rhetoric or the putative institutional dynamics of Islamic insurgencies.[14] What little academic and political debate there had been about the authors and logics of the violence in 1990s Algeria became another victim of the 9/11 attacks and the overreaction of the North Atlantic world.[15] Within a short period, the discursive Islamization and terrorization of Algeria's massacres was so complete that world-renowned scholars accepted it as a casual fact.[16]

The strange certainty surrounding Algeria's violence—that much of it undoubtedly constituted mass Islamic terrorism—is likewise visible in the most important technology of truth used in the conflict sciences today: the dataset. One of the most important such datasets is produced by the National Consortium for the Study of Terrorism and Responses to Terrorism. Founded in 2005, this US consortium produces the Global Terrorism Database, the preeminent catalogue of a number of variables associated with discrete terrorism events from 1970 to the present. It lists some two thousand terrorist events in Algeria between 1990 and 2005. This figure constitutes a quarter of all the terrorism events in the dataset for the Middle East and North Africa region, and more than 5 percent of the worldwide total during that same period. Algeria's contribution to Middle East terrorism thus appears to be quite significant in the years leading up to 9/11. Yet the perpetrators of nearly half the events listed in this dataset for Algeria are identified as "unknown." Roughly another quarter of the events are attributed to "Algerian Islamic Extremists," "Algerian Moslem Fundamentalists," "Islamic Extremists," "Muslim Extremists," "Muslim Fundamentalists," "Muslim Guerrillas," "Muslim Militants," "Muslim Rebels," and a host of other generic identifiers. The rest of the events are attributed to several named groups, mainly the FIS, the GIA, and the organization that largely continued the insurgency following the demobilization of the AIS and the collapse of the GIA in the early 2000s: the Groupe Salafiste pour la Prédication et le Combat (GSPC, or Salafist Group for Preaching and Combat). In terms of motive, a quarter of the cases list the attack's logic as unknown or use such phrases as "it is suspected" or "specific motive is unclear." In half the cases, the alleged motive for the attack is simply left blank.[17] Algeria has thus come to represent a conflict in which the violence could be described as terrorism despite any certainty as to the identity of the agents behind most of the violence or to their motivations.

This consolidation of understanding is even more striking when one considers the myriad ways in which Algeria's violence was viewed—and contested—in the years leading up to 9/11. Human rights organizations were the most vocal in the expression of concern about the massacres and their putative authors. Reports and statements issued by Amnesty International, Human Rights Watch, Reporters Without Borders, and the Fédération Internationale des ligues des Droits de l'Homme (International Federation for Human Rights) often questioned the Algerian state's apparent indifference to the massacres.[18] Sometimes these reports even provided evidence of its complicity.[19] As these groups have documented in the years since, the Algerian government has not taken any steps to shed light on the violence of the 1990s. This is particularly the case when it comes to the major massacres of 1997 and 1998, their perpetrators, and the motivations behind the slaughter of dozens, sometimes hundreds, of civilians in a single episode.[20] Indeed, the Algerian government made independent or foreign inquiries into the violence of the 1990s illegal as part of the national reconciliation measures adopted in 1999 and 2005.[21] Though foreign government officials most often took their cues from Algiers and characterized the violence in Algeria as Islamic terrorism, this monolithic account began to break down in 1997 as the plausibility of any single-actor narrative became increasingly untenable.[22]

Area and country experts tended to view such simplistic or one-sided accounts of Algeria's violence with some skepticism. As the violence escalated in 1995, renowned sociologist Pierre Bourdieu—at the urging of his colleague François Burgat—began to suggest that, contrary to prevailing accounts, the violence in Algeria could not be attributed solely to, or explained solely by, Islamic actors and beliefs.[23] Luis Martinez, who conducted research on the conflict in the early 1990s, expanded on this notion. He explained, "In the majority of cases, we no longer know who kills whom. There's a feeling of an immense settling of scores on a national scale."[24] These feelings of uncertainty and ambivalence were carried into the international debate surrounding the identity of the massacres' perpetrators in 1997 and 1998. Some leading North Africanists (such as Bruno Étienne, Joe Stork, Ahmed Rouadjia, Clement Henry, and Dale Eickelman) alleged various degrees of state complicity in the massacres, from direct and covert authorship to indirect facilitation.[25] Others, such as Lahouari Addi, Claire Spencer, and Mary-Jane Deeb felt that other actors, beyond the insurgency and the state, were involved in the massacres.[26] Gilbert Grandguillaume, Michael Willis, and John Entelis suggested that civilian self-defense militias, criminal organizations, and private business interests (all of them possibly linked to the regime, the insurgency, or both) were likely contributing to the massacres for obvious and less obvious reasons. One of those reasons, many suspected, was the accumulation in some provinces of local-level vendettas from the days of FIS rule in the early 1990s, or more profoundly, from the war of independence and its bloody aftermath.[27] As the massacres began to subside in 1998, Barbara Smith concluded, "There are, for now, no clear answers."[28] Recent political histories of 1990s Algeria have continued to express a profound sense of confusion and ambivalence when addressing the massacre debate.[29] In his 2005 historical survey of jihad as a concept and practice in Islam, religion scholar David Cook concluded with respect to the Algerian massacres, "The question remains unresolved."[30]

An examination of the broad parameters of the debate surrounding the 1997–1998 massacres shows a complex arrangement of hypotheses, many of them overlapping or interactive. Most attention was focused on the insurgency and its putative strategic or ideational reasons for perpetrating the massacres. The viability of this singular and totalizing understanding began to collapse as the massacres escalated in frequency and intensity in late 1996 and early 1997. The Algerian government's demonstrated inability to prevent or interrupt the repeated and escalating massacres began to raise difficult questions about the government's incompetence, if not its indifference. The appearance of Algerian whistleblowers in the fall of 1997 began to raise a whole new set of concerns. These whistleblowers were former and serving members of the security, military, and intelligence agencies, and they began to make claims of direct and indirect state complicity in the massacres. Others suspected that the massacres had little to do with the contest between insurgents and the state. Though far less prevalent, notions of privatized violence taking hold in Algeria were voiced. This violence was private either because it was motivated by rationales outside the politics of the state-insurgency struggle, or because the economics of the violence was rooted in local, regional, or national struggles over commerce. Figure 1 summarizes the various theses about the massacres' agents and logics at the height of the crisis in 1997–1998, when the massacres were at their most lethal and most subjected to threats of international humanitarian intervention.

Within a short period, this complex web of understandings was reduced to one dominant and unquestioned account of the Algerian massacres: fanatical Muslim insurgents had perpetrated all of the massacres in Algeria. What is interesting about this transformation is the relative abruptness of the change, which has yet to be explained. What is also interesting is the change itself and what it tells us about the role of terrorism and counterterrorism in the science and management of conflict today. Though Algeria's violence is often treated as a central case study in the emergence of terrorism as a global security issue, what the violence of 1990s Algeria actually reveals is the strangeness of terrorism as an organizing problem for a field of social scientific expertise and so the

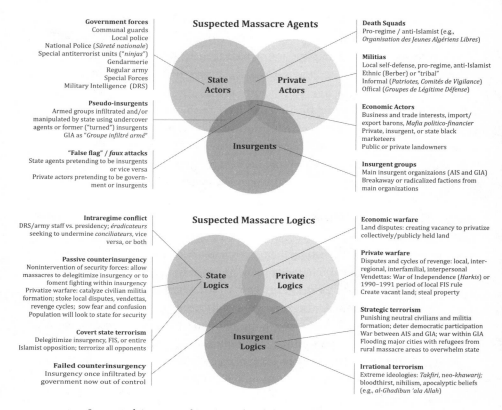

Figure 1. Suspected Agents and Logics Behind the Algerian Massacres

NOTE: This figure summarizes various theses regarding the massacres compiled from news reports cited in Chapters 3, 4, and 5. It is not an exhaustive list of all possible combinations of agents and logics. For example, it is not impossible that armed opposition groups could have played a role in "land interest" massacres or that state agents had a role in "vendetta" massacres involving Harkis. Such arbitrary boundaries were imposed by outside understandings of the violence, for reasons that Chapters 3 and 4 attempt to explain.

strangeness of counterterrorism as the dominant framework through which global security has come to be managed today.

Critical histories of terrorism and counterterrorism have already problematized terrorism's ascent to preeminence in matters of global security. Two central insights have been generated by these critical studies. First, counterterrorism, a school of conflict science and management that began to emerge in the 1970s, has played a profound role in the production of the conditions that enable the very thing it seeks to defeat—terrorism. Second, much of what we call terrorism today would have been called something else just one, two, or three decades prior. As a species of warfare, terrorism is ostensibly distinct from other forms of armed violence, though its normative character, as always already illegitimate violence, haunts efforts to subject it to scientific understanding. An increasing tendency to view all forms of asymmetric warfare as terrorism contributed to the tendency to understand and manage such violence as apolitical phenomena. Scientifically, this antipolitical approach to understanding terrorism has led to correlative analysis (rather than to historiographic and ethnographic approaches) and, in the field of terrorism's management through security, has led to militarized, eliminationist strategies (rather than to traditional forms of conflict resolution utilizing negotiations and reconciliation).[31] Though these insights are important, a reading of the relationship between the Algerian massacres and 9/11 instructs us to rethink how to approach a critical history of terrorism and counterterrorism. Contemporary counterterrorism doctrine cannot be understood solely in relation to its evolution from the 1970s to the present. It must also be understood genealogically, as an assemblage of actors, ideas, and violences whose powers include the power to embed historical significance in the distant and recent past. A critical history of what counterterrorism has made is insufficient. We must also understand what it has unmade. Counterterrorism, an antipolitical framework for thinking about conflict in the world and so managing it, made Algeria one of its preeminent exemplars of horrific jihadi violence by unmaking what the violence actually was.

The terrorization of Algeria's violence, which easily followed from its Islamization, spoke not only to the massive and spectacular power of 9/11 to produce its historical context, but also to the antipolitics of counterterrorism as one of the preeminent strategies for understanding and managing violence today. When Algeria's violence was viewed as a complex problem of civil war, the conflict was rendered unmanageable within the evolving framework of humanitarian intervention in the 1990s, the framework that would become the R2P project in the 2000s. As a civil war, the Algerian conflict also proved difficult to understand and, more important, manage via traditional methods of international diplomatic and financial intervention. That is to say, when viewed as a civil war, Algeria's violence was not very useful to the regimes of knowledge and practice that tried to manage it as such, that is, as a civil war. As a simplified problem of terrorism, however, Algeria's violence was more comprehensible and thus more useful to the post-9/11 antipolitics of global conflict management. This understanding of Algeria's violence, as terrorism, was, however, largely produced in retrospect. By 9/11 it was too late to do anything about the 1997–1998 massacres except to memorialize them as acts of Islamic terror and to vow *never again*. The reinscription of the violence of 1990s Algeria as the most profound instance of Islamic terrorism prior to 9/11 nonetheless lent strength to new strategies of managing terrorism globally through uncompromising eradication. One of the ironies of using Algeria's violence in this way was its incongruity with the Algerian regime's actual approach to national reconciliation. Compromises were made to achieve peace with violent, radical jihadis, ostensibly implacable enemies who in the 1990s had allegedly committed some of the worst crimes against humanity.

TERROR CARTOGRAPHY

To make Algeria's massacres useful to counterterrorism required framing them in particular ways. First and foremost, the massacres had to be one thing rather than many things. In the post-9/11 sciences that study radicalization and jihadism, as well as in the managerial strategies of counterterrorism into which these sciences feed, the mass civilian killings in 1990s Algeria are treated as an inter-articulated series of events—events tied together by a distinct and singular set of actors and motives. This assumption, rarely stated and never interrogated, is common in all efforts to explain Algeria's massacres. These episodes of mass violence were implicitly systematized prior to their explicit systematization. The result is often question-begging accounts whose conclusion—the logic behind the massacres—is already an operational assumption.[32] There is otherwise no *a priori* basis on which to see commonality across all of the massacres apart from naming them as such, that is, as massacres.

   Discussions of Algeria's massacres in the 1990s overwhelmingly focused on the largest ones—that is, the massacres with reported death tolls of one hundred or more. These occurred mainly on the periphery of Algiers, on the Mitidja agricultural plain, and in the nearby foothills. The sites of the Bentalha and Raïs massacres in August and September 1997 were the most visited by journalists and hence these massacres have been the most scrutinized, followed by the January 1998 Sidi Hamed massacre in the same region. The late December 1997 and early January 1998 massacres in the western Ouarsenis Mountains in the Tiaret, Tissemsilt, and Relizane provinces were likewise massive in scale and widely reported, though no foreign journalist, and very few Algerian ones, ever visited those killing sites. Three important studies of the massacres simply fail to incorporate into their analysis the major Ouarsenis massacres at all.[33]

More generally, these extraordinary massacres in the Mitidja and Ouarsenis came to represent all massacre activity, though they were actually outliers. Most of Algeria's massacres in the 1990s, according to the two efforts to document all of them,[34] were of one to two dozen people. (Table 2, by contrast, lists only the most widely reported massacres.) Though most hypotheses claimed to explain all of the massacre activity in Algeria, basic data and survivor accounts exist for only a small number of the most extreme cases.[35]

Table 2 Nonexhaustive List of Widely Reported Massacre Episodes in Algeria (1996–2002)

Approx. End Date	Min. # Killed	Max. # Killed	Approximate Locality	Province	Notes
8/17/96		63		M'Sila-Batna	Highly disputed faux barrage road attack
9/4/96		18	Towards Tunisian border	Batna	Faux barrage attack
9/6/96		12		Ghardaia	Faux barrage attack on road
11/5/96		31	Sidi Kebir	Blida	
1/12/97		14	Tabainat	Blida	
1/19/97	30	49	Beni Slimane, Sidi Abdelaziz	Médéa	
2/1/97		21	Médéa	Médéa	
2/17/97		31	El Karrech	Blida	
3/4/97		52	Thalit	Médéa	
3/19/97		32	Ouled Antar	Médéa	
4/14/97		30	Boufarik	Boufarik	
4/22/97	47	93	Bougara	Blida	
4/23/97		42	El Omaria	Médéa	
5/15/97	30	32	Chebli	Blida	
6/14/97		13		Alger	
6/16/97		50	Dairet Lebguer	M'Sila	
7/13/97		44	Ksar El-Boukhari	Médéa	
7/23/97	37	56	Yemma M'ghita and Benachour	Blida	
7/25/97	28	38	Hadjout	Tipaza	
7/28/97	50	51	Larbaâ	Blida	
7/30/97		41	Aïn Defla	Aïn Defla	
8/21/97		63	Souhane	Blida	
8/26/97		64	Beni Ali	Blida	
8/29/97	98	300	Sidi Raïs	Alger	Officially 98
8/30/97		42	Maalba	Djelfa	Often dated 28 Aug
9/6/97		63	Algiers (Béni Messous)	Alger	

(*continued*)

Table 2 Nonexhaustive List of Widely Reported Massacre Episodes in Algeria (1996–2002) (*continued*)

Approx. End Date	Min. # Killed	Max. # Killed	Approximate Locality	Province	Notes
9/20/97		53	Beni Slimane, Tablat	Médéa	
9/23/97		250	Bentalha	Alger	
9/27/97		30	Sfisef	Sidi Bel Abbes	
10/13/97	43	54	Sig	Mascara-Oran	Attack on bus
12/18/97		31	Djiboulo, near Larbaâ	Blida	
12/21/97		30	El Bordj	Tlemcen	
12/24/97	48	120		Tiaret	Two attacks
12/26/97		27		Tiaret	
12/27/97	25	30	Safsaf	Mascara	
12/31/97	78	412	Souk El Had (area)	Relizane	Three to four villages attacked
1/3/98		117	Meknessa	Relizane	
1/4/98	153	500	Had Chekala (area)	Relizane	
1/5/98		62		Relizane	Several attacks reported
1/11/98	103	400	Sidi Hamed	Blida	
3/27/98		47	Oued Bouaicha	Djelfa	
4/28/98		28	Arzew	Oran	
12/8/98	55	81		Chlef	
8/15/99		29	Beni Ounif	Bechar	
12/24/99		30	Khémis Meliana (area)	Aïn Defla	Faux barrage attack
2/28/00		24		El Bayadh	
5/4/00		23		Médéa	Faux barrage attack
1/18/01		23		Chlef	
1/28/01		25		Chlef	
2/11/01		27		Berrouaghia	
27/9/01		22	Larbaâ	Blida	
5/30/02		23		Chlef	

SOURCES: AFP, "Les principaux massacres en Algérie depuis le début des troubles en 1992," August 19, 1996; "Bombs Shatter Safety of Big Cities, Muslim Fundamentalists in Algeria Take Violence to Urban Areas in Heightening Conflict," Reuters/Globe and Mail (Canada), January 23, 1997; Le Monde, "Plus de 700 morts depuis juillet," September 1, 1997; Sud Ouest, "Un terrible bilan," September 24, 1997;"Algerian Rebels Kill 54 in Night of Bloodshed," Reuters/Toronto Star, October 15, 1997, A12; "Following Is a Chronology of Some of the Worst Known Massacres of 1997," AFP, December 31, 1997;"Les massacres les plus meurtriers en Algérie depuis le début de l'année," AFP, December 31, 1997; "Major Massacres of Algerian Insurgency," Associated Press, January 3,1998; "Worst Massacres in Algeria in the Past Year," AFP, January 7, 1998; "Algérie. Deux ans de violences sans précédent," La Croix, December 12, 1998; "Dix ans de violence en Algérie," AFP, January 9, 2002; "Les attentats les plus meurtriers en Algérie depuis trois ans," AFP, July 5, 2002.

Reports of massacre activity prior to 1996 are difficult to corroborate. Algerian historian Mohamed Harbi, citing a high-level source, said that state agents had massacred "hundreds" of civilians in Ouled Asker (Jijel province) in 1992, a claim for which there are no other accounts.[36] Dissident Algerian activists recorded allegations of state-authored massacres as early as 1993, though these have never been independently confirmed, nor are they supported by any contemporaneous sources.[37] In his memoir of life in the Algerian special forces, Habib Souaïdia recalls unwittingly taking part in a state-authored civilian massacre in March 1993 in a place called Douar Ez-Zaatria (or Zaâtria), a massacre that, according to Souaïdia, the Algerian press blamed on Islamists.[38] Problems arose with Souaïdia's description of the massacre when a leading Algerian newspaper editor denied that such stories had ever been reported.[39] Then two French journalists visited the putative site of the massacre; villagers there said there had never been any such thing.[40] Most reports of massacres between 1992 and mid-1996—apart from the Berrouaghia prison massacre of November 1994 (ranging from 12 to 500 prisoners killed) and the Serkadji prison massacre of February 1995 (in which 109 prisoners were reportedly killed)—are highly contentious.[41]

Indisputable is the fact that public bombings caused a significant number of fatalities before and after 1996 and continued to haunt security in Algeria into the first decade of the 2000s and beyond. Though both bombings and massacres caused a great number of injuries and deaths, most studies of the Algerian massacres have either explicitly[42] or implicitly[43] distinguished between bombings and other forms of mass killing. Classifying bombings as random massacres and face-to-face killing raises some problems as well. Impersonal or at-a-distance bombings—as opposed to "suicide" bombings—are not likely to be as selective as face-to-face killing, but public at-a-distance bombings in Algeria frequently appeared to have specific targets, from civilian to military, and therefore had in mind specific victim populations as well. It would be a mistake, however, to assume the logic or identity of bombers on the basis of the victim population. Much the same goes for face-to-face massacres. Allegations of deliberate victim selection has often been treated as a key variable in the massacres. A number of massacres occurred in false checkpoint (*faux barrage*) situations, in which armed actors established barricades on roads, pretending to be either security forces or insurgents, in order to engage in terror, racketeering, or both. In these cases, the perpetrators were less selective about the victim population than those who committed a raid on a village or neighbor-hood. *Faux barrage* massacres were much smaller in scale compared to others. In much the same way that labeling all antigovernment violence as terrorism falsely constellates the actors and logics of violence, giving a common label—*massacre*—to the murder of four, fourteen, forty, and four hundred people has the effect of implying dubious commonalities, particularly in terms of the per-petrators' identity and motives.

The lack of disaggregation in studies of the massacres is not the only prob-lem. For obvious reasons, there is significant variance in the basic figures asso-ciated with Algeria's massacres. Totals range from a low of 66 massacres (from November 1996 to August 2001)[44] to a high of 335 massacres (from December 1993 to December 1998).[45] Whereas the former calculation uses a threshold of fifteen deaths, the latter uses five. Ignoring the more controversial massacre re-ports from 1993 to 1995, these studies suggest that roughly 3,000 to 6,500 Algeri-ans died in face-to-face massacres from late 1996 to the end of 1998.[46] The most detailed record of the massacres that occurred after 1998 documents nineteen massacres in 1999 (297 killed), thirteen in 2000 (174 killed), thirty-two in 2001 (356 killed), and thirty-three in 2002 (375 killed).[47] Massacres were reported in a large number of provinces, though very few in the Saharan areas or, be-fore 1999, in the eastern provinces. The highest concentration of massacres oc-curred in the central north region: Algiers and the adjacent provinces of Blida, Médéa, Tipaza, and Aïn Defla (see Map 1). The second highest concentration was in the northwestern provinces.[48] Compared to the total number killed in acts of armed violence since 1992, estimates of which range from 50,000 to 200,000, the number of massacre victims appears to account for a relatively small fraction of total war-related fatalities.[49] Algeria ostensibly suffered the most jihadi violence of any country in the 1990s, yet the vast majority of the Is-lamists' alleged victims cannot be accounted for in the most basic terms (that is, who died, how, and where?)

What helped make the massacre crisis of August 1997 to January 1998 an international crisis in the first place was the deterioration of the official nar-rative that had been constructed to explain the massacres. The Algerian gov-ernment, most of all, insisted that all reported massacres, big and small, were the work of the insurgency, even though it refused to recognize some of the massacres independently reported in the Algerian or foreign press. The wide-spread insistence on rebel culpability became increasingly difficult to main-tain in the face of several confounding claims. Two commonly reported facts

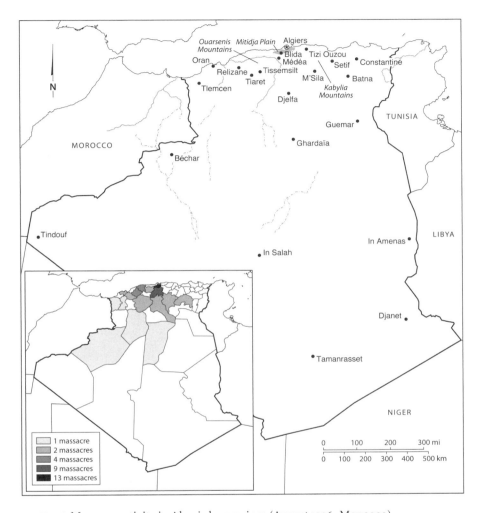

Map 1 Massacre activity in Algeria by province (August 1996–May 2002)

KEY: #. Province (Number of massacres): 1. Alger (4), 2. Blida (13), 3. Médéa (9), 4. Tipaza (1), 5. Aïn Defla (2), 6. Chlef (4), 7. Relizane (4), 8. Batna (2), 9. M'Sila (2), 10. Djelfa (2), 11. Tiaret (2), 12. Mascara (2), 13. Oran (2), 14. Tlemçen (1), 15. Sidi Bel Abbes (1), 16. El Bayadh (1), 17. Ghardaia (1), 18. Bechar (1).

NOTE: This map should be treated only as a cartographic representation of Table 2. It is not intended to be a comprehensive or accurate representation of the actual geographical distribution of all suspected or confirmed massacre activity in Algeria since 1992.

about the political and security geography of the massacres, particularly the massacres of August and September 1997, raised a number of questions. First, the massacres seemed to be occurring in areas that had been dominated by the FIS in the local elections of 1990 and the aborted national elections of 1991. This suspected correlation prompted questions as to why an insurgency would slaughter its own supporters. "There seems to be no logic to the carnage," wrote a US journalist in a report from Paris. "The villages targeted by the extremists of the Armed Islamic Groups have included traditional fundamentalist strongholds."[50] Following the massive Bentalha massacre of September 1997, the *Economist* likewise asked, "Why would Muslim rebels attack in an Islamist area?"[51] There was also a relationship, albeit of a different kind, between the massacres, the 1996 constitutional vote, and two elections in 1997, one national and one local: massacre activity decreased significantly, almost to zero, when those three votes took place.[52]

Second, the security geography of the massacres was said to be as puzzling as their political geography. The major massacres of April, August, and September 1997 often occurred in areas where police, military, and gendarmerie units were close by, or in locales that ostensibly had self-defense militias, some of them recently armed by the state. The government's failure to protect civilians in situations where security installations were visible from the sites of the killing raised further questions about the agents of the massacres and their motivations. French journalist Jean Hatzfeld, writing after the Raïs massacre, wondered "how two to three hundred killers can operate in an area normally under tight police and military surveillance on the outskirts of the capital."[53] *Libération*'s José Garçon also noted, "The authorities have never been known to intervene in the four or five hours it takes to wipe out a village."[54] As the massacres peaked in January 1998, Patrick Baudouin, president of the Fédération Internationale des ligues des Droits de l'Homme, asked, "Why do the massacres happen in Algiers or in the suburbs, near military barracks or police outposts, but without military or police intervening in favor of the victims?"[55]

The problem with making such inferences about the logic or agents of the massacres on the basis of these two features of their geography is the general unreliability of the data and, again, a failure to appreciate all classes of massacres, not simply the largest. Like all aspects of the massacres, the geographical features have been subject to much confusion and conjecture. The common failure to include the western Ouarsenis massacres in an analysis of the massacres is a related problem. Indeed, death tolls reported at the time of the killing easily suggested that the Tiaret, Tissemsilt, and Relizane massacres were far more devastating than the intensely scrutinized massacres in the Mitidja just months prior.[56] There is also a case to be made that major massacres like Raïs and Bentalha, with their exceptionally high death counts, should be treated as anomalies rather than as the norm. Less than 10 percent of re-ported massacres saw more than fifty people killed and only 3 percent appear to have exceeded one hundred fatalities between November 1996 and Decem-ber 1998. Though massacre activity seems to have been heavily concentrated in the three provinces that encompass the Mitidja, more than a dozen other provinces also reported massacres. The five major massacres in the Algiers-Blida-Larbaâ region—at Bougara, Raïs, Bentalha, Béni Messous, and Sidi Hamed—span an arc of just thirty kilometers. Opinion has thus been divided on whether or not the Mitidja had become an exemplary space of conflict[57] or merely an exceptional one.[58]

Interpreting the spatial dynamics of the violence in 1990s Algeria was all the more difficult because the data were of such poor quality. Basic distinc-tions between rural, urban, and suburban massacre settings were often ig-nored or confused. As this chapter and the following make clear, universal claims about the massacres—such as their alleged intimate proximity to, or extreme distance from, military and security installations—do not hold up to scrutiny. The infamous "triangle of death" (triangle de la mort) in the Mitidja is emblematic of the spatial caricatures that haunted coverage of the massa-cres. According to some observers, the triangle was constructed without clear limits or points; it was a "zone,"[59] a "theatre,"[60] or "the Algiers region,"[61] if not all the farmlands of the Mitidja[62] or even all the lands between Algiers and the Atlas Mountains.[63] More specific renderings constructed the triangle out of three cities—Algiers, Blida, and Larbaâ.[64] Depending on the account, Lar-baâ was a "point" on the triangle,[65] an "edge" of the triangle,[66] or the "heart" of the triangle[67]—a designation (au coeur) it shared with the massacre site Raïs six kilometers away in Algiers.[68] The mid-1997 massacre in Larbaâ, sev-eral reports noted, had been focused on the specific locale of Si Zerrouk, vari-ously described as a "hamlet,"[69] a gehucht (hamlet or township),[70] a "village near Larba,"[71] "a settlement on the outskirts of Larbaâ,"[72] and a quartier[73] or "district."[74] The post-9/11 terrorization of Algeria's violence has thus been grounded in a distorted understanding of the numerical and geographical scope of the 1997–1998 wave of massacres. This transformation of exceptional violence into exemplary violence has been made possible through processes of categorization and geographical homogenization. These processes unified and homogenized the massacres so they could be treated as a singular phenomenon with a singular explanation.

VOODOO COUNTERINSURGENCY

A degree of analytical and geographical reductionism is to be expected in any effort to account for a set of mass killing episodes spanning hundreds of miles and incorporating thousands of murders. This reductionism nonetheless had two important effects: it invited a singular reading of the massacres and, in so doing, allowed a particular reading of the massacres to exclude all others. That the Algerian massacres came to be seen as entirely encompassed within a logic of Islamic terrorism is, on one level, a testament to the historiographic power of the massacres' horror over the scientific imagination of those who claim to understand them. On another level, it is also a testament to the historiographic powers of the spectacle of 9/11 over the imagination of those who would seek to understand and so prevent something similar from ever happening again. To appreciate the powers of such horrific and spectacular violence, it is worth understanding the depth and breadth of debate surrounding the Algerian massacres, particularly in late 1997 and early 1998. That the massacres represented a campaign of state-initiated or state-condoned terror was the dominant counternarrative. The state's alleged nonresponse to the massacres and the peculiar features of their geography began to raise suspicions about the conditions that allowed, and the forces that drove, the mass killings. Grounded in these suspicions, direct and indirect state complicity in the massacres first gained purchase.

The purported failure of Algerian security forces to prevent or interrupt a single major massacre in 1997 and 1998 was central to concerns that the regime might be playing a role in the massacres. Given the brutal reputation already associated with Algeria's counterterrorism effort, it was often a small leap to assume a state role in the massacres. Torture, disappearance, summary executions, arbitrary and prolonged detention, as well as masked special counterterrorism units of the police and military (the *ninjas*) had all become part of the security landscape. How the violence escalated, seemingly beyond anyone's control, is illustrated in a 1994 interview with an exiled former officer of Algeria's military intelligence, the Département du Renseignement et de la Sécurité (DRS, or Department of Intelligence and Security): "When the terrorists started to massacre young conscripts, repression moved up a level. Fearing desertions,

the hierarchy decided to strike blow for blow. It was then that the reprisals became systematic: combing a district as soon as an offence was committed, summary execution of three, four or five young people selected at random."[75] By
1996, a leaked report of the French Defense Ministry bluntly stated, "The strategy of counter-guerrilla warfare utilized by the [Algerian] armed forces is the
fairly simple technique of terrorizing the population."[76] Some members of the
security forces also expressed fear of being killed by special police, military, and
intelligence units designed to root out and eliminate anyone suspected of being
Islamist or critical of the counterinsurgency effort.[77] In such a context, it was
not difficult for many to think that elements of the regime were playing some
role in the massacres.

The question, for some, was the extent of state involvement in the massacres.
The most generous interpretation of the situation suggested that the regime
had decided not to intervene in the massacres, even when they were taking
place within visual range of security installations. Here the idea was often that
the regime was simply allowing an intra-insurgency conflict to play out, or that
elements of the regime might even have had a hand in provoking or manipulating internecine AIS-GIA fighting and the GIA's own fratricidal purges.[78]
Elements of Algeria's military and intelligence were proud of their efforts to
manipulate, and so discredit, the FIS and the insurgency in the early 1990s—
years before the insurgency allegedly began massacring entire villages.[79] The
logic of allowing or stoking civilian massacres was thus quite simple: even if
the population blamed the government for not intervening, the government
would still come out on top once the insurgency had exhausted and delegitimized itself. Moreover, the victims of the massacres were those who had voted
for the FIS and supported (or at least tolerated) the Islamist guerrillas in their
midst. As an Algerian veteran of the war against France suggested, the GIA "terrorists are a weapon used by the authorities to justify the absolute power of the
army here, as well as discrediting the opposition Islamic parties. They do not
perpetrate the massacres themselves, but they do little to stop them and use
them as a reason to oppress any voice of criticism."[80] Theories of state complicity in the massacres grew even more ominous as the crisis became increasingly internationalized in 1997–1998. It was alleged that Algeria's intelligence
services, through various means (such as informants, traitors, undercover op-
eratives, double agents, and propaganda), were controlling or directing groups
within the rebellion to carry out the massacres. A related thesis saw the massacres as the unintended consequences of a very dark counterinsurgency effort, a

phenomenon known in the intelligence world as *blowback*. State efforts to infiltrate, disrupt, and otherwise manage the insurgency had haphazardly resulted in a more radicalized and uncontrollable insurgency when these agents eliminated more moderate actors. Finally, another set of theses held that the massacres were in fact part of a war within the regime, that one or all sides of this struggle were orchestrating massacres for political gain or manipulating elements of the insurgency to do it for them.

Allegations of state indifference and inaction vis-à-vis the massacres became widespread, yet the actual picture being reported at the time was more confused. Concerns were raised by the fact that the Mitidja massacres occurred largely in the First Military Region (also known as the Centre or Blida military region), the most heavily militarized zone in the country.[81] Disputed reports then appeared that said the military had been placed on the highest alert following the Béni Messous massacre,[82] or that the leadership had stopped all nighttime troop movements in August 1997 without direct authorization from the Army's Chief of Staff, General Mohamed Lamari.[83] But not all massacres were near military installations. Notably, the Ouarsenis New Year's massacres of 1997–1998 took place in isolated rural locals, far from military installations.

To defend the government against international accusations, officials often cited the impossibility of staging a careful intervention in time to disrupt a massacre without collateral damage.[84] The sheer brutality of the insurgency was also cited as a reason for the security forces' inability to intervene,[85] though the Algerian government made a media spectacle of its post–Bentalha counterinsurgency operations and shake-ups in the relevant military command.[86] In the Ouarsenis massacres, the state's failure to intervene was instead explained by Algeria's vast size. Though the massacres were taking place almost entirely within Algeria's Mediterranean north, one report nonetheless noted, "The 130,000-strong Algerian army is relatively underrepresented for the size of the territory, which is five times the size of France."[87] The US congress was similarly reminded by the Algerian ambassador that "Algeria is about four times the size of the State of Texas."[88] General Kamel Abderrahmane, commander of Algeria's western military region, likewise lamented, "The state cannot put a solider in front of every house."[89]

Similarly inconsistent were reports that state forces had intervened or been active at the time of the massacres. The Interior Ministry initially claimed that the Bougara massacre had been interrupted once officials were notified of the attack.[90] Two reports claimed that the Béni Messous massacre was brought to an end when security forces arrived.[91] These claims were contradicted by others.[92] There were also contradictory accounts of the role played by the local militia in the Sidi Hamed massacre, and of whether or not there was even a militia there in the first place.[93] In late 1997, an Amnesty International report cited two cases in which Algerian security forces blocked civilians from leaving a massacre site and prevented a local militia from attempting to come to the rescue.[94] After visiting several massacre sites, one reporter believed that the evidence pointed toward "some collusion between the attackers and the security forces."[95] According to residents of Bentalha, security forces had been visibly active on the edge of the attack during the hours of killing.[96] One survivor's story was recounted by a British reporter:

> According to Ahmed, the army sent tanks to the very edge of the town while a helicopter circled overhead. No one else contests the essence of his version but some, more circumspect, found justifications for the army's non-intervention. [. . .] Ahmed said that it was from the roof that he saw the tanks. And he insisted they were tanks, not just armoured cars. In fact the traces of tank tracks are still clearly visible—they end just 200 yards from his house. It was from the roof that he also saw the helicopter.[97]

Other survivors of the Bentalha massacre told a reporter that some of the actors involved had been military or members of the government-armed militia.[98] A survivor in Sidi Hamed likewise said that the military had arrived within fifteen minutes of being notified of the massacre but had not entered to stop the killing. "It is clear that many in Sidi Hamad fear some kind of complicity," one reporter claimed.[99]

Accusations of even more direct and active forms of state complicity began to circulate as the massacres reached their zenith in late 1997. Several Algerian dissidents, including ousted President Ahmed Ben Bella,[100] former Prime Minister Abdelhamid Brahimi,[101] and former diplomat Mohammed Larbi Zitout,[102] had been making such allegations for several years.[102] And this was not just the opinion of an exiled elite; similar suspicions circulated among common Algerians. "Terrified civilians whisper of special execution brigades, dressed in civilian clothes, that roam the country hunting down and murdering Islamists," claimed one 1995 report.[103] "In 85 percent of the cases," an Algerian in Blida told a US reporter, "It is the state."[104] Another journalist claimed, "In Algiers, taxi drivers and human-rights lawyers alike will tell you: '*Le terrorisme? C'est le pouvoir.*'"[105] Terrorism? It's the regime.

By the time Raïs had grabbed global attention, there was already international suspicion that special units within the security forces were playing a role in the vicious spiral of violence engulfing the country.[106] Alleged members of those units began talking to the French and British press soon after the massacres of August and September 1997.[107] A problem with these accounts was that they were outdated: none of these insiders could really speak to the major massacres near Algiers in 1997. Alleged state participants in the more recent massacres finally stepped forward in January 1998, after international interest in Algeria's turmoil was reignited by the Ouarsenis massacres.[108] For example, *Der Spiegel* carried an interview in January 1998 in which a deserting intelligence officer corroborated some of the accounts of state complicity in the massacres. He alleged that small-scale collective killings had been carried out by undercover military-intelligence units (dressed as Islamists) in the suburbs of Algiers in 1994 and 1995. But the recent massacres, he claimed, had been the indirect fault of the security forces' efforts to infiltrate, manipulate, and ultimately subvert the GIA.[109]

The GIA was essentially painted as an out-of-control counterinsurgency Frankenstein by the former and acting members of security forces who gave interviews to various European media outlets in late 1997 and early 1998. In some cases, the massacres were purported to be a combination of state-authored violence and violence conducted by infiltrated insurgent groups.[110] These agents' elimination of moderates within the insurgency allegedly led to increasing levels of radicalization.[111] Voices within the Algerian opposition expressed similar theses. Even before the massacres, union leader Abdelhak Benhamouda had already sourced the violence to "implanted and corrupt politicians who are pushing terrorists to kill Algerians."[112] Several years down the road, Saïd Sadi, head of the Kabylia-based Rassemblement pour la Culture et la Démocratie (RCD, or Rally for Culture and Democracy), similarly alleged that the Algerian regime was allowing the massacres in order "to immunise society from religious extremism."[113] Yassir Benmiloud, an Algerian columnist, posited an even more complex thesis: "The plan may have been to infiltrate the rebel groups in order to track them and better fight them. But the 'infiltrators' were quickly seduced by the rustic and decadent lifestyle of the terrorists: raping of women, theft of money and jewelry, pedophilia followed by mutilation and free food. In short, life with the rebels was much better than what the Algerian Army could offer."[114] Officials with the FIS entertained a number of theses about the massacres, all of them positing a degree of state complicity.[115] When the AIS unilaterally declared a truce after the Bentalha massacre, the organization said it was doing this "so that the enemy hiding behind abominable massacres can be unveiled, as well as the GIA criminals and those hiding behind it."[116]

Other accounts of the massacres suggested that the true war being waged was between elements of the regime rather than between the government and an insurgency. The massacres were thus theorized as a proxy war between two or more groups contending for control over the state. Supposed divisions within the regime were often articulated as conciliators versus eradicators. The *conciliateur* or *dialoguiste* branch ostensibly represented Algerians who favored dialogue with the outlawed opposition, perhaps the rehabilitation of the FIS (in its old form or another), and even engagement with moderate elements of the insurgency. The hardline *éradicateurs* were said to be those seeking to keep any semblance of the FIS out of government and looking for a military solution to the problem of the insurgency. Traces of talk about an *éradicateur/conciliateur* split dated back to at least the first months of the conflict in 1992.[117] Woven into this thesis, as the massacres were increasing in tempo and size in 1997, were contemporary reports of ongoing negotiations between the presidency and the FIS-AIS. General Mohamed Lamari, the Chief of Staff, suspected leader of the hardline *éradicateurs*, was allegedly seeking to undermine Zéroual's peacemaking efforts.[118] Another thesis proposed a tripartite system in which the intelligence services, led by DRS chief Mohamed "Tewfik" Mediène, formed a pivotal third group that could be swayed to one side or another.[119] An even older discourse of clans—interest groups based on geography, family, financial stakes, political party, military service, and contribution to the war of independence—surfaced in writing on the Algerian conflict and the massacres.[120] Several weeks after the massacre at Bentalha, a US academic speculated, "The recent upsurge in murders so vicious as to guarantee international media attention is part of efforts to derail such a process by hard-liners on both sides."[121] A French expert on Algeria concurred: "these latest attacks appear to be the work of one faction of the military junta that refuses, contrary to another faction, to negotiate with the [FIS]."[122]

INTERMEDIATE SCENARIOS

Also effaced in the wake of 9/11 were suggestions that actors outside of the state/rebel dichotomy might be the authors of some of the massacres too. Like the other theses presented in this chapter, the "privatized" violence thesis involved a number of claims about the true agents of the massacres and their motivations. The main drivers of violence in Algeria, according to these various theses, had little to nothing to do with the putative conflict between the government and the armed opposition groups. The violence had become private either because it was not related to national politics or because it was economic. Motives could be based in local politics, historical legacies, personal vendettas, regional issues, financial interests, land disputes, trade monopolies, and a whole range of other "intermediate scenarios," as one French expert called them.[123] Like other hypotheses of the massacres, some of these intermediate scenarios were considered rational or self-promoting, whereas other massacres were seen as driven by darker, illogical forces embedded in the Algerian polity.

Several ways were suggested in which Algeria's violence had become *privatized*. First and foremost, the privatized violence thesis referred to the significant *privatization* of the Algerian state's war-fighting capacity vis-à-vis self-defense militias. Early on, these militias had formed autonomous of any state encouragement or support. They had armed themselves with rifles, shotguns, handguns, and crude weapons, drawing on the knowledge of those who had experienced military service, seen action in the war of independence, or recently left the Islamist *maquis* (the insurgency). As the war dragged on, the Algerian state began to arm and train these militias, and offered moral and material support for other communities to do likewise. By the time of the massacres, civilian militias—ostensibly allied to the government—were the largest fighting force in the country, far outnumbering the largest estimate of the insurgency's peak strength.[124] A short-lived controversy in the spring of 1998, known in Algeria as the Hadj Fergane affair, which involved alleged abuses committed by Fergane's militia in Relizane, brought some foreign scrutiny to Algeria's militias and their possible role in the massacres.[125] By that time, however, international security concerns had largely moved to other conflicts as Algeria's massacres subsided and no longer seemed to warrant intervention.

French historian Benjamin Stora was one of the main proponents of the privatized violence thesis. He believed that Algeria's "peasant militias" were engaged in cycles of violence that pitted "village against village, family against family."[126] French journalist José Garçon was likewise intrigued by this thesis, whether applied to small massacres[127] or large ones.[128] One of the more prominent cases to trigger this line of speculation was the massacre of more than forty people at El Omaria only a day after the larger Bougara massacre in April

1997.[129] The following month, Pierre Sané, secretary-general of Amnesty International, blamed the escalating massacres on the Algerian state's "deliberate strategy" of creating civilian militias. This privatization of violence, when combined with the fragmentation of the armed opposition groups, created a dangerous combination, Sané argued.[130] One Algerian suggested that the problem was not just that the state had armed so many civilians, but that the security forces had primed the population for tribal war by pitting one group against another.[131] Others presented a much more simple logic. A report from Bentalha suggested that the rebels decided to organize the massacre simply because some locals took weapons from the government.[132]

Property rights and claims over prime agricultural land were also thought to be driving the massacres in Algeria. These issues were rendered in prosaic and local logics, as well as in grand, national, and conspiratorial ones. Survivors of the Ouarsenis massacres near Oued Rhiou and Souk El-Had said the attackers were simply their neighbors trying to take their houses.[133] "Even government officials admit that some of the violence is related to banditry rather than political motivation," noted a *Financial Times* reporter. "In rural areas south of Algiers, there is talk of disputes over land generating some of the attacks."[134] A grander thesis related the massacres to the government's continuing efforts, initiated in the 1980s, to privatize state-held properties. One of the last major assets was farmland, ostensibly socialized since the 1971 agrarian revolution.[135] Contradictory laws adopted in 1987 and 1990 brought claims of title into conflict between pre-1971 owners and those who had occupied and worked the land from 1971 onward.[136] The massacres were thus theorized as efforts to scare off the tenants; vacant or abandoned plots could be sold at a better price, particularly to larger interests in the financial, import-export, real estate, and agricultural sectors.[137] As one British expert argued, "The clearing of rural areas through the threat of renewed massacres opens the way for some to control and benefit from the abandonment of valuable land. The maintenance of a certain level of violence averts scrutiny, particularly from abroad, of a range of shady financial interests that many at the top undoubtedly operate."[138] The agents of the massacres were either those in government who were selling the land, those in the private sector who were seeking to buy it, or a combination of the two.[139]

The most important actors in the privatized violence thesis were often hybrids—actors with a foot in the state and another in the private sector—and even, at times, a third foot in the insurgency. They were called a variety of names ("mafia politico-financiere[s],"[140] or "gangsters posing as Muslim holy warriors"[141]) and accused of various untoward activities ("mafia-style gangsterism"[142]). An instructor at the Institut National d'Agronomie described the escalation of privatized violence in the Mitidja in the following way: a "mafia" of business interests related to agriculture had targeted union activists who were organizing locals during the early years of the violence. Because this syndicate failed in its efforts to privatize the land, large-scale massacres were then sponsored by "wholesalers and importers, mostly from the region of Blida."[143] "This is a war for land and wealth," Luis Martinez said in a press interview in mid-1997.[144]

History and culture also factored into privatized violence theses. This kind of warfare was private because it was intimate and localized. It drew on and recirculated private grievances with both shallow and deep genealogies. Vendettas were frequently cited as drivers of private violence in Algeria at the height of the massacre crisis. These vendettas could have been incurred during the two years of local Islamist government (1990–1992) and in the early years of the conflict, culminating in the mass atrocities of 1997 and 1998.[145] Or they could date back to the 1954–1962 war in which France had mobilized and armed Algerians in its fight against the independence movement.[146] Known as the *Harkis*, these French auxiliary forces composed of native Algerians were said to be a factor in the bloodshed of the 1990s, if not responsible for the conditions that led to the warfare in the first place.[147] The killing in Algeria was likely a countrywide "settling of accounts," suggested anthropologist Gilbert Grandguillaume. The war in the 1990s allowed many Algerians to attend to the unfinished business of the war of independence.[148] For others, the massacres were a manifestation of a cultural history of violence.[149] This "war of tribes"[150] did not have to be catalyzed by state manipulation; it was latent within the Algerian polity.

As were all other hypotheses of the violence in Algeria, particularly the massacres, the privatized violence thesis was just that—a thesis. There was no more or less evidence to support this thesis over the others, and the evidence for privatized logics driving the violence was as scattered and incoherent as the evidence for all other accounts. Almost no new information on the Algerian massacres has come to light since then. Despite this paucity of information, there is widespread consensus, particularly within the new sciences of terrorism, that the Algerian massacres can be understood within the logic of radicalized Islamic extremism. The reification of this thesis into fact can now be seen in the unproblematic constellation of Algeria's massacres with 9/11 and, more recently, the jihadi Muslim-on-Muslim violence witnessed in Iraq after 2003 and Syria after 2012.

WAR'S "OTHER"

What Algeria reveals to us is the strange power of the counterterrorism framework. This power is not underwritten by any superior capacity to illuminate the unseen mechanisms of contemporary mass violence, nor does it seem to offer a superior method of managing armed conflict worldwide. More than a decade after 9/11, so called jihadist movements were stronger and more widespread than ever. What had once been a small network of Islamists in Afghanistan and abroad, Al-Qaida, had rhizomically spread to West Africa, the central Sahara, the Horn of Africa, Yemen, Iraq, Syria, and Pakistan. All of this occurred in tandem with significant US military interventions and occupations in Iraq and Afghanistan, and the relentless pursuit of a more irregular war strategies globally—mass surveillance, the permanent presence of US drones in some regions, and special forces operating with little respect for traditional notions of state sovereignty. Trillions of dollars have been spent fighting terrorism, as well as researching it, with little to show for it. Despite the stunning failure of terrorism studies and counterterrorism doctrines, counterterrorism has become one of the organizing principles of global security. This is a strange paradox. As a strategy for understanding armed conflict and managing it, the new terrorism framework has proved to be disastrously inadequate. Yet no other approach to understanding and managing conflict after the Cold War has achieved as much institutional success. To understand this paradox, one has to understand the antipolitical function of terrorism studies and counterterrorism doctrine.

To render Algeria's violence in such a way as to make it useful to the post–Cold War science of terrorism and the post-9/11 techniques of confronting terrorism, these frameworks of understanding and management made as much as they unmade. But the ability of contemporary counterterrorism to impose its imagination on Algeria's violence has much to do with forces beyond its control. The inadequacy of other frameworks explains the success of the terrorism framing in Algeria. As examined in earlier and subsequent chapters, Algeria's violence fit with neither the civil war framework nor the genocide framework of the new humanitarianism of the 1990s. Where there was minimal consensus was on the fact that Algerian civilians were being terrorized on a massive scale. That no one could account for who was behind this terror-ism—the state, the insurgency, or other actors—is also one of the reasons that the terrorism framework succeeded in appropriating Algeria's violence. Science abhors a vacuum. And then of course there were the events of 9/11, which rad-ically changed the discourse on the Algerian massacres. This debate did not disappear entirely after 9/11; legal proceedings in France, initiated before 9/11, would represent the last major push to shed some light on the horrific violence in Algeria. In the end, the court in Paris deferred the question of the Algerian massacres to history, as if history writes itself (see Chapter 6).

That the history of the Algerian massacres became a story of Islamic ter-rorism testifies to the power of violence to create pasts that make the present understandable, and to make actions to control violence imperative. What were otherwise serious and credible understandings of the Algerian massa-cres (as state terrorism or privatized violence) became footnotes, marginalia, or rejected conspiracy theories in the new sciences of terrorism, radicaliza-tion, and jihadi violence after 9/11. The consolidation and hegemony of the Islamic terrorism thesis was not arrived at scientifically; rather, it was arrived at because of the way in which contemporary counterterrorism—as a new field of study that coordinates with a set of conflict management strategies—labors to produce a past, present, and future for itself but does so in ways for which it cannot account. These processes are not unlike those described by Benedict Anderson in his analysis of nationalist ideologies, in which episodes of past mass violence are understandable only in relation to more recent ones: "World War II begets World War I; out of Sedan comes Austerlitz; the ances-tor of the Warsaw Uprising is the state of Israel."[151] Or as Said would have it, meaning is determined largely by the explicit and implicit conceptual frame-works brought to bear on a problem; even basic description is embedded in invisible theories.[152] The history of contemporary terrorism, in which Alge-ria plays a significant role, is the product of the contemporary geopolitics of counterterrorism, not vice versa.

From their humble origins in the 1970s, terrorism studies and global coun-terterrorism doctrine grew to become central to how global security is managed in the first decade of the new millennium. To understand the power of terror-ism discourse today, one need only look to the world's largest military budget, that of the United States, which has become increasingly articulated in terms of counterterrorism. But that terrorism constitutes an actual threat to the security of powerful states is possible only because counterterrorism has made it so.[153]

What terrorism has come to represent is the Other who produces the legitimacy of efforts to understand, control, and eliminate violent resistance to the contemporary geopolitical order. Terrorism now stands as the Other relative to neoliberalism's way of war in a world where war appears to be disappearing. What "war" exists these days is recoded as peacekeeping, humanitarian intervention, and counterterrorism. The antipolitical function of terrorism studies and counterterrorism doctrine is to maintain a category of violence that automatically justifies efforts to eliminate it.

In a listening mode: US ambassador Cameron Hume (*third from right*) tours the site of the Sidi Hamed massacre on January 17, 1998. Photograph by Souhil Baghdadi. Courtesy of the *El Watan* archive, Algiers.

5 HUMANITARIAN INTERVENTION AND THE RESPONSIBILITY TO PROTECT

United by Our Absence of Knowledge of What to Do

FOR FOUR DECADES, the Libyan regime of Muammar Gaddafi had been quite useful to the West, right to the regime's bitter end. Under Gaddafi's rule, Libya became an important laboratory for various international conflict management strategies. What now seem like natural parts of the global security environment often found purchase for the first time in the confrontation between the antagonistic geopolitical visions of Washington and Tripoli. Libya was an early test case for unilateral and international responses to the idea of state sponsors of terrorism. There was the Reagan administration's punitive 1986 air raid against the Gaddafi regime for its ties to a Berlin discothèque bombing that killed several people. And then there were the protracted sanctions enacted by the UN Security Council after the Gaddafi regime was tied to the bombing of Pan Am flight 103 over Lockerbie, Scotland, in 1988. Post–Cold War, the Gaddafi regime also became central to emerging security doctrines that aimed to contain "pariah states."[1] These doctrines seemingly were vindicated, as was the George W. Bush doctrine of preventative intervention, when the Gaddafi regime suddenly agreed to meet all international demands for sanctions to be lifted, mere months after the US invasion of Iraq in 2003.

Gaddafi's final contribution to the science and management of conflict was to the Responsibility to Protect (R2P) project. In September 2001, the idea of a global R2P doctrine appeared to be one of the victims lying in the ruins of the twin towers. Ten years later, the R2P project's key intellectual and policy architects hailed the humanitarian intervention of the North Atlantic Treaty Organization (NATO) into the 2011 Libyan civil war to be a resounding success.[2] Never again would the international community have to say "never again." But it was a pyrrhic victory for R2P in Libya. Questions were raised about the UN Security Council's ostensible humanitarian warrant to authorize military action to protect civilians in Libya.[3] On the ground in Libya, NATO did little to protect civilians but did much to advance the military objectives of the rebellion, especially in the final months prior to the regime's decapitation. Legitimated and protected by NATO and the Security Council, Libya's rebels went on to commit the very kind of mass atrocities that the intervention was said to have prevented—ethnic cleansing, massacres, mass rapes, and other crimes against humanity.[4] What had been a foreign policy coup for the Obama administration became an albatross. As post-revolutionary Libya struggled to form a new polity, an attack on a US intelligence compound in Benghazi claimed the life of the US ambassador on September 11, 2012. In short order, Washington's freedom fighters had once again become terrorists.

The R2P project was also put into question by the international response to what had become a far bloodier civil war in Syria. Constrained by a skeptical Russia and China after NATO's overreach in Libya, the Council essentially tolerated in Syria some of the worst war crimes and crimes against humanity documented in the twenty-first century, so long as the international taboo against chemical weapons was not broken. When that taboo was broken in late 2013, the United States openly threatened to mount a unilateral intervention in the name of protecting Syrian civilians, with or without UN blessing. For any student of the history of humanitarian intervention and the R2P project, the irony of these unilateral threats was striking. The R2P project had been formulated in the wake of another unsanctioned intervention, when the United States and the United Kingdom used military force against Serbia in 1999 allegedly to stop Serbian atrocities being committed in Kosovo. Unwilling to see another Srebrenica massacre tarnish their legacies, US President Bill Clinton and British Prime Minister Tony Blair acted in the Kosovo crisis without UN Security Council approval because of the alleged humanitarian nature of the intervention. Though the multilateral body of NATO was the vehicle for their humanitarian ambitions in the Balkans, the military intervention into the Kosovo War caused immense global controversy. It threatened to undermine what little progress had been made since the end of the Cold War toward a new consensus on the legitimacy of humanitarian intervention—that is, a consensus on the conditions under which the United Nations could authorize military intervention into situations that did not seem to constitute threats to international peace and security but nonetheless were constituted by conscience-shocking violence—if not outright genocide—that morally warranted action. That the United Nations had actually *withdrawn* in the face of events in Bosnia and Rwanda—events that were later determined to have been acts of genocide—further reinforced the need for a new consensus on humanitarian intervention. In the wake of the contentious intervention against Serbia in 1999, the R2P project sought to lay the foundations for this consensus. It would be built by those who ostensibly had learned the key lesson of the 1990s: that mass atrocities could not be allowed to occur or to go unpunished. That lesson was built on histories of the 1990s that documented repeated international failures to stop the decade's worst crimes. Those failures are meticulously catalogued and autopsied in the founding documents of the R2P project,[5] as well as in the works of key intellectual activists such as Samantha Power's *A Problem from Hell* and Gareth Evans's *The Responsibility to Protect*.[6]

In these and related studies, Algeria's massacres and the international response to them are never mentioned. Given the explosion in analytical and normative research on the R2P project, it is surprising that the international outcry generated by Algeria's violence has been ignored or forgotten. This absence might initially be explained by two features of the Algeria case. One, the violence could not have been reasonably described as resulting from either a collapsed state or genocide, the two situations that R2P seeks to regulate. Two, the violence was actually Islamic terrorism perpetrated against civilians in the context of a fully functional, if negligent, state.[7] Though these two reasons might suffice as *post hoc* explanations, they ignore an important fact: the Algerian conflict was subjected to increasing levels of internationalization in late 1997 and 1998, such that preliminary forms of humanitarian intervention were being seriously considered in the North Atlantic world. The warrant for such interventionary claims was precisely that it had become impossible to be sure who was killing whom. Algeria thus represents a case of failed humanitarianization. It is not a failure in the same sense as Rwandan or Bosnia—that is, a failure to stop genocide. It is rather a failure to appreciate the ways in which Algeria's violence could not be understood or managed by humanitarian thought and action after the Cold War.

Only one major study has ever examined the international reaction to the Algerian massacres of 1997 and 1998. In fact, it does so in comparison to the international military response to the Kosovo crisis of the following year. In that study, Helle Malmvig is uninterested in the apparent hypocrisy in the two responses; instead, she uses the cases to explore synchronic variances in the nature of sovereignty.[8] Malmvig's exploration of the heterogeneous patterning of sovereignty reveals much about the nature of global power today, though it does so by explicitly refusing to account for the failure of humanitarian thought and action vis-à-vis Algeria's massacres. Efforts to understand and manage Algeria's massacres through the new frameworks of humanitarianism developed after the Cold War failed for several reasons. First, foreign interest in Algeria's conflict was responding to the levels of violence; once the violence retreated to acceptable levels, the interest disappeared. Second, interventionary talk was driven by concerns about the perpetrators of the massacres and about whether or not the Algerian state was complicit. These concerns created a paradoxical situation. To establish whether or not a humanitarian intervention was necessary for Algeria required answering the question that no one could answer: Who is killing whom? An intervention to protect Algerian civilians from mass slaughter thus became contingent upon an intervention to establish the truth of Algeria's atrocities (that is, an international commission of inquiry). Finally, there is also the brute fact that Algeria is Algeria. The failure of humanitarian thought and action in Algeria in 1997–1998 has to be understood in relation to the histories of colonial, anticolonial, and postcolonial Algeria. That is, how Algeria's particular geopolitical character was elaborated by and within several shifting international orders helps us to understand the response to the massacres of 1997–1998.[9] This inability to appreciate and engage geopolitical specificity is a particular deficiency in contemporary humanitarian thought and action. As far as the R2P project is concerned, Benghazi in 2011 was a replay of Srebrenica in 1995. Darfur in 2004 was Rwanda in 1994 all over again.

Indeed, the intellectual and policy architects of the R2P project have steadfastly refused to draw any lessons from the Algerian massacre crisis of 1997–1998. That Algeria is absent from the scientific and institution-building labors of the R2P project is not a mere accident; it is indicative of the project's antipolitical nature. Proponents of an international norm or doctrine like R2P claim that such an implication would apply only to the most challenging phenomenon in international conflict management: genocide. Yet genocide is, in another sense, the easiest problem to manage. On paper, at least, genocide is a neat, transparent, and bifurcated situation, one that rarely, if ever, obtains in actual conflicts. To label something *genocide* strips it of its political content and, just as important, ends political debate about what to do in response. Intervention is the only response to genocide. Yet the importance of stopping genocide, and the means to confront it (the 1948 Genocide Convention), had already been recognized more than six decades before the R2P project was initiated. There is also no geographical limit on what kinds of situations the Security Council can declare a threat to international peace and security; internal crises, wars, and humanitarian situations have long been managed by the Council's coercive powers. Sovereignty has never been sacrosanct—neither before the end of the Cold War nor after. That the intervention in Libya prevented a counterfactual (that is, an imaginary) genocide, and so signified the "end of the argument" concerning the use of military force to protect civilians,[10] is suggestive of the antipolitics of the R2P project. That political leaders should be able to use military force without question, even in the face of genocide, should be recognized as a dangerous idea for democratic polities to adopt. That contemporary humanitarian thought and action are informed by easy cases (Rwanda and Srebrenica) instead of by the most difficult (Algeria) is utterly apparent when one considers the international community's failure to stop mass civilian killing in Darfur and Syria, as well as in post-R2P Libya.

FUNDAMENTALLY, NOBODY KNOWS WHAT TO DO

Calls for intervention to stop the killing in 1990s Algeria were at their most frequent and intense during the major massacres of late 1997 and early 1998.[11] Though the suspension of constitutional norms in early 1992 had been cause for much international concern, few parties proposed concrete international action to restore to power the FIS, a political party whose democratic credentials were unknown.[12] By contrast, the foreign response to the massacres saw serious calls for intervention take shape in late 1997. The extent of the humanitiarianization of the Algerian conflict is revealed in the parallels casually drawn with other recent cases—cases in which international military force had been used belatedly or preemptively to stop atrocious violence or to repair war-torn societies. Bosnia and Rwanda, which would feature prominently in the formulation of the R2P project, became key points of reference in the discourse on Algeria as well, particularly after the Raïs massacre.[13] It was even suggested that the violence in Algeria was far worse than what had previously been declared internationally intolerable in those other cases. An official with the Red Cross suggested that the brutality of the massacres in Algeria made the Rwandan genocide seem clean and efficient by comparison.[14] Bentalha was described as a game-changing event like the Srebrenica massacre in Bosnia. It was a killing so massive that the world could no longer ignore the conflict that had generated it.[15] Similar sentiments found expression after the New Year's massacres of 1997–1998 in the western provinces[16] and the Sidi Hamed massacre.[17] In this context, the words *genocide*[18] and *holocaust*[19] found purchase. Algeria's massacre sites were also termed "killing fields"[20] and the perpetrators were compared to the Khmer Rouge[21] or the Nazi regime.[22] An editorial, citing Hannah Arendt's *Eichmann in Jerusalem*, speculated that the international community was paralyzed by the violence in Algeria because "sometimes the scope of evil seems too great for the human mind to deal with."[23] The fact that the violence in Algeria had become genocidal was, for other observers, the exact reason not to intervene.[24]

Arguments against intervention in Algeria often made implicit or explicit reference to notions of failed or collapsed states. What set Algeria apart, for some, was the fact that its government was still very much in control of the country.[25] During the Relizane massacres, Joe Stork of Human Rights Watch, one of the groups leading the charge for international action, admitted that intervention would be difficult. He argued that "unlike, say, the situation in Rwanda—essentially without a government for this period of genocide—the [Algerian] government is very much in control, particularly in the areas that count."[26] The question driving interventionary interest, after all, was whether or not elements of the Algerian regime were playing a role in the massacres. A Western diplomat suggested that, even in the face of allegations of state complicity in the massacres, the Algerian government had become more, not less, central to a solution: it "is the only authority in the land that can prevent the chaos worsening."[27] Though the R2P project would later redefine state failure to include the failure to protect civilians from mass atrocities, the apparent stability of the Algerian government in late 1997 and early 1998 often had the effect of ruling out intervention entirely. This was particularly acute when intervention was defined solely in terms of military action. Witness assertions such as "Fundamentally, nobody knows what to do," from Washington think-tank regular Andrew Pierre,[28] and "We are united by our absence of knowledge of what to do," from Dominique Moïsi of the Institut Français des Relations Internationales.[29] Not knowing what to do depended on tacitly knowing what had been ruled out.

States and international bodies helped reinforce the humanitarian framing of Algeria's escalating violence through statements of concern, expressions of moral outrage, declarations of impotence, and eventually demands for transparency. The change during and after the massacres of August and September 1997 is noticeable. In February 1997, French Foreign Minister Hervé de Charette was asked about the "shocking silence" of France toward the violence in Algeria and opposition calls for a more active French policy on the issue. De Charette's response suggested that even commenting on the violence in Algeria was tantamount to neocolonial interference. "Algeria is not France; that has to be understood and admitted once and for all," he explained. "It is a sovereign nation. It is up to Algeria to solve its problems, and up to the Algerian people to decide their fate."[30] Even the Bougara massacre of April 1997, in which more than one hundred persons were reportedly killed, had little effect. The Clinton administration, pointing its finger at the Islamist insurgency, condemned the massacre and called for "an end to the violence," though without saying how Algeria or the international community could actually accomplish this.[31]

The Raïs massacre in August 1997 not only seemed like a new scale of killing in Algeria, but also followed a succession of atrocities over the previous weeks. In the months after the April massacre at Bougara and during the campaign season for the June 5 parliamentary elections (the first such elections since 1991 under the new 1996 constitution), massacres were initially less intense and frequent. Mid- to late July then saw several reported massacres in the Blida and Aïn Defla provinces. Reports tallied one hundred to four hundred killed in all of these episodes combined. In the week leading up to the Raïs massacre, there were reports of two massacres in the Médéa and Blida provinces, each totaling more than sixty killed. Admittedly, the international response to the Raïs and other late-summer massacres was attenuated by another global event: the death of Princess Diana. This fact was not lost on some observers.[32]

The mitigated response to the Raïs massacre nonetheless followed the same script as was laid out in the response to previous massacres in Algeria: condemnation of the violence and calls for a domestic solution to the conflict. The new UN Secretary-General, Kofi Annan, was quick to express his dismay and regret at "the continuing loss of life," which had surpassed a "horrendous level." His statement also continued to frame the issue as an internal political matter in which "the Algerian people" would have to find a solution for themselves.[33] The new French government of Lionel Jospin shared this attitude. As Jospin's foreign minister, Hubert Védrine, told Le Monde, "Algerians have to find a solution to their problems themselves."[34] Even France's President Jacques Chirac ventured a rare comment on Algeria, pronouncing his "indignation at these acts of barbarity."[35] The US State Department, while acknowledging that the massacres had "reached yet another astonishing threshold of barbarity," towed the same line as France, placing its hopes in the Algerian "political system" so that the "Algerian people can work their way back towards some modicum of civility and of peace." When asked if the United States would support a UN inquiry into the violence, the State Department spokesperson suggested that Washington would if the Algerian government agreed to it.[36] The Vatican, on the other hand, criticized the international community's nonresponse to this "unprecedented crisis."[37] Pope John Paul II described it as "unheard-of violence."[38]

Suggestions that there should be an international inquiry were not the only sign that the Raïs massacre had changed the international dynamic around Algeria. Two days after the massacre, the UN Secretariat's position seemed to shift as well. Annan gave reporters an off-the-cuff statement while attending the Venice Film Festival; he suggested that the killing in Algeria was of such an order that the international community could no longer remain indifferent: "The killing has gone on far too long. [. . .] We are dealing with a situation which for a long time has been treated as an internal affair, and yet as the killing goes on and the numbers rise it is extremely difficult for all of us to pretend it is not happening, that we don't know about it and we should leave the Algerian population to their lot."[39] Annan's intimation that it was time to internationalize the Algerian conflict elicited a strong rebuke from Algiers and even from the French government. Védrine asserted that no foreign actor could make a useful contribution to the crisis in Algeria.[40] Indeed, Annan soon admitted that Algeria was the exact opposite of a failed state: any international initiative depended on the full cooperation of Algerian authorities.[41] But the clamor was difficult to silence after Raïs. Editorials in *Le Monde* and the *New York Times* called for more international pressure to stop the killing.[42] The *Economist* supported an inquiry: "The West should insist on finding out what is happening."[43]

Strong reactions followed the Béni Messous massacres as well. Citing a recent photograph showing the heads of decapitated Algerian children in a bucket, Lisbet Palme of the UN Children's Fund urged the world to pay attention to the "bloodbath."[44] Though Amnesty International did not specifically call for an international inquiry, the rights group took a position that would strongly resonate with the R2P project today: "With tens of thousands killed, it is high time for the Algerian authorities to acknowledge that human rights protection is not an internal affair and to take concrete measures to protect the civilian population."[45] In the wake of Raïs and Béni Messous, Algeria's violence was now understood as an international humanitarian problem in which intervention was increasingly being framed in terms of *how*, not *if*. For reasons of history and geopolitics, the burden of managing the humanitarianization of the Algerian conflict would fall on the shoulders of Paris and Washington.

PLATITUDES FROM THE PODIUMS

Caution prevailed. After the massacre at Béni Messous, a White House spokesperson described the latest massacres as "stupefying" and as breaking "yet another astonishing threshold of barbarity."[46] The outgoing US ambassador to Algiers, Ronald Neumann, during his last meeting with President Zéroual, told the Algerian president that the US government "support[s] military measures that are consistent with the rule of law to protect civilians." This comment was read in two ways: first, Washington was signaling its support for a more aggressive counterinsurgency effort to stop the massacres; second, Washington was implicitly acknowledging international concern that the Algerian security, military, and intelligence agencies were grossly negligent vis-à-vis the massacres, if not somehow complicit in them. Most important of all, Neumann was acknowledging that intervention in any form, including diplomatic efforts to reconcile the regime and the Islamic opposition, would happen only if Algeria allowed an initiative in the first place. As an unidentified US official explained, "Any kind of mediation within the international context would have to be in agreement with all the parties. We haven't really gotten into this question."[47]

The European Union followed with roughly the same response. It expressed collective "shock" at these new massacres, condemned the "terrorism and indiscriminate violence," and encouraged the ongoing process of political and economic reforms in Algeria.[48] EU President Georges Wohlfahrt, Foreign Secretary of Luxemburg, also expressed "concern," but he reiterated the idea that "Algerians must find for themselves a solution to the serious crisis afflicting their country."[49] Other actors within the European Union, however, were pressing for more engagement. The idea of sending an *ad hoc* EU delegation to the Algerian parliament surfaced in mid-September. One of the key architects of the proposal in the EU Parliament, Daniel Cohn-Bendit of Germany's Green Party, favored a more aggressive joint European policy. For obvious historical reasons, he felt that France should not be looked to for international leadership on this issue, because it was unable to call a spade a spade (*appeler un chat un chat*). As elsewhere, increasing reports of Algerian state indifference and possible participation in the massacres were driving interventionary talk in the European Union.[50] French MEP (member of the European Parliament) André Soulier, chair of the EU parliament's subcommittee on human rights, also backed the proposal, but only as a means to "start down the road to peace." There was also an effort to frame the initiative within the ongoing negotiations over an EU-Algeria association agreement and the reforms that Algeria was undertaking to make it happen. That is, it would neither be an intervention nor be motivated by the massacres. Soulier tried to make this concept as clear as possible: it "will be necessary to avoid Algeria thinking we are going to become involved in its internal affairs."[51] The EU parliament thus adopted a resolution on September 19 in support of sending a delegation to Algiers in the name of dialogue between parliamentarians. Though carefully framed as a dialogue rather than as a fact-finding missing, the interparliamentary initiative would nonetheless be characterized in the media as an intervention.

The following day delivered news of some fifty people being massacred near Tablat in the Médéa province. Two days later was the Bentalha massacre, with reported death tolls equivalent to Raïs if not greater. Again, the international response was anguished cries of outrage and impotence. Védrine was quick to express his "revulsion" at the "monstrous," "absolutely heartrending" massacres. He also stated that any intervention without the Algerian government's permission remained unrealistic. "We cannot do nothing. But what can we do?"[52] British Foreign Office minister Derek Fatchett likewise condemned the killing but refused to support anything other than an Algerian solution.[53] Klaus Kinkel, Germany's foreign minister, equated such inaction with indifference. "How long can the international community look away?" he asked.[54] The German opposition went even further, urging France and Germany to engage the UN Security Council to resolve the crisis.[55] At the United Nations, the High Commissioner for Human Rights, Mary Robinson, met with Algerian Foreign Minister Ahmed Attaf to discuss the massacres. A post-meeting UN statement stuck close to the script of expressing concern and calling for an internal solution to an internal problem.[56] Departing from this script, Robinson later told reporters, "Human rights have no borders. [. . .] The situation in Algeria cannot be considered an internal matter." The Algerian government quickly "deplored" her "selective" remarks.[57]

Once again, eyes turned to Paris and Washington for action. Responding to the Bentalha massacre, an anonymous White House official said that the US executive was "outraged by the savagery of the attack" and supported what they called "national reconciliation."[58] This call was echoed by President Chirac during a visit to Moscow.[59] At the United Nations, Védrine and then US Secretary of State Madeleine Albright met on the sidelines of the General Assembly. Over breakfast they agreed to meet again to discuss a joint policy toward the Algeria crisis.[60] A fortnight after the massacre at Bentalha, a journalist, citing the "almost genocidal [. . .] proportions" of the violence of the massacres, interrogated the Clinton administration about whether the US government would go beyond "platitudes from the podiums" in its response to Algeria. The State Department's spokesperson, James Rubin, pointed to the UN meeting between Albright and Védrine as action. When he was subsequently asked if there was a threshold for intervention, Rubin evaded the question and reiterated the Franco-American pledge to work together. When finally asked to state what the current US policy toward Algeria was, Rubin admitted that he did not know the specifics.[61]

Implicit in this promise of a joint French and US initiative was the fact that, after Bentalha, Algeria's violence was almost entirely understood, and so increasingly managed, through a humanitarian framework. This transformation did little to resolve the impasse in thought and action vis-à-vis Algeria; in fact, it raised new problems. A European official summed up the impasse in the following terms: "The EU defers to the French, and the French are paralyzed. [...] I don't say that critically, because nobody including the United States pretends to have an idea of how to tackle the problem. We are all groping for answers, and there is a real paucity of ideas."[62] This paucity of ideas was evident in a statement issued following a meeting of EU foreign ministers at the end of October 1997. The statement again anticipated the rhetoric of the R2P project. It expressed solidarity with the Algerian people and underscored their right to be protected by their government from mass atrocities. "Obviously, it's not a declaration that will have any immediate impact," said Luxemburg's Jacques Poos, the host of the meeting.[63]

More aggressive measures were off the table. A UN peacekeeping force, for example, was rarely given explicit consideration except to dismiss it or, as noted in earlier examples, to draw a dichotomy between absolute inaction and military intervention. Bill Richardson, US ambassador to the United Nations, went as far as to assert, by evoking bitter US memories of failed peacekeeping in Somalia,[64] that the violence in Algeria was far worse than anything the United Nations had yet tackled. An unnamed Western official in Algiers even suggested that a diplomatic initiative would fail for the same reason: "I'm not sure outsiders can play a constructive role. [...] As long as the situation on the ground is so fractious and so murky, I mean, whose heads are we supposed to be banging together?"[65] For prominent international human rights groups, the course of action after Bentalha was clear: to address the conflict's opacity head on. In a joint statement, several leading groups called on the UN Commission on Human Rights to hold a special meeting on Algeria. They also called for an investigation "to ascertain the facts, examine allegations of responsibility and to make recommendations in respect of the massacres and other abuses by all sides in Algeria."[66] As Prime Minister Jospin admitted on French television in early October, the major problem facing an international response to the massacres was the lack of reliable information.[67]

The situation became even more unclear in the weeks after the Bentalha massacre. Though massacre activity diminished in October as Algeria approached nationwide elections for municipal and provincial governments, conflicting reports continued to emerge from the August and September massacres. It became increasingly difficult for the Algerian government to maintain the impression that the massacres had been the sole work of terrorist gangs.[68] As detailed in Chapter 4, this narrative had already been subject to growing criticism resulting from several disturbing features of the massacres. The failure of the government to prevent or interrupt any massacres was often contrasted with the proximity of local security installations (civilian militias, police, military, gendarmerie) to the killing sites. The inability of Algerian journalists, foreign journalists, and international monitoring groups to access these sites and interview survivors was likewise troubling. The reliability of the accounts that did emerge in the Algerian and international press, whether through independent reporting or via the Algerian government's official state news agencies, was impossible to evaluate. The impenetrability of Algeria's conflict zones abated briefly when the government began issuing special journalist visas for the elections. Wanting to control international perceptions of the conflict, the Algerian government organized press junkets for foreign reporters to access some of the massacre sites, mainly Bentalha and Raïs, under close supervision. From the reports, an even more complex and confusing picture of the massacres emerged.[69]

Then, in late October and early November 1997, even more disturbing accounts of the massacres appeared in the French, Irish, and British press. A number of former and active Algerian state agents gave interviews in which they claimed to have participated in massacres or to have firsthand knowledge of the regime's complicity in them. One of the most dramatic interviews, in terms of its international effect, was someone going by the name Hakim, allegedly a serving DRS officer, who was interviewed in *Le Monde*. He seemed to corroborate claims that the Algerian intelligence services were responsible for some of the massacres directly (that is, as commandos disguised as insurgents) and for others indirectly (that is, by manipulating the insurgency). Shortly thereafter, the French Socialist Party backed calls for an international inquiry. "It is the duty of the international community to establish what is happening in Algeria," said a party official.[70] The Algerian government vehemently rejected the idea of an inquiry, and received support for this rejection from the Arab League.[71] Amnesty International, on the other hand, charged Algeria with intimidating its critics and called on the United Nations to press for an investigation.[72] In what was reported as an Algerian effort to head off such initiatives, Foreign Minister Attaf met with EU President Poos in Luxembourg and then with the EU Parliament's Committee on Foreign Affairs in Brussels on November 26 and 27.[73] At the United Nations, Commissioner Robinson continued to press for an inquiry into the massacres and claimed that negotiations for a mission were under way. Algiers denied this and seemed to be lobbying strongly against such a mission.[74] One of the problems facing support for an inquiry was the relative drop-off in spectacular massacre activity following Bentalha. As Le Monde reporter Jean-Pierre Tuquoi noted, Algeria no longer constituted an international humanitarian problem because it was no longer front-page news.[75] That was about to change.

WE'RE NOT GOING TO SEND IN THE MARINES

The humanitarianization of the Algerian conflict peaked in January 1998. Between December 31, 1997, and January 6, 1998, reports of a new mass killing spree in western Algeria reached international audiences. This time the sites were in the Ouarsenis mountains in the province of Relizane. Conservative estimates put the number of lives lost in the hundreds. A week before, there had been vague reports of massacres in the adjacent Tiaret and Tissemsilt provinces. What initially seemed like an anomaly in Tiaret and Tissemsilt (large-scale massacres in the western region) became a trend after the reports from Relizane. The Ouarsenis massacres also led some observers to conclude that the violence in the Mitidja had been pacified by the Algerian military, but such speculation was proved false by reports of a massive slaughter in Sidi Hamed, not far from Algiers, on January 12. The cumulative civilian mortality of the past fortnight had, by several accounts, topped one thousand. As before, international condemnation, expressions of support for the Algerian people, and calls for intervention naturally followed.[76]

Germany was one of the first governments to propose action. On January 4, Foreign Minister Kinkel suggested that an EU "troika"—the past, current, and future holders of the EU presidency—visit Algeria to discuss humanitarian aid to the victims and cooperation in the fight against terrorism.[77] The idea was to inject neutral foreign aid workers into the killing zones to shed some light on who was behind the rolling atrocities in Algeria, or at least to prevent more killings by acting as observers. Such an initiative, however, would require French backing. Paris initially responded to the January massacres with boilerplate condemnation ("atrocious and horrible"), expressions of "solidarity," and calls for "reconciliation" in Algeria.[78] But soon the French government joined with the Portuguese government in support of the German proposal, which Foreign Minister Védrine described as "very useful."[79] The British government, which then held the EU presidency, suggested a more limited response: humanitarian aid and services to the victims under the auspices of the Algerian government.[80] Prime Minister Jean Chrétien of Canada dispatched his own envoy to Algiers to make the same offer of aid.[81] Secretary-General Annan's office, which did not react until after the Sidi Hamed massacre, diplomatically asserted that Algerian civilians needed to be protected.[82]

The problem, as always, was that nobody was sure *from whom* Algerians needed to be protected, though it was utterly clear that the Algerian state was incapable of providing such protection or, more disturbing, unwilling to do so. Implicitly recognizing these facts, the US government announced on January 5 its support for having UN human rights experts visit the country. In justifying its position, the US State Department claimed that the Algerian government was willing to accept such a visit.[83] Apparently, however, this was not true. Not only did Algeria deem France's support for Germany's troika to be "unacceptable,"[84] but it also saw Washington's position as simply intolerable. Cameron Hume, the new US ambassador in Algiers, was quickly called in to the Algerian Foreign Ministry to be "reminded" of Algeria's "categorical rejection" of "an international commission of inquiry, no matter where it comes from or whatever its form or nature."[85] The provocative aspect of this new US position was the way in which it openly questioned the Algerian government's narrative of the massacres. An inquiry was necessary, Rubin explained, because it could help "get to the bottom of some of these issues to determine the extent of the massacres, perhaps begin *to pin more clearly the blame for them*."[86] The following day he added, "Let's remember that the facts of many of these massacres are often unclear. *The perpetrators are sometimes unclear*."[87]

After Hume's dressing down in Algiers, the State Department changed its approach and Rubin adopted friendlier language: "Let's focus first on the culprits. These terrorist attacks must be condemned in the strongest possible terms. The terrorists must be condemned by the entire international community."[88] By the end of the week, reporters felt that Rubin was playing a semantic game with them. He insisted that the US government had never called for an international commission of inquiry but had encouraged a visit by special UN rapporteurs.[89] Even on the question of rapporteurs, Algeria's position remained absolute. The

Algerian ambassador to the United Nations, Abdallah Baali, reiterated, "We have said repeatedly that the United Nations has no role to play in Algeria." Robinson's desire was to have either Senegal's Bacre Ndiaye, UN expert on summary and arbitrary executions, or Nigel Rodley of Britain, UN torture expert, visit Algeria. These options were nonstarters as far as Algiers was concerned.[90] Even a modest investigation "would mean there are doubts over who is responsible for the massacres," Baali explained, "while everyone knows who they are."[91] In the wake of the Ouarsenis massacres, the contradiction became clearer, though no one seemed to recognize it: to establish whether or not intervention was necessary, the international community would somehow have to intervene.

A significant constraint on humanitarian thought and action vis-à-vis the Algerian massacres had been the implicit rejection of military intervention. After Relizane, the scope of the massacres forced this rejection to become explicit. "I'd like to see the first country that will send its military there," commented Eric Derycke, Belgium's foreign minister.[92] The top Democrat on the US Senate's Foreign Relations committee, Lee Hamilton, bluntly echoed this sentiment: "We're not going to send in the Marines."[93] There was broad consensus that Algeria's violence was indeed conscience shocking, but there was little consensus as to whether or not it threatened international peace and security.[94] For the French government, a multilateral UN force was out of the question unless the Algerian state collapsed.[95] Others shared this view as well. The question of intervention pivoted not on the scale of deliberate violence against civilians but on whether or not there was a functional state. Even at the height of the massacres, the Algerian state appeared to be far healthier than it had been just two to three years prior. From the perspective of international oil corporations and the governments that supported their activities in Algeria, the massacres in the Mediterranean north had very little to do with their day-to-day extractive operations hundreds of miles away in the Sahara.[96] A report by the *Economist* Intelligence Unit suggested that the major concern of energy companies in January 1998 was not the violence *per se* but rather the extent to which their investments in Algeria could come into play as international leverage against the Algerian regime's intransigence on the question of an inquiry.[97]

There was also a competing view on the question of state collapse and intervention. Here the argument was the opposite: intervention should be considered to prevent Algeria from falling apart. Humanitarian experiences in the former Yugoslavia and Rwanda were cited as examples of similar crises in which floods of refugees led to spillover violence in neighboring territories. Algeria's crisis was no longer an internal matter, it was suggested, because it now threat-ened pan-Mediterranean security.[98] Britain's Foreign Secretary Robin Cook advocated for a more concerted European response to the Algerian massacres on the basis of an argument for preventative intervention. This argument was couched, however, in terms of preventing terrorist safe havens instead of pre-venting refugees from overwhelming neighboring states. "If you allow terrorism to take growth and take root in any one country," Cook argued, "it very quickly can get exported to the rest of the international community."[99] That the inter-national community was responsible for preventing terrorist safe havens was an argument that would come to dominate post-9/11 counterterrorism discourse. Here we see an early formulation of this global counterterrorism doctrine in the humanitarian debate about Algeria's violence in the late 1990s. Needless to say, Cook's arguments largely fell on deaf ears.

Whether or not one considers the visit of the EU troika an intervention, it was undoubtedly brief. On January 8, 1998, Algeria agreed to host a delegation from the European Union, but with the proviso that its mandate was to talk about Algeria's "fight against terrorism."[100] It was not to be described as an in-quiry.[101] The European Union and Algeria first had to negotiate the right diplo-matic level of the delegation, which was eventually composed of three deputy foreign ministers: Derek Fatchett of Britain, Benita Ferrero-Waldner of Austria, and Georges Wohlfahrt of Luxembourg, respectively representing the current, future, and past holders of the EU presidency. They set out on January 19 and joined EU Commission Vice President Manuel Marin in Algiers. The delega-tion's itinerary was also modest. It included meetings with Foreign Minister Attaf and Prime Minister Ouyahia, several opposition parties and newspaper editors, and representatives of official humanitarian and human rights bodies. At the outset, Marin stated his hope that the breadth of the discussion would be "quite wide." He also stressed the need for the dialogue to be "careful and con-structive" so as not to "delegitimise" Algerian authorities.[102] Before leaving for Algiers, the leader of the mission, Fatchett, told the BBC that part of their aim in going was to convince the Algerian government to become more transparent about the massacres: "It would help their case," he argued, "if we had a very clear statement and a clear understanding of the cause of these events, who's respon-sible for them."[103] The visit concluded the following day, January 20, with no new light shed on the massacres, nor any signs of a forthcoming international inquiry. The troika nonetheless asserted in their departing statements that the visit had had a positive effect.[104] During the troika's visit, thirty-three people were killed in various attacks across the country, according to news reports. In the hills above Algiers, for example, a bus had been ripped apart by a bomb.[105]

Given the cooperative tone of the troika's final statement, it was surprising that a subsequent meeting of the EU foreign ministers under Cook's chairmanship produced a more antagonistic statement on the massacres. The EU "demanded" that Algeria allow an inquiry, "regretted" Algeria's refusal to allow UN investigators, and "hoped" it would allow them in the future.[106] Though the statement blamed "terrorist groups" for the violence, the EU Ministerial Council pressed Algeria for "greater transparency."[107] Pierre Moscovici, France's Minister for European Affairs, went further and threatened that the European Union "has its limits."[108] The Algerian government naturally blasted these calls for an inquiry. Communications Minister Habib Chawki Hamraoui suggested on Al Jazeera that all such efforts aimed "to control Algeria."[109] Cook even admitted that it was entirely up to Algeria to accept or reject any international initiative. By this time, the violence in Algeria had tapered off from the peak intensity of early January. Only half a dozen massacres were reported between Sidi Hamed and the release of the ministers' statement. None of those massacres appeared to top twenty deaths.

As Algeria's violence declined, so too did international enthusiasm for a humanitarian intervention. The next international foray into Algeria occurred in mid-February 1998, when an EU parliamentary delegation, first proposed in September 1997, finally arrived. The nine-member delegation—five of them French—met with Algerian officials, politicians, and members of civil society. Though frequently framed in the international media as an extension of EU efforts to establish an inquiry (if not as an outright fact-finding mission in its own right[110]), the visit was actually unrelated to, and predated, the troika's initiative. The invitation had ostensibly come from the MEPs' counterparts in the Algerian parliament several months prior, though as noted earlier the idea had come about in Brussels in late 1997 in the wake of the Raïs and Bentalha massacres. The head of the delegation, André Soulier, was adamant that the visit was not an investigation nor would they seek to convince Algerians to accept one.[111] For most of their visit, the MEPs were cloistered in the isolated Djenane El-Mithak hilltop state residence. Foreign journalists accompanied them but were placed in a separate hotel and similarly restricted in their movements. Media, officials, personalities, and activists who met the delegation were ferried to the EU parliamentarians' redoubt. MEP Daniel Cohn-Bendit, in a small act of defiance, regularly absented himself from the daily press conferences. He even threatened to quit the delegation if they were not allowed to tour a massacre site and visit still-imprisoned FIS leaders, but he never made good on the threat.[112] Toward the end of the mission, Soulier dramatically tore apart an unopened letter from the FIS at one of the press briefings. It had been delivered to the MEPs by Abdennour Ali-Yahia, head of Algeria's oldest independent human rights group, the Ligue Algérienne de Défense des Droits de l'Homme. Whether the letter was an invitation to meet or, as claimed by the FIS, simply an assessment of the situation in Algeria, this "consensus" act of the MEPs reportedly pleased the Algerian government as much as it pleased Algeria's anti-Islamist press.[113] Back in Brussels, Soulier attempted to defend the mission's neutrality: "We are supporting neither the Algerian Government nor the opposition. [. . .] We support democracy." As for an inquiry, Soulier rejected the idea: "Who is killing who?" he asked rhetorically. "Nobody, when speaking to us, pointed the finger at the army."[114] As the mission departed Algiers, a string of bombs exploded in the central neighborhoods of Birkhadem and Bab El-Oued.[115] In the final two weeks of February there were four reported massacres, claiming a total of more than fifty lives.

Outside of Algeria, legislative committees in the United Kingdom[116] and the United States held hearings that did little to shed new light on the massacres.[117] It was clear from the latter that what little enthusiasm there was in Washington for an inquiry had all but disappeared by March. This was abundantly clear when former ambassador Ronald Neumann, along with Martin Indyk, the new assistant secretary of state for the Near East, toured the Maghrib, meeting with Attaf and Ouyahia in Algiers in mid-March. It was officially a regional orientation trip for Indyk, but they carried a message from Clinton to Zéroual expressing the United States' desire to have better relations with Algeria. Indyk reportedly told his Algerian interlocutors in private that allowing some kind of foreign inquiry would help disperse the clouds of doubt hanging over the massacres in Algeria. Indyk's public statements, on the other hand, were lauded by Algerian state media as a 180-degree turnaround from the low point of early January.[118] Back in Washington, a State Department official boasted to the Washington press corps that Algeria had committed itself to a new "process of openness and transparency." When pressed on what exactly that meant, the US official could not provide any specifics except for one fact: "They don't want a U.N. Human Rights Commission special rapporteur to come in. All right?"[119]

By the time of the fifty-fourth session of the UN Commission on Human Rights, which ran from the end of March 1998 through most of April 1998, it was clear that dramatic international action on Algeria was not going to materialize. Coincidentally or not, massacre activity in Algeria had substantially subsided in the face of the international outrage witnessed in January and February. Leading rights groups nonetheless urged the Commission to press Algiers to allow UN special rapporteurs into the country, something the Algerian government had allegedly agreed to "in principle."[120] Both the US and European delegations signaled their support for an independent examination of the massacres, preferably a UN rapporteur, but a rumored US resolution never materialized.[121] During the Commission's session, which celebrated the semicentennial of the Universal Declaration of Human Rights, more than eighty resolutions were adopted. These included, for example, resolutions on Sudan, Burma, Rwanda, Haiti, Palestine, the Democratic Republic of the Congo, Iran, and the former Yugoslavia. The situation in Algeria was not even officially listed on the Commissions agenda. An official from Human Rights Watch lamented, "Algeria was the main topic in the hallways and the cafeterias [. . .] but in the meetings, it couldn't be mentioned." As the body's session came to an end on April 26, Amnesty International strongly condemned the Commission's inaction on Algeria: "During its six-week session, thousands of people were killed or injured in Algeria, yet the Commission did nothing. If a blind eye is turned to such blatant and often publicized abuses, what hope can victims not in the international spotlight have."[122] Though the claim of "thousands" was hyperbole, there were eight reported massacres in March and April; together their suggested death toll was 170 victims. Among these massacres, the slaughter of some fifty people in Bouira Lahdab in the Djelfa province on March 27 was the largest reported massacre since Sidi Hamed.[123]

Given the outcome at the Commission on Human Rights and the relative decline in massacre activity, further UN action might have seemed unexpected. On June 29, however, Annan announced that Algeria had invited a UN "panel of eminent persons" to "gather information on the situation in Algeria." The panel would have "free and complete access to all sources of information necessary for the panel to exercise its functions, in order to have a clear vision and a precise perception of the reality of the situation in all its dimensions."[124] As a panel organized by the UN Secretariat, its work would be independent of other UN bodies, including the UN Human Rights Committee, which met on July 20–21 to discuss Algeria's performance under the International Covenant on Civil and Political Rights. For two years, Algeria had failed to deliver its periodic human rights self-assessment.[125] Facing the Committee, the Algerian government was forced to address the touchy subject of the massacres and state-armed militias.

The Committee's findings, vigorously denounced by the Algerian government, were clearly limited given the paucity of information available on the conflict's violence. According to the Committee's chair, French jurist Christine Chanet, their interaction with Algeria had been a "dialogue of the deaf."[126]

The UN Secretariat's *ad hoc* panel succeeded in eliciting more cooperation largely because Algerian authorities had dictated its mandate. Touring the country between July 22 and August 4, the panel met with a wide variety of Algerian politicians, officials, personalities, and members of civil society. They also met with the families of "disappeared" persons and with a paramilitary self-defense group in the Kabylia mountains, and they visited the sites of the Béni Messous massacre and a more recent massacre in Aïn Khelil in the Tlemcen province that occurred on July 25 and resulted in twelve reported deaths. Leading the mission was former Portuguese president Mário Soares. He was supported by former prime ministers Inder Kumar Gugral of India and Abdel Karim Kabariti of Jordan. Former US representative to the United Nations Donald McHenry was also a member, along with Amos Wako, Kenya's attorney general, and former EU president Simone Veil of France.

The panel's report admitted that Algerian authorities did not permit the panel's members to meet with FIS leaders, whether imprisoned (Madani and Benhadj) or released (Hachani); nor were they allowed to visit the house of the recently assassinated Kabyle singer Lounès Matoub or to interview Algerian activists struggling for the rights of Algeria's Berber-speaking minorities.[127] Under such heavy constraints, the panel admitted that "we had neither the means nor the mandate to conduct investigations of our own." The final report refrained from criticizing the Algerian government directly. It "concluded" ("recommendations" to the Algerian government were explicitly not allowed under the panel's mandate) that "efforts to combat terrorism must take place within the framework of legality, proportionality, and respect for the fundamental human rights." This statement, however, was not an implicit criticism of Algeria's dirty war against the insurgency. As the report stated, the Algerian government's "efforts to combat this phenomenon" of terrorism deserve "the support of the international community."[128]

Amnesty International was quick to denounce the Panel's report as a "whitewash."[129] Soares did not agree. "We listed evidence of human rights abuses by both sides," he argued. But any thought that the report was using the terms *terrorism* and *terrorists* in an ambiguous way (so that state terror could be included) was quickly dispelled by Soares: "We didn't put them on the same level:

the terrorists' slitting of children's throats is not the same as torturing detainees or holding people in prison without charge."[130] After the panel's report was released, Human Rights Watch expressed concern that it would be seen "as a substitute for an in-country investigation by U.N. human rights experts."[131] As the final UN statement on the massacres, the report became just that.

WHO PROTECTS WHOM?

The Irish rock band U2 held a concert in Sarajevo, Bosnia, on September 23, 1997. The reported attendance was fifty thousand. The group's vocalist, Bono, a celebrity icon of transnational humanitarian advocacy, said that the concert signified a return to normalcy after years of bloodshed in the heart of former Yugoslavia.[132] On the other side of the Mediterranean, Algeria awoke to news of another massive killing spree. As victims were shuttled to the Salim Zmirli Hospital in the El Harrach neighborhood of Algiers, Hocine Zaourar, an AFP photographer who had already visited the massacre site at Bentalha, found at least a hundred women waiting outside the hospital for information on those being treated inside. He captured one woman, a mother, in a moment where she appears to be succumbing to grief after reportedly discovering that her eight children had died in the massacre. The following day, the photo, which *Le Monde* labeled the "Madonna in Hell,"[133] appeared on the front pages of several major newspapers worldwide, including *L'Humanité, Libération, Le Parisien, El País*, the *L.A. Times*, the *International Herald Tribune*, the *Guardian*, the *Sun*, and *Newsday*.[134]

The director of Agence France-Presse's photography department, Jean-Francois Le Mounier, later explained that the image had "immediately gone around the world because it expressed better than any words the emotion aroused by the horrible massacre at Bentalha."[135] Yet the power of the image transcended Algeria. Commentators often drew comparisons with some of the most famous images in the history of photojournalism. "It was one of those photographs, like the little Vietnamese girl with her skin in napalmed tatters, that send reverberations round the globe."[136] "Just as Robert Capa's dying Republican soldier epitomised the Spanish Civil War [. . .] Hocine's photograph has become Algeria's icon."[137] The following month, the Italian magazine *Rivista del Cinematografo* awarded the photo its top prize, calling it "a symbol of the struggle against barbarism and for the promotion of peace between men."[138] Among the several other accolades it earned was the 1998 World Press Photo award, considered the top prize in photojournalism. In choosing this photo, the World Press Photo jury reminded the world that "there are very few pictures on the

El Watan photographer Souhil Baghdadi captures the "Madonna of Bentalha" at almost the same moment as AFP photographer Hocine Zaouar, whose arm is visible on the left side of the frame. Photo courtesy of the *El Watan* archive in Algiers.

Algerian tragedy, a tragedy that nobody understands."[139] In winning this award, Hocine's photo haphazardly elevated the Algerian conflict to an infamous pantheon. From its early days in the Cold War to the 1990s, the history of the World Press Photo award often reads like a catalog of the international community's durable and fleeting humanitarian concerns. Through Hocine's image, Algeria had become another Yugoslavia (photos of which received awards in 1990, 1998, and 1999), Somalia (photo awarded in 1992), Rwanda (photo awarded in 1994) and Chechnya (photo awarded in 1995).

With these award-winning photos and other archives of global concern, the R2P project created a history of the 1990s in which there were many failures of international humanitarian concern.[140] These failures are attributed not to the indifference and inequities of geopolitics but rather to the global south's cynical efforts to defend their postcolonial sovereignty from Western interference, even at the cost of tolerating genocide.[141] One would assume from this history that humanitarianization is a natural feature of geopolitics. It either happens or it does not. Intervention is either warranted or it is not.

Compared to these idealized notions, the career of the Algerian massacres in the history of international humanitarian thought and action is strange and ephemeral. The massacres emerged as an object of intense international humanitarian attention in late 1997 only to disappear in the spring of 1998. It required human effort and imagination to render Algeria's violence as intelligible vis-à-vis crises that had elicited far more intense international responses, even military intervention in some cases. It also required human effort to disable the processes that would have otherwise led to a confrontation between Algiers and key members of the Security Council. This situation tells us that humanitarianization does not just happen. It is a process fostered, sustained, disempowered, remembered, and forgotten by human thought and action. The same month in 1998 in which President Clinton apologized to Rwanda and promised never to forget its massacres, his administration allowed a similar bureaucratic inertia—the kind of inertia that kept Washington from seeing the Rwandan genocide until it was too late—to undermine any international initiative to investigate Algeria at the UN Commission on Human Rights.

The R2P project's failure to recognize its participation in these processes of humanitarianization and dehumanitarianization—particularly the forgetting of Algeria's massacres—is an aspect of the "new politics of protection"[142] that the R2P project claims to represent. This new politics of protection is, in fact, an antipolitics. The R2P project seeks to establish, by framing the humanitarian intervention debate in the 1990s in particular and incomplete ways, a world in which there is no debate about the use of military force to stop mass atrocities. This framing is largely preoccupied with the simplest ontology of mass violence—genocide. Genocide itself is likewise a vehicle for these antipolitical tendencies insofar as genocide is now viewed as a violence without politics and a violence whose international response should not be polluted by politics. Purposeful ignorance of more complex, opaque, and indeterminate forms of mass violence—like those witnessed in Chechnya and Algeria in the 1990s—explain two important, recent failures of the R2P project: the invention of a genocide to justify intervention into Libya, and the subsequent conceptual and practical paralysis of the R2P project in the face of the far bloodier Syrian civil war. That the R2P project is utterly inapplicable to mass atrocities in situations where it would run against the current of geopolitical forces—US occupied Iraq or Israeli campaigns in Gaza in 2008–2009 and 2014—suggests its antipolitical function in global conflict management today.

In the late 1990s, in the tradition of Argentina's Madres de Plaza de Mayo, Algerian families began holding weekly vigils for their family members who had been "disappeared" by state agents. Algeria's national reconciliation policies have offered compensation but have steadfastly refused to investigate the thousands of persons who "disappeared" in the 1990s at the hands of state agents and armed rebel groups. Photograph by Souhil Baghdadi. Courtesy of the *El Watan* archive, Algiers.

6 TRUTH, RECONCILIATION, AND TRANSITIONAL JUSTICE

History Will Judge

THE END OF THE COLD WAR reanimated a long dormant form of conflict management: the international criminal tribunal for war crimes and crimes against humanity. The wars in former Yugoslavia and the mass atrocities in Rwanda were the first to receive this treatment; hybrid domestic-international courts for Sierra Leone, Cambodia, and Lebanon followed. The proliferation of UN war prosecutions in the 1990s coevolved with increasing assertions of universal jurisdiction by various states and international bodies. Together they helped engender the International Criminal Court (ICC) around the turn of the millennium. Since then, the ICC has launched several investigations and proceedings, all of them related to conflicts in Africa. The Court's geographical selectivity has elicited growing accusations that the gaze of transnational justice is an extremely biased one. Others have voiced concern that the international community's increasing criminalization of wars came at the expense of their depoliticization. The danger was that trials rather than negotiations were becoming the preferred strategy to manage mass violence, particularly in Africa.[1] In this way, international criminal proceedings and demands for the transnationalization of justice had the effect of advancing the antipolitics of late conflict management as well.

But what about the ostensible alternative—transitional justice mechanisms designed to advance the cause of peaceful, nonpunitive national reconciliation? Since the 1970s, dozens of countries have engaged in various acts of national reconciliation: truth commissions, commissions of inquiry, and other state-sponsored mechanisms whose primary function is to manage the production of historical knowledge. Their mandates ranged from the austere to the ambitious. Some were produced by revolutions; others were nothing more than a tyrant's whitewash.[2] Above all, it was South Africa's Truth and Reconciliation Commission (TRC) that tamed this constellation of political experiments into a routinized set of universal procedures for postconflict management. Supporters of the TRC's restorative approach to justice suggest that it produces a unified polity of mutual survivors rather than a divided one of victors and losers. Though the ICC presents itself as a neutral instrument of transnational justice, its critics suggest otherwise. They say it represents nothing more than the latest instantiation of the kind of hypocritical victor's justice embodied in the Allies' Nuremberg and Tokyo tribunals after WWII. Today the victor is neoliberalism, the recolonization of Africa is its conquest, and the ICC is its preferred instrument of legitimation.[3]

The problem with this critique of transnational justice, and with its reliance on transitional justice as an ostensible alternative, is the critique's failure to recognize similar shortcomings in the TRC model. On what grounds the TRC deserves to become the model for treating the ills of all contemporary war-torn societies is not obvious. The rapid transformation of the TRC from contingent necessity in South Africa into a generic regimen for all other conflicts came well before the TRC's effects on the post-Apartheid polity could be reasonably evaluated.[4] The TRC ostensibly produced the citizen as survivor by making a public spectacle of victims' suffering and perpetrators' misdeeds. But only 10 percent of victims on file with the TRC were actually allowed to speak at the public hearings.[5] The TRC's organizers carefully selected testimonies and confessions on a dramaturgical basis rather than on juridical grounds. Entertainment value guided which survivors and which perpetrators would be staged, heard, watched, or otherwise transmitted, recorded, and recirculated. Like the Nuremberg and Tokyo tribunals, the contemporary truth commission is also a morality play. The only difference is the ending. Instead of the good vanquishing the evil, the good redeems the evil.

Whether in the form of commissions of inquiry or actual trials, most forms of transitional justice, in their efforts to manage postconflict environments, are guided by a key underlying assumption: a firm belief in the ameliorative power of history, a history that most often takes the form of an official consensus narrative of the violence or the tyranny that gripped the polity, a narrative peppered with oral histories of victims, perpetrators, collaborators, and bystanders. This faith in history is related to an even deeper assumption found throughout contemporary discourses of postconflict management: an insistence that the denial, suppression, and cynical manipulation of a conflict's history is not only *prima facie* bad but also likely to contribute to recidivism in the future. Champions of truth and history also claim to be champions of victims' right to speak, to be heard, and to be remembered for what they suffered. But, as just noted in the paradigmatic case of the TRC, in the model on which most national reconciliation processes are now based and judged, most victims' voices are silenced by truth commissions, not enabled by them. Those voices that are mobilized to retell tales of horror are not always volunteered, and those that do speak are selectively chosen for rationales that have little to do with simple truth-telling. As Holocaust scholar Gulie Ne'eman Arad proposes, the natural response to trauma is to try to move beyond it and, ultimately, to forget it—not to revive and relive it day after day, year after year. If a story of mass trauma is being kept alive, and if victims are compelled to speak by institutional forces, it begs the question why.[6] This question is particularly pertinent when the narrative bears the imprimatur of state or international power. Remembering is no more innocent than forgetting is guilty.

These conflicting attitudes toward the role of history—remembering and forgetting—in the enabling and disabling of mass violence reflect ambivalence between the science and the management of warfare today. History generates conflict through momentous nonhuman forces and imagined human narratives; but only an official, staged, and otherwise selective history of a conflict can truly end it once and for all. That is, only when a polity becomes the master of its own past can it escape the tragedy of it. Analyses of Algeria's violence in the 1990s and criticisms of Algeria's approach to national reconciliation in the 2000s reflect both of these pathologies in the science and management of late warfare. The intensity of the violence, particularly in the mid-1990s, elicited explanations that could understand such atrocities only as tectonic in nature— as underlying, massive, ominous, and beyond human capacity to manage or fully comprehend.

The ominous relationship between Algeria and its histories of violence was explicitly called into question during a defamation trial in Paris in 2002. The precise question posed to the court was whether or not the true masters of Algeria's eruption of killing in the 1990s had been secret elements within the military. That is, the court confronted head on the debate that had threatened to internationalize the Algerian conflict because of humanitarian questions about the agents and logics of the massacres in 1997–1998. Moreover, the location of this trial had the effect of highlighting the often-alleged imbrication of colonial and postcolonial violence in Algeria. Indeed, questions of historical justice were part of the rationale behind the Algerian regime's amnesty and in-demnity approach to national reconciliation: if such policies were good enough for the French after the 1954–1962 war, then they were good enough for Algeria after the warfare of the 1990s. This related to another question of justice and history: to what extent was Algeria's violence in the 1990s the direct or indirect result of French colonialism and, in particular, its bloody climax? Historicized accounts of Algeria's violence in the 1990s were most often framed as indict-ments of French rule. Other frames were even more sweeping indictments of a particularly Algerian culture of violence, with antecedents in Ottoman, and even deeper Islamic, histories.

HISTORY WILL JUDGE?

A brief defamation trial in the summer of 2002 is the closest Algeria has ever come to a public inquiry into the events of the 1990s. Not only was the trial about who had really caused the conflict (the regime or the Islamists), but it even touched on the issue of the massacres of 1997 and 1998. The plaintiff, the defendant, and most of the witnesses were Algerian, but the courtroom was in Paris. Seventeen months before these proceedings, a small but sensational book, *La sale guerre* (The dirty war), had been published in France. Its author, Habib Souaïdia, was a former officer in the Algerian military who had won political asylum from French authorities. Souaïdia's memoir of life in the Algerian coun-terinsurgency hit the bookstands on February 8, 2001, and quickly sold more than seventy thousand copies within three months.[7] An appetite for Souaïdia's allegations had been whetted by several developments, as well as by the fact that the authorship of the major massacres in 1997–1998 remained an open ques-tion for many. That said, the *Qui tue?* debate had significantly abated since the depths of January 1998, and all momentum for an international inquiry had largely dissipated with Algeria's declining rates of violence and the events of 9/11.

Prior to the book's release, a preview of *La sale guerre*'s revelations appeared in an interview with Souaïdia in *Le Monde*. Like the other Algerian government officials who came forward at the height of the massacres in late 1997 and early 1998, Souaïdia recounted witnessing torture and other atrocities committed by his fellow soldiers. But an important difference seemed to make Souaïdia's account more credible. Unlike the former and serving members of Algeria's security, military, and intelligence forces who gave anonymous interviews in the French, Irish, and British media in 1997 and 1998, Souaïdia was willing to use his real name and show his face in public.[8] This openness initially provided his "serious allegations"—in the words of Amnesty International[9]—with more integrity. And unlike the public claims of Algerian dissidents (such as former civil servants Lakhdar Brahimi and Mohamed Zitout), Souaïdia's experience in actual counterterrorism operations seemingly provided his first-person testimony of Algerian state abuses, including secret military involvement in civilian massacres, with a credibility that other informants lacked.

La sale guerre also seemed preordained to cause controversy because of another book, *Qui a tué à Bentalha?* (Who killed in Bentalha?), which had appeared just months beforehand. Coauthored by Nesroulah Yous, eyewitness to the Bentalha massacre, and Salima Mellah, operator of the dissident Algeria Watch website, it was published in October 2000.[10] Though not without controversy of its own,[11] *Qui a tué à Bentalha?* provided a thickly textured background to what had already become the most internationally scrutinized Algerian massacre of the 1990s. Not only did Yous's account corroborate some of the more disturbing claims made by Bentalha's survivors in 1997, but more important, Yous, like Souaïdia, did not remain anonymous. He defended his claims publicly, including his accusation that the Algerian security forces had played a role in the massacre. When *La sale guerre* hit the shelves in early 2001, the market was primed for a narrative that could provide more than just circumstantial evidence of state complicity in the massacres. A pivotal claim in Souaïdia's narrative is an alleged 1993 massacre near Douar Ez-Zaâtria. Though he did not perpetrate or even witness the killing firsthand, Souaïdia recalls having played a supporting role in the massacre. His unit supported a special group of Algerian commandos who, disguised as Islamist rebels, carried out the actual slaughter of many civilians. Critics noted a number of problems with Souaïdia's account, including the fact that no one could corroborate the Douar Ez-Zaâtria massacre.[12] But what landed Souaïdia in a French court were not the many holes in *La sale guerre*'s narrative. Rather, it was a war of words between Souaïdia and former HCE member Khaled Nezzar.

The first salvo came when Souaïdia, expressing his willingness to testify before an international inquiry, suggested that the concentration of power in the hands of ten senior military officers, including Nezzar, was the source of Algeria's troubles. Souaïdia accused them of collectively robbing the nation of its wealth.[13] In an interview in *Le Figaro*, Nezzar shot back, alleging that Souaïdia was a convicted criminal, an "impostor" who had never been in the Algerian Special Forces, and a co-conspirator in the Islamists' international campaign to attack the Algerian military.[14] Nezzar then traveled to Paris in April 2001 to defend the actions of the Algerian military and to publicize his new memoirs. While he was there, it was revealed in the French press that several complaints of torture had been lodged against him in French courts. Nezzar was forced to leave quickly, before French prosecutors could question him.[15] For some, Nezzar's escape from France bore echoes of former Chilean dictator Augusto Pinochet's recent ordeal in England. Pinochet had been detained in 1998 under a Spanish arrest warrant for crimes against humanity, a warrant premised on notions of universal jurisdiction. He was released in 2000 and quickly fled back to Chile, where he was ostensibly protected by local amnesty measures.[16]

Nezzar, undeterred, announced his intention to sue Souaïdia in France. Nezzar allegedly had the full backing of his colleagues in both politics and the military.[17] Nezzar's complaint was not against *La sale guerre* but against statements Souaïdia had made on a French television program, *Les Droits d'Auteur*, in May 2001. Marc Tessier, president of La Cinquième, the French public television channel in question, was also named in the case.[18] From the outset it was clear that the lawsuit had two intentions: to undermine Souaïdia's credibility and to confront the international chorus of accusations facing the Algerian state vis-à-vis the massacres.[19] But the defamatory statement in question seemed to have much more to do with the Algerian war of independence than with the warfare of the 1990s: "I cannot forgive French generals [Jacques] Massu and [Paul] Aussaresses for their crimes as I cannot forgive General Nezzar. (...) They are cowards who have profited." These "crimes," Souaïdia claimed, included the killing of "thousands of people for nothing."[20]

The key provocation was less Souaïdia's allegations of Algerian state abuses in the 1990s and much more that Nezzar's actions were comparable to the actions of French officers who infamously led the torture program against the FLN in the Battle of Algiers. The timing of Souaïdia's comparison was equally provocative. At roughly the same time as the publication of *La sale guerre*, Aussaresses had released a memoir in which he defended his use of torture against Algerians.[21] Then, in June 2000, Louisette Ighilahriz, a former female FLN guerrilla, published her own memoir, in which she accused Massu and others of physically and sexually torturing her over the course of several months.[22] Late in life, Massu seemed to have reconsidered the utility of torture. Aussaresses, on the other hand, was unapologetic. The Franco-Algerian context in which *La sale guerre* appeared was also tense because President Chirac had requested a national day on which to commemorate the *Harkis*—the Algerians who had fought on the side of France during the 1954–1962 war.[23] Roughly three weeks after Nezzar announced the lawsuit, civilian aircraft were flown into the World Trade Center in New York and into the Pentagon in Washington, DC.

The Nezzar-Souaïdia trial was initially set for February 2002 but was postponed until July. The first day of the proceedings featured the testimonies of Souaïdia and Nezzar. Subsequent days featured alternating testimonies from both the plaintiff's side and the defense. Testifying in support of Nezzar were two members of the HCE, former prime minister Sid Ahmed Ghozali and former human rights minister Ali Haroun; two former ministers with intellectual backgrounds, Ahmed Djebbar and Leïla Aslaoui; Kamel Razzag-Barra, former head of Algeria's human rights monitoring body; Mohammed Sifaoui, a journalist who initially was the coauthor of *La sale guerre* but later denounced Souaïdia and his editor, François Gèze;[24] author Rachid Boudjedra; a militia leader from Bentalha; the founder of a pro-government civil society group; and six survivors or family members of survivors allegedly victimized by armed Islamist groups. Among the last group, Mohamed Daho testified that his son, Ali, was killed by insurgents, not burned alive by soldiers as Souaïdia alleged in *La sale guerre.*[25] Hadda Chaouche ("Khalti Aïcha") and Hamid Bouamra, two residents of Bentalha, seem to have been presented to refute Yous's *Qui a tué à Bentalha?* rather than Souaïdia's *La sale guerre.*

Souaïdia's side boasted an impressive list of personalities: dissident Algerian figures Hocine Aït Ahmed and historian Mohammed Harbi;[26] two former Algerian government officials (Ghazi Hidouci and Omar Benderra) selected to testify on the issue of finance and corruption ; journalists José Garçon, Salima Ghezali, and Nicole Chevillard; two political refugees in Europe, Colonel Mohammed Samraoui and Captain Ahmed Chouchène (Chouchane), who had served in the Algerian military; human rights activists Patrick Baudouin (of the Fédération Internationale des Ligues des Droits de l'Homme) and Nassera Dutour (of the Collectif des Familles de Disparu(e)s en Algérie), who believes that her son was "disappeared" by state agents; an Algerian victim of torture; and MEP Hélèn Flautre of the French Green party.[27]

The trial was also attended by civil society figures, including activists straddling both sides of the *Qui tue?* debate in Algeria. One of the attendees, Chérifa Kheddar, cofounder of Blida-based Djazairouna (*Jaza'iruna* or Our Algeria), an advocacy group for victims of nonstate terrorism, hoped that the proceedings might lead to some answers and accountability: "For the first time, a real trial is taking place about the question of who is killing whom. [...]. It's no longer an impersonal question from the media, but real questions by lawyers in a real jurisdiction."[28] Reviving the *Qui tue?* debate was the precise problem with the proceedings, charged *L'Humanité*'s Hassane Zerrouky. He argued that the proceedings, in focusing too much on the question of the spectacular massacres, would have the effect of whitewashing the crimes of the insurgency.[29]

Expectations were particularly high for Samraoui, who had served in Algeria's military intelligence (DRS), the branch of the security forces most often accused of opacity and excess in the fight against terrorism. More than any other witness, Samraoui was in a position to lend some credibility to Souaïdia's most sensational claims about government participation in atrocities. More precisely, had Algerian soldiers dressed as Islamists and carried out massacres in order to discredit the FIS and the other rebel groups? Samraoui's first media appearance was in early 2001, though he had lived in Germany since deserting and receiving asylum in early 1996. After Souaïdia's book was published, Samraoui was interviewed on the Al Jazeera Arabic satellite channel to discuss the merits of *La sale guerre*. One of his more dramatic claims was that the DRS had created the GIA in the summer of 1991—months before the cancellation of elections in January 1992—in order to subvert the Islamist movement.[30] At the *La sale guerre* trial, Samraoui recounted in more detail how, from March 1990 onward, he had been on the frontlines of the DRS's efforts to monitor, penetrate, and ultimately subvert the Islamist movement. "Our mission was to break the FIS, infiltrate it, disperse [*disloquer*] it, attribute violent actions to the Islamists," he testified. He also reaffirmed, "The GIA is a creation of the Algerian security services."[31]

Though Samraoui's testimony and character seemed unimpeachable,[32] his account suffered the same chronological problem as Souaïdia's. By late 1996, when the intensity and frequency of civilian massacres began to escalate, Souaïdia was in prison and Samraoui was in exile. Neither could provide firsthand confirmation of whether or not the state had been involved in the massacres of 1997–1998; they could only conjecture on the basis of previous state atrocities. Nor was this deficiency in the testimonies of Souaïdia and Samraoui corrected by the testimony of Chouchène. A political refugee in Britain at the time of the 2002 trial, Chouchène's superiors had allegedly offered him the job of helping to infiltrate the Islamist movement in order to carry out high-level assassinations of FIS leaders. When he reportedly asked why they did not go after

GIA leader Djamel Zitouni, Chouchène was told, he claimed, that Zitouni was "our man."[33] Shortly thereafter, Chouchène escaped to Europe, meaning that he was not in a position to speak about the 1996–1998 massacres firsthand either.

By the end of the proceedings, the French court began to realize that it was being assigned a much larger task than to render a simple verdict on defamation. To decide whether or not Souaïdia's comments held sufficient warrant to be labeled defamatory was to tempt the court to determine the reality of events that seemed irreducibly ambiguous, in order to clear the fog of war hanging over 1990s Algeria. In her concluding statements, the public prosecutor, Béatrice Angelelli, argued against going down that road. "This week, two theses, two truths have clashed," she noted, recommending that Souaïdia ultimately not face any punitive measures, even if he was found guilty. "History will judge," she concluded. This was an explicit reference to Nezzar, who defended his actions in the 1990s with the same claim, *L'histoire jugera*.[34]

The court refused to judge history. Its September 27 verdict found that Souaïdia's claims were uttered in good faith and therefore rested well within the boundaries of France's speech laws.[35] A brief Algerian state radio broadcast noted simply that Nezzar's evidence of slander had been "insufficient."[36] Nezzar opted not to pursue an appeal, claiming that the trial had served its purpose.[37] The trial's ambiguous outcome, coupled with the events of 9/11, seemed to demobilize all interest in an international inquiry into the Algerian massacres. The publication of Samraoui's own memoir, though it was far more authoritative and penetrating than *La sale guerre*, was a virtual nonevent when it appeared the following year.[38] In Algeria, the government's war against the insurgency continued to simmer. It is suspected that between 2000 and 2002 several thousand Algerians were added to the conflict's death toll.[39] The Algerian presidency had already publicly embraced a figure of one hundred thousand dead by 1999, while small-scale massacres of civilians continued into 2002. On the same day that a French prosecutor declared that only history will judge, Algeria celebrated forty years of independence from France. These celebrations were marred by a bomb placed in a pile of garbage in Larbaâ that killed roughly three-dozen people.[40]

AN EXTRAORDINARY CULTURE OF VIOLENCE

The role of history in Algeria's *décennie noire* was not only that of judge but of executioner as well. Among the forces that were said to account for Algeria's violence (identity, scarcity, *hogra*, *le pouvoir*, Islam), history was frequently considered the most powerful force tearing the Algerian polity apart. It was also frequently suggested that only an honest confrontation between Algeria and its history—perhaps involving France as well—could heal the polity.

The ambivalent role of history in 1990s Algeria is illustrated in an international reference to one particular massacre that occurred on a small hilltop settlement on the southern side of the Kabylia mountain range. Victims had been slaughtered with guns, knives, and other rudimentary implements. The *International Herald Tribune* reported 302 deaths—almost all the men in the village. "In one house 35 bodies were piled on one another. It was the bloodiest single incident that observers here can ever recall in the modern history of Algeria." Officials denounced the attack as a "nameless massacre." The circumstances of the massacre were initially unclear. It was suspected that it had resulted from rivalries within the insurgency and possibly the authorities' countermobilization of the population into an armed militia.[41]

What was different about this massacre was its location in time. The Mélouza massacre of May 1957 became one of the most infamous acts of mass terror in the 1954–1962 war. Four decades later, Mélouza returned to haunt understandings of the violence in 1990s Algeria.[42] For some, Mélouza was proof that Algeria's violence in 1997–1998 was not unprecedented—neither in its scale nor in its logic. It was a demonstration of the continuity of particular "methods" of resistance.[43] For others, Mélouza was proof of discontinuity; the violence of the Algerian rebellion in 1957 paled in comparison to that of the massacres in 1997.[44] The ghosts of Mélouza could be invoked to problematize calls for international intervention into the massacres of 1997–1998. The massacres in Mélouza, like those in Bougara, Raïs, and Bentalha, were manifestations of the Maghrib's "traditional forms of cruelty," which the international community could do little about.[45] Mélouza was also used to rally international sympathy for Algerian civilians in the 1990s. It was constellated in a series of massacres— Guelma and Sétif in 1945, Mélouza in 1957, the Mitidja in 1997, the Ouarsenis in 1998—whose roots all traced back to the violence of French colonialism.[46]

In the international debate about the 1997–1998 massacres in Algeria, one historical event, the 1954–1962 war, most often came to the fore as the alleged origin of the violence of the 1990s. There were utterances of a "second Algerian war,"[47] a "new Algerian war,"[48] and a "new battle of Algiers."[49] There was also the alleged return, appropriation, and redeployment of particular practices and vocabularies of repression and resistance. Torture, assassinations of intellectuals, public bombings, and civilian massacres were not always read as the self-rationalized operations of strategic actors in 1990s Algeria. These were instead uniquely Algerian "repertoires of violence" whose source was uniquely Algerian as well.[50] "How little Algeria's suffering had changed," wrote a journalist from the scene of Bentalha's massacre, remarking on a history textbook found in one of the victimized homes.[51] A line in Albert Camus's letter to a young Algerian revolutionary—"Algeria will be a land of ruins and of corpses that no force, no power in the world, will be able to restore in our century"[52]—became a fifty-year-old prophecy revealed in several accounts.[53]

Algerians often corroborated and promulgated these historical linkages. "Beheading and mutilation of women and children seem atrocious, they are atrocious," a serving Algerian military officer told the London Times in late 1997, explaining, "but it is no more than a predictable evolution of violence in Algeria, seeded in our war with the French."[54] It was often remarked that the FIS was the offspring of the FLN. When pronounced in French, FIS sounds like fils, meaning "sons." When the FIS first emerged, it was the "sons" of the FLN's hogra, the contempt expressed by the elite toward the masses, which structurally manifested as deep inequality in Algeria. But Algeria's dispossessed masses were also the children of the FLN maquisards (those who fight in the maquis or bush). What the FIS represented was a generation of young men in Algeria raised on tales of revolutionary valor, earned in the crucible of urban and rural warfare against unjust rule. The veteran socialist guerrillas of the FLN begot the Islamic jihadists of the AIS, the GIA, and others. The Algerian regime responded to the insurgency of the 1990s with the use of disappearance, torture, and ratissage (combing operations), as the French had done in the Battle of Algiers and the longer rural war that followed in the maquis. Within Algeria's political elite, there emerged in the 1990s a discourse of "eradication" not unlike the discourse used by those in the French government who had prosecuted the war against the FLN. The Islamists could not be reasoned with, the eradicators alleged; they could only be eliminated on the field of battle. Insurgents characterized their opponents as pied noirs (French colonials) and all sides referred to the other as Harkis or children of Harkis.

Indeed, it was often alleged that vendettas by and against Harkis were an important vector through which the 1954–1962 war helped to realize the violence of the 1990s. Harki has come to mean, generically, any French collaborator during the war of independence and, more specifically, native Muslim auxiliaries of the French army. Of the suspected 250,000 Algerians in this latter category, tens of thousands fled to France or were killed—sometimes in massacres—in

1962 as the war of independence began to wind down.[55] Dormant, repressed, and sublimated anger, whether harbored by *Harkis* and their children or maintained by others against them, was a main driver of the conflict in the 1990s according to some accounts. In the 1990s the Algerian press often recirculated government claims that captured or eliminated "terrorists" were the children of *Harkis*.[56] One Algerian academic's unsympathetic study of the Islamist rebellion draws our attention to the alleged geographical coincidence between some of the most violent provinces in the 1990s and those with the most *Harkis* participating in the insurgencies there.[57] This view has even found expression in fictional literature. Algerian author Mohammed Moulessehoul, writing under the pen name Yasmina Khadra, tells the story of a small town torn apart by the insurgency of the 1990s. At the apogee of the narrative, a *Harki* family's secret desire for revenge is the *deus ex machina* behind all of the conflict and violence, including the book's climactic massacre.[58]

Outside of Algeria, these connections were drawn more obliquely. After the Bentalha massacre, a Canadian journalist noted, "The throat-slitting, disemboweling and beheading described by survivors of recent massacres have been seen before in Algeria. The war of independence from France in the late 1950s was marked by the same kind of unspeakable atrocities. And the massacre afterwards of thousands of 'harkis,' or pro-French collaborators, was also coldly barbarous."[59] The mass killings of 1962 and 1997 were also framed in terms of a specific Algerian vocabulary or dramaturgy of violence, rather than according to cause and effect.[60] For others, the logic of the 1990s violence was simple: "Scores are being settled today whose origins lie in conflicts resulting from Algerian independence in 1962, such as the massacre of 60,000–100,000 *harkis* that took place only months after independence."[61] It was allegedly in the nature of counterinsurgency warfare like that practiced by the French in Algeria to produce these kinds of vendettas.[62]

The forces of history were, more often than not, much more vague than the vendetta thesis. For some, the role of history in Algeria's violence was as a kind of wardrobe for reenactments of the past. Algeria's history of violence had become "analogy" and the present mere "mimicry."[63] History was thought to be less of an occult or subliminal force acting on the polity and more of a vocabulary of references to the past redeployed in the pursuit of both petty and grand economic ambitions.[64] That a police torture room in the 1990s was described in the very same terms as a French torture room of four decades prior was a piece of the puzzle of Algerian violence for one journalist.[65] For one analyst, Algeria's "mythology" of a violent and glorious past was much "more than a tradition"[66] because it was manifesting before the world's eyes in the 1990s. As French sociologist Bruno Étienne insisted, "It's an extraordinary culture of violence."[67] The suspected origins of this culture were manifold, but its means of reproduction were never given much clarity. French colonialism, particularly the 1954–1962 war, was always front and center in debates about the origin of Algeria's violence of the 1990s.[68] Others felt it had a deeper genealogy, with Ottoman rather than European roots.[69] Algeria's *imaginaire de la guerre* was accused of fabricating and then drawing on a lineage of violently rebellious figures—Ottoman corsairs, colonial *qa'ids*, anticolonial Moudjahidine, and Islamist *amirs* of the 1990s insurgency.[70] Algerian public education and the mass media were suspected as much as the FLN regime itself of being complicit in the transmission of these violent traditions.[71] And whether or not this historically conditioned culture of violence could be transformed was another dividing point. Just as applying the term *civil war* to Algeria justified calls for and against intervention into the conflict of the 1990s (see Chapters 1 and 5), historicizing Algeria's violence was used as a reason for more active international engagement with the conflict[72] and as a reason to abandon Algeria to its predetermined fate.[73]

Efforts to constellate and contextualize Algeria's violence as historical and cultural often elicited cries of determinism and reductionism. The emerging historiography of Algeria's *décennie noire* of the 1990s has been divided on these issues. On the one hand, Algeria's violence has been difficult to explain without history as a guide. It would otherwise be difficult to decode the meaning of Benhadj's 1989 insistence that the 1954 jihad had to continue[74] or the significance of self-defense militia leaders in Relizane touting their and others' experiences as veterans of the 1954–1962 war,[75] or to make sense of the Algerian government telling Human Rights Watch that the problem of the "disappeared" in the 1990s paled in comparison to the number who had disappeared during the 1954–1962 war of independence.[76] How else would it be possible to understand the irony of the Pentagon screening Gillo Pontecorvo's 1966 film *La Battaglia di Algeri* to educate itself on how to fight a growing insurgency in Iraq in 2003?[77] As much as there were insistences that Algeria's violence could not be understood without identity (see Chapter 4), there were also insistences that Algeria's history had to be taken into account.[78] On the other hand, historical and cultural framings of Algeria's conflict in the 1990s, like exclusively economic, political, or humanitarian framings, threatened to efface important aspects of the violence as observers searched for an elegant, parsimonious account of the conflict's origins—Martinez's *imaginaire de la guerre* thesis being the most controversial. Dissenting from these reductionistic tendencies, James McDougall argued that it was wrong to view of the violence of 1990s Algeria as "the instinctive reiteration of culturally entrenched patterns of political behaviour," patterns "dictated by some inflexible, metahistorical fate."[79] Others agreed,[80] though there was fear of "throwing out the baby with the bathwater."[81] As with most aspects of Algeria's violence in the 1990s, historical framings often seemed less about making sense of the facts coming out of Algeria and more about compensating for the lack of coherent and reliable facts. This problem is not exclusive to Algeria, however. Looking at the phenomenon of mass violence more globally, historian Dominic LaCapra has suggested that mass violence is still beyond our intellectual and political capacities to understand and control.[82]

History played many roles and served many functions in 1990s Algeria. It was context, cause, costume, discourse, pretext, and prophecy. It was reconciliatory and retributive, caustic and curative, judge and executioner. History was the force that had divided the polity and had the power to heal it. Historicizing the warfare served to mark Algeria as a forbidden space in geopolitics, a place where good intentions would go to die, a no man's land for humanitarians and diplomats alike. History was also used to mobilize the conscience of outsiders, to call into question—once again—the true nature of the debt that France owed to Algeria. History was able to do all of these things to, with, and against Algeria's violence because history is not one thing. These conflicting characterizations and mobilizations of history reflect how historicizations of Algeria's violence were produced by the violence itself as much as history was said to have produced the violence. The power of violence in 1990s Algeria was not its putative ability to tap into a hidden reservoir of Hobbesian malice latent in the minds of Algerians but its ability to make so many see such reservoirs as necessary, if not sufficient, conditions for the ongoing horrors. The *imaginaire de la guerre* thesis was an effect of the very violence it purported to explain.

PERFORMING NATIONAL RECONCILIATION

At the end of the Souaïdia-Nezzar trial, it was said that history, not courts, would judge those responsible for Algeria's violence. But it was very unclear in July 2002 how this history would be written. Indeed, Algeria's violence was largely seen as ongoing, if somewhat reduced, in 2002. What was clear in the summer of 2002 was that the Algerian state, most of all, was not going to participate in the writing of the history of the 1990s. The first decade of the new millennium was one in which the Algerian regime continued to be at war with itself as President Bouteflika staked his reelections in 2004 and 2009 on his signature national reconciliation initiatives, the 1999 Concorde Civile and the 2005 Charte pour la Paix et la Réconciliation Nationale.[83] The steady decline in violence after its peak in January 1998 ushered in a long dénouement that saw civilian massacres dissipate into the new millennium. Divided, decapitated, or demobilized, the insurgency seemed a spent force. What was left of it took to the remote, untouchable, and forsaken parts of Algeria, notably the Kabylia mountains and the Sahara desert. For a brief moment in April 2001, massive protests, in Kabylia and then Algiers, suggested that fear of the regime and the insurgency had passed, and that the project of the October 1988 protests could be renewed. But this Mouvement Citoyen (Citizens' Movement), driven by the enduring forces of *hogra,* faced a renewed state helmed by a stunningly resurrected FLN whose coffers were saturated with hydrocarbon revenues. As quickly as it appeared, this nonviolent insurgency was co-opted and divided. Instead of becoming a vehicle for a new national politics, the Mouvement Citoyen instead revealed the intense localization of Algerian politics. Demands for education, jobs, and housing were no longer made via formal national politics. Youth riots became the primary means through which locales communicated to the bureaucracy of the state, vis-à-vis elite intermediaries, whether to register grievances, call for reforms, or demand goods and services.[84]

The Algerian regime was willing to accept this social contract in which the sphere of governance was largely the domain of technocratic and security elites. State-society relations were dominated by questions of management and the allocation of rents. Where politics seemed most ferocious was at the top. With the international legitimacy afforded to him by his long absence from Algerian political life and his embrace of the US global war on terror, Bouteflika set about dispatching his rivals in the FLN (such as Ali Benflis in the 2004 elections) and in the security establishment (for example, Chief of Staff General Mohammed Lamari). Bouteflika compensated those in the latter group with a blanket amnesty in 2005. All actions taken by the police, gendarmerie, military, civilian militias, and intelligence forces in the 1990s were rendered legal under the 2005 amnesty, including acknowledged crimes such as the "disappearance" of thousands of civilians by government agents. Under Bouteflika's watch, there would be no going back to 1988 or 1998. Twenty years after Boudiaf's assassination there were still daily reminders of the persistence of the *décennie noire*, long after that decade was over, from turmoil in the Malian Sahara and a random-kidnapping epidemic in Kabylia to suicide bombings and IEDs (improvised explosive devices) targeting Algerian security officers and installations. Some of these reminders were spectacular enough to make global headlines, such as an unprecedented attack on a major natural gas production facility in eastern Algeria in early 2013. Other reminders of the 1990s were more intimate, such as the small weekly protests by Algeria's mothers of the "disappeared." Of the many appellations given to both the French-Algerian war and the violence of the 1990s, the title *guerre sans fin* (war without end) seems as fitting as any other.

The history that would condemn or vindicate Souaïdia and Nezzar was not going to be authored, authorized, or allowed by the architects of Algeria's national reconciliation policies. The Concorde and, even more so, the Charte were, above all, efforts to incentivize rebel demobilization (and, implicitly, depoliticization) through amnesty and stipends. Amnesty was also given to state agents, who ostensibly had done nothing wrong during Algeria's long "national tragedy." Victims of state and nonstate terror were offered compensation, but almost no official information was released on these indemnity programs, nor were families ever told what happened to their missing relatives. It was this latter aspect—the Algerian state's refusal to offer any kind of narrative, whether to individual victims or to the nation at large—that drew the most criticism internationally. The basis of this criticism was an emerging global consensus. It held that national reconciliation could not be achieved without the government organizing, licensing, or simply allowing the construction of an official narrative of the country's suffering. The refusal of Algiers to do so meant it would run afoul of this consensus within the international conflict management community.[85] Even a deeply flawed, state-engineered commission designed to produce a certain truth so as to legitimate a certain regime of power, such as the Instance Equité et Réconciliation (Equity and Reconciliation Commission) organized by the regime in neighboring Morocco in 2004–2005, was viewed as better than no truth commission at all.[86] Still, the gold standard for truth commissions (as noted earlier), has become and remains South Africa's TRC, the standard by which Algeria and other postconflict societies are now implicitly or explicitly judged. This standard has more to do, however, with the mythology that now surrounds the TRC than with any demonstration of its efficacy. Like Algeria's, South Africa's national reconciliation process was born of politics and neither victims nor perpetrators would get all of what they wanted or derserved.[87] That said, the mythology of the TRC, as entirely constituted by heart-wrenching public hearings, is largely mistaken. The majority of victims were not allowed to face their perpetrators in public testimony in the TRC; the vast majority of testimonies of Apartheid's victims were relegated to the library of texts that the TRC produced.[88]

The power of the TRC was not just the mythology that every victim and every perpetrator would face off. The TRC's most interesting power was its ability to convince so many people of its efficacy, and so its portability, so quickly. As Bouteflika spearheaded national reconciliation efforts in 1999, soon after his election, the TRC strangely became an important model in international discussions on Algeria's way forward. The TRC's work had barely been finished and analyzed in 1999, and its ultimate impact is still far from being objectively assessed. But South Africa's TRC is by far the most thoroughgoing and transparent experiment in national reconciliation yet enacted. By virtue of these facts alone, the TRC, regardless of its efficacy, has become *the* model for postconflict and postauthoritarian polities to adopt. In retrospect, the velocity of the TRCs success is all the more surprising. The new and old challenges that faced South Africa ten years after the end of *de jure* Apartheid raised many questions as to what exactly the TRC had accomplished.[89]

When asked by *El País* in 1999 why Algeria would not adopt the South African model, Bouteflika countered, "The situation [in Algeria] is far more complex than it was in South Africa. [. . .] The Truth Commission would be justified in a relationship of colonizer to colonized, such as France to Algeria or Spain to Western Sahara. [. . .] And if my memory does not betray me, you [i.e., Spain] have never needed a commission to achieve democratic transition."[90] When confronted by several mothers of Algeria's "disappeared" at a public meeting, Bouteflika made a more blunt argument: "How are you going to leave this war behind if you don't forget?"[91] Bouteflka's amnesty and indemnity approach to national reconciliation was criticized internationally for being a top-down effort to sweep the country's dark secrets under the rug in the name of turning the page. But popular referenda in 1999 and 2005 suggested significant, if not broad, support for these initiatives. A man in charge of the polling station for the 2005 referendum on the Charte—a polling station at the site of the massive 1997 Raïs massacre—told a reporter, "People who have been so hurt hesitate to pardon. [. . .] It is so easy to say 'sorry' but in reality here it is difficult to swallow."[92] Criticism urging Algeria to adopt the South African model paid no attention to the fact that most Algerians seemed favorable to these policies. To understand this situation is to understand the powerful role of shame in Algeria—not just the shame that a polity feels toward itself for allowing two decades of governance by *hogra*, but also the shame it feels for letting itself slide into a bloody morass of murder, rape, massacres, and innumerable other atrocities.

Algeria's experiment in national reconciliation nonetheless seems to run contrary to recent trends in international conflict management that have attempted to standardize the South African TRC model. Critics, particularly international human rights groups, have claimed that the deviant path forged by the Algerian regime constitutes an antipolitical effort—one that denies the polity's right to a history of the national trauma of the 1990s. Specifically, these groups have taken issue with provisions in the 2005 Charte that outlaw all activities that might contribute to the independent formation of some kind of account of the 1990s. These national amnesia provisions make it seem all the more clear that postconflict reconciliation in Algeria has been a massive cover-up in which the *quid pro quo* is indemnity and amnesty for silence.[93] There are several problems with these criticisms. First of all, there is the confounding fact that Algerians voted in two referenda (1999 and 2005) to support the amnesty, indemnity, and "amnesia" approach lamented as antidemocratic by the self-appointed international technocracy of conflict and postconflict management. More important, however, is that criticisms of Algeria's national reconciliation policies were problematically grounded in assumptions that prior experiments in truth commissions, mainly in South Africa, were transparent, uniformly applied, and effective. Such assumptions bear little resemblance to the actual lives and legacies of truth commissions. What these assumptions actually reveal is the normative convictions of those who would seek to intervene and manage postconflict polities; how those convictions become ideationally elaborated by taming the heterogeneity of postconflict reconciliation experiments into a thing called transitional justice; and then how these norms and ideas become materially elaborated in actual postconflict environments by postconflict managers. Finally, criticisms of Algeria's national reconciliation policies have been based on the assumption that the denial of history is Algeria's problem, as if history in and of itself is never problematic. Yet the very problem that Algeria faced in the 1990s, according to many observers, was history.

Given the global decline in rates and intensities of armed conflict, there is a growing certainty among conflict and postconflict managers that the code of peacebuilding has been cracked.[94] Central to late peacebuilding is a curious fetishization of memory and history. Champions of truth commissions often tout the therapeutic and remediative effects of such procedures at the individual and national level.[95] They "break the cycles of hatred" that ostensibly drive so many conflicts and thus perform an important preventative function vis-à-vis recidivism.[96] But there is, as yet, no research that establishes even a correlation between truth commissions and nonrecidivism, let alone any convincing hypothetical arguments beyond the simplistic and deterministic platitude that those who forget history are bound to repeat it. This antipolitical faith in history, that war-torn societies should subordinate their political needs to international norms and procedures of postconflict management, should raise questions as to the other functions that transitional justice and national reconciliation mechanisms serve. One of those functions is to use the power of history—that is, to have control over it—to forge the postconflict environment in the first place. In an age when wars rarely have official endings, transitional justice and national reconciliation produce that which is otherwise ambiguous and contested—war's end. Once the postconflict environment has been proclaimed, it can then be realized by those who claim mastery over it: the techno-managerial experts of contemporary peacebuilding whose strategies render postconflict (read *pliable*) nation-states into a more geopolitically intelligible form.[97] Truth commissions help terraform the neoliberal peace.

THE NIGHTMARE OF TRADITION

Where will histories of Algeria's *décennie noir* come from if not from French courts, an international fact-finding mission, or a national truth commission? The potential archives for this history making are not difficult to find, and the records often emerge in unexpected ways. An archivist with one of Algeria's leading newspapers showed me a portfolio assembled by the interior ministry in the mid-1990s. He kept it hidden in his desk. The cover read, in both Arabic and French,

wahshiyyah al-tatarruf fi al-Jaza'ir

1995

La barbarie de l'extremisme en Algerie [sic]

1995

Inside were photos of severed heads, decapitated or dismembered bodies, gaping throat wounds, charred remains, bloated corpses, and matching case details for each victim: men, women, children, infants. The purpose of this portfolio

had been to help convince Algerian and foreign journalists that the armed opposition groups were truly immoral.[98] Yet the violence in Algeria would get
much worse in the months and years after those photos were assembled.

In the El Harrach neighborhood of Algiers, where many repentant terrorists were given employment in exchange for their surrender, I visited a small
legal office. There an Algerian lawyer struggled to deliver a modicum of justice
to the victims of the rebellion. His office occupying the first floor of a concrete
building, typical of the post-independence construction boom of the 1970s, was
modest. The reception area smelled of mildew and the ceiling was rotted out
with water damage. A small patch had already collapsed, exposing guilty pipes.
The reception area consisted of a small desk for his assistant and two school
chairs with no seats, so I had to balance precariously on their metal tubing. The
lawyer's own office was a little nicer, with a sturdy wood desk and the requisite
bookcase of legal texts behind it. I asked him if it was true that there were a significant number of Islamists in this neighborhood. "Certainly," was his response.
A number of the shop owners on the same street, he elaborated, were Islamist
guerillas in the 1990s. Having accepted the government's offer of *rahmah* (clem-
ency), they quit the *maquis* and returned to civilian life. No questions were asked
of them (at least publicly) and they received a decent monthly stipend from the
government to seal the deal. The tension I felt between this young, secular lawyer and the Islamist shop owners outside was more than just philosophical or
theological. This lawyer and his organization wanted to see those men outside
in their little shops held responsible for any crimes they might have committed.

Less than an hour from Algiers, the provincial capital of Blida lies on the
other side of the farmlands of the Mitidja plain, quaintly nestled at the foot
of the Chréa Mountains in the Tell Atlas. The Mitidja witnessed some of the
most intense and atrocious violence in the entire country during the 1990s.
Several of Algeria's most infamous massacres of 1997 and 1998—Bougara, Raïs,
Bentalha, Sidi Hamed—occurred in this zone between Algiers and Blida. These
were massacres in which a hundred to several hundred perished in hours of un-
interrupted slaughter. To get to Blida from Algiers, one normally passes right
through what was called the "triangle of death." Ten years later, there was nothing remarkable about the journey, nothing to indicate that the Mitidja had been
the heart of a war. At the height of the killing in Algeria, between late 1996 and
early 1998, when collective massacres stretched from the hills of Algiers across
the Mitidja to the slopes of the Atlas, venturing this journey on public transpor-
tation would have been considered suicidal for a foreigner. Now the only dan-

ger is the national epidemic of highway collisions. The parts of Algeria that do look like former war zones could just as easily be evidence of a different kind of war. Without detailed knowledge of intimate, local histories, how can one differentiate between damaged caused by armed violence and damage caused by decades of structural violence? The road between Algiers and Blida, like many roads across the country, is populated with ruined buildings, abandoned construction, neglected agricultural plots, bricolage dwellings, and entrepreneurial ingenuity. These things that stream past the bus window could easily be the effects of terrorism, if not the effects of postcolonial development, hydrocarbons, structural adjustment, authoritarianism, or sheer neglect. Even when one pours over video and photo archives of Algeria in the 1990s, it is difficult to find contemporary warfare's more telltale signs—pockmarks from a million bullets, smoke-charred buildings, perfectly round holes from shelling, concrete buildings pancaked by aerial bombing, tanks burning on the side of the road. Mary Kaldor's contention that the terrain of late warfare is now corporeal rather than terrestrial or infrastructural seems to have some validity in Algeria.[99]

In Blida I found the headquarters of an advocacy organization that supports victims of nonstate terror. It was located in an apartment building in need of a good paint job and a more diligent superintendent. Whether out of modesty, lack of funds, local political sensitivities, or the government's known hostility toward their work, there were no signs on the outside of the building advertising the offices to the public. Up several flights in an unlit stairwell, the organization operated out of a residential flat converted into office space. I met several of the officers, staff, and volunteers—all women—working on various projects, including an electronic database that cataloged and quantified the excesses and depredations of the insurgency. Of the roughly two thousand files they had collected, I was allowed to scroll through the six hundred that had been digitized so far. Countless victims' names, killing sites, suspected attackers, and surviving family members all streamed before my eyes. A burgeoning library, part of a *Markaz Dhakirah* (Memory Center) funded by the European Union, was opened to me. In what would normally be a bedroom or living room, a group of apprehensive men sat in plastic chairs, filling the air with cigarette smoke as they conversed quietly. Later, I was told that they were part of a support group for people who had been attacked or lost family members to the armed groups. Sometimes local psychologists and counselors volunteered their time to help the children, women, and men who came to this organization seeking help that they could not or would not get from the government.

Downtown Algiers hosted a similar memory site, one that was just off its most prominent boulevard. Here too there was little to indicate, from the outside, what was inside those offices—Algeria's most famous victims' rights organizations, working out of a tarnished old colonial building. This group collected data on the alleged abuses of government agents, particularly on the sensitive issue of state-sponsored "disappearances." Visiting their offices, I was shown several bookcases full of binders containing thousands of incident reports collected by this organization. Each binder had several dossiers on individuals that provided case details for each claim of state-sponsored disappearance. Most cases had an identity photo attached. Flipping through, I saw children and women but mostly men. They were various ages, looking serious, playful, or aloof. They sported haircuts and numerous styles of dress—casual, Western, traditional, business, military, "Islamist," or "Afghan."[100]

From its founding in the late 1990s, this organization demanded an international inquiry into the "disappeared." Worn down by the regime's own antipolitics machine, it settled for a national initiative, so long as it was independent of the government. What they got was an "*ad hoc* mechanism" within already existing state structures to address the problem. In 2005, the government first admitted to disappearing 6,146 of its citizens; this number increased to 8,000 in 2010.[101] These figures did not result from an intensive investigation by the government but were drawn directly from the painstaking labor of this human rights organization. That is, the *ad hoc* mechanism simply accepted the majority of this association's dossiers without investigation. Each family was offered roughly ten thousand Euros for their loss. Other major victimized groups that constitute Algeria's "national tragedy"—an official euphemism for the conflict—have been met with similar offers: either one-time cash payments or diminishing monthly payments. These constituencies include the families of those "disappeared" by state agents, families of armed opposition members ("terrorists," in official parlance) killed by the state, families victimized by "terrorists," the "terrorists" themselves, and Islamists who lost their government jobs in the 1990s because of their alleged political affiliations. The means by which the Algerian government determined who received amnesty and compensation, particularly when it came to former guerillas, has never been explained. The lawyer in El Harrach summarized the process to me as "very opaque."

A weekly struggle against the tyranny of this opacity was often staged in Addis Ababa Place, a roundabout midway between downtown Algiers and Bir

Mourad Raïs. The Algerian government's human rights monitoring body, the CNCPPDH, is located there in a gorgeous Moorish building bathed in white-wash and perched overlooking the bay of Algiers. On Wednesdays, a handful of women, and sometimes a few men, would hold a silent vigil in front of that building. Some carried sheets of paper with enlarged identity photos printed on them; sometimes there was a sign in Arabic or French. These women were Algeria's version of the Madres de Plaza de Mayo (Mothers of the Plaza de Mayo). Yet unlike their Argentine counterparts, Algeria's mothers of the "disap-peared" have been denied the right to know what happened to their children. The Algerian government acknowledged that it was responsible for disappear-ing some eight thousand of them and offered compensation. But so far the government has refused to compensate many other Algerians for their loss and suffering, such as those chain-smoking men in the Blida support group.

The profound injustice that one feels in the face of Algeria's national rec-onciliation policies might be assuaged when one considers the arc of justice in other postconflict sites. Recently Argentina prosecuted former dictators Jorge Rafael Videla and Reynaldo Bignone, as well as several other high-level officials, for crimes—including torture and murder—committed during their 1973–1983 dictatorship. Brazil has similarly examined repealing a 1979 amnesty law cover-ing state abuses during the 1964–1985 dictatorship, including torture and disap-pearance. The country's top federal prosecutor has even asked the government to offer an official apology for the crimes it committed during that period. A special Cambodian court indicted four leading officials of the Khmer Rouge re-gime for crimes against humanity and increased the sentenced for one official to life imprisonment for his actions during the genocide (1975–1979). South Af-rica began considering an additional 149 cases of pardon for crimes committed during Apartheid (1948–1994) that were not addressed by the TRC. Internal and external investigations have been launched into crimes committed during the Franco regime in a direct challenge to Spain's 1977 amnesty laws.[102]

What these struggles, from the high politics of Franco-Algerian diplomacy to the grassroots struggles of Algerian victims' rights advocates, suggest is that the war over Algeria's history, like all history and all wars, is never ending. But within the historiography of Algeria's violence—colonial, anticolonial, and postcolonial—there is a problematic tendency to view Algeria as a victim of its own history.[103] The latest iteration of this tendency can be found in the inter-national peacebuilding regime of transitional justice. Central to this regime's *raison d'être* and *mission civilisatrice* has been the international regulation of postconflict polities through the contemporary morality play of the truth commission. The Algerian rejection of this approach was widely denounced by human rights and transitional justice organizations, the new technomanagerial experts who claim epistemic mastery over postconflict environments and peacebuilding processes. Criticism of Algeria's failure to live up to their standards was automatic; they did not wait to evaluate the effects of either the Concorde or the Charte. By comparison to Morocco's truth commission, Algeria's approach to reconciliation has also elicited a cold reception from key North Atlantic powers. Much of the criticism directed at Algeria is based on the assertion that there now exist international standards and norms of transitional justice for postconflict and postauthoritarian societies to follow. The origins of these standards has little to do with an objective assessment of whether or not truth commissions and other related mechanisms are actually effective. What these standards represent is the emergence of an international peacebuilding regime that manages postconflict environments through judicial and history-making processes. In so far as this regime cares little about the actual politics of history in postconflict societies, and instead pushes its vision of history making on polities, the antipolitics of transitional justice largely functions to expand the globalizing and totalizing horizon of the neoliberal peace.

September 1997: A boy takes a break from digging graves near the site of the Bentalha massacre. Photograph by B. F. Zohra. Courtesy of the *El Watan* archive, Algiers.

CONCLUSION
Conflict Science, Conflict Management, Crisis

THE EXTENDED CRISIS of 1990s Algeria exposed the weaknesses of contemporary understandings of late warfare and the international strategies that seek to manage it: from the centrality of the January 1992 "coup" in narratives of the conflict to the repeated financial interventions of the IMF and other bodies; from the failure of the diplomatic peacemaking initiatives, such as the 1995 Rome Platform (see Chapter 2) to the failures to understand the massacre crisis of 1997–1998 and the emergent postconflict environment. Few had bothered to truly understand Algeria's violence in the 1990s, yet many were quick to draw and deploy lessons from it. Algeria's violence continued to be paradoxically misunderstood and instrumentalized even as the killing declined after 1998 while the insurgency retreated to the Kabylia mountains and the southern border region shared with Mauritania, Mali, and Niger.[1] A postconflict environment emerged in Algeria, one characterized by a permanent state of unease, a polity suspended between armed conflict and national reconciliation, between democracy and authoritarianism. The Algerian regime saw its new mission in life as guaranteeing that there would be no going back to the horrors of the 1990s. But the cost of this security was high: there would also be no going back to the false hope and promises of the democratic opening that followed the October 1988 protests.

The international reaction to an attack on a gas production facility near In Amenas, deep in Algeria's Sahara on the border with Libya, in January 2013 was further indication that understandings of the prolonged crisis in Algeria were still impoverished, even twenty years after the events of the January 1992 "coup" and the assassination—still unexplained—of Boudiaf five months later. What the 2013 In Amenas attack called into question was one of the most obvious but rarely examined features of the violence in Algeria: oil. Throughout the 1990s and the early 2000s, Algeria's copious hydrocarbon production and distribution infrastructure, much of it exploited in coordination with foreign companies, had seemingly never been under threat until it was brazenly attacked in 2013. This fact alone should have been interesting; Algeria's insurgents had never targeted the state's Achilles heel in more than two decades of conflict. But as with so many elements of the conflict in Algeria, the situation was never subjected to intense scrutiny. In the end, Algerian special forces brought the brief In Amenas hostage crisis to a dramatic conclusion after a few days, killing some of the hostages and several of the attackers in the process. Longtime observers of Algerian affairs, both inside and outside the government, were, as always, left with more questions than answers.[2]

Though little understood, the crisis of 1990s Algeria became a productive case study for the science and management of conflict after the Cold War. Algeria's violence was contorted to fit new understandings of civil wars developed in the 1990s and early 2000s. These understandings not only devised new economic accounts of civil wars that stripped them of their political, historical, and ideational content, but also fed into neoliberal strategies of conflict management and prevention by addressing armed conflict as a problem of development rather than diplomacy. Similarly, Algeria's violence of the 1990s was rendered in such a way as to make it a pivotal case in new understandings of Islamic terrorism, jihadi violence, and (de)radicalization that came of age after the Cold War and effloresced after 9/11. Algeria of the 1990s also contributed to new understandings and doctrines of humanitarian intervention by not contributing at all. The absence of Algeria allowed the R2P project to narrate itself and the killing fields of 1990s in such a way as to avoid the difficult task of developing tools to understand and manage the kinds of complex and indeterminate forms of mass violence that Algeria's massacre crisis represented in 1997–1998. More recently, Algeria has likewise contributed to understandings and strategies of postconflict management by being a bad example. Algeria's failure to follow the South Africa model of staging a national truth and reconciliation commission becomes a possible explanation for the persistence of violence and authoritarianism.

These various framings of Algeria's violence reveal the antipolitics driving contemporary efforts to systematically understand and so manage late warfare. This antipolitics is best understood—and clearly manifests in understandings of, as well as interventions into, Algeria's violence—as a scientific and managerial attitude in which questions of power, space, and history are absent or highly circumscribed. Central concepts in international security today, such as civil war, terrorism, genocide, and the postconflict environment, have come to be understood, and so acted on, in new, reimagined ways since the Cold War. These reimaginings of conflict reflect the triumph of neoliberalism and the growing antipolitics that neoliberalism came to represent and enact in the world through globalization, democracy promotion, and international conflict management. Civil wars were reimagined as economic phenomena to be addressed through schemes of development rather than traditional forms of diplomacy. Terrorism, once thought of as a tactic arising out of strategic adaptation, became an irrational, ahistorical, apolitical identity that could be managed only through elimination. Mass atrocities likewise were deemed no longer tolerable after the Cold War, but the underlying justification relied on the racialized concept of genocide rather than on the more profoundly humanitarian concern for the systematic killing of any civilians regardless of their identity or the perpetrators' identity. Necessary conditions for atrocities to take the form of genocide have since come to include either a foreign military intervention in the name of stopping genocide (for example, Libya in 2011) or at least a geopolitical predisposition among key states on the UN Security Council to use military force for such humanitarian purposes (as in Darfur from 2002 onward). Transitional justice, through the ICC or truth and reconciliation commissions, has increasingly transformed postconflict justice into a morality play that has obfuscated history and power in the name of neoliberal peacebuilding.

Some of these scientific framings and managerial strategies drew on Algeria's violence and were applied to Algeria with varying degrees of accuracy and self-defined success; others used Algeria by not using it as a case—by avoiding the ways in which Algeria's violence would otherwise complicate the ability of neoliberal conflict management to understand and intervene in mass violence and postconflict environments. This critique of contemporary conflict science and management elucidates some of the reasons for the international community's paralysis vis-à-vis the violence in 1990s Algeria. It also provides some leverage for understanding both the productivity and the incapacity of contemporary conflict management and science vis-à-vis more globally distressing issues.

The career of conflict science and management after the Cold War is animated by several crises of thought and action. The first crisis is the end of the

Cold War itself, which called into question the epistemological regimes that had positioned themselves as the primary interpreters of the US-USSR rivalry and all of the politics that derived from it. The failure to predict the collapse of the Soviet Union was most often laid at the feet of international relations theory as well as sectors of government, notably intelligence.[3] Nonetheless, this epistemic crisis quickly became the occasion for bountiful debate on the shape of things to come, whether in its optimistic "end of history" variant or its pessimistic "clash of civilizations" form.[4]

Shortly after the end of the Cold War, another crisis in conflict management and science emerged. The genocidal acts in the former Yugoslavia and Rwanda raised serious questions about international capacity to understand and so control episodes of mass internal violence. The response to this post–Cold War crisis—as with the response to the end of the Cold War itself—was likewise bountiful in terms of its discursive production (such as debates about "new wars" and humanitarian intervention) and equally problematic in terms of its limits, blindspots, and misprisions, as this study has demonstrated. Nonetheless, boycotts of conflict minerals such as "blood diamonds" were linked directly to the new science of civil wars; thanks to the R2P project, efforts to "save Darfur" became the largest globally oriented social movement on US college campuses in the 2000s. The irony of these movements was the way in which their expressions of concern hinted at the depoliticization—and economization—of social activism against war through boycotts and calls for sanction. Another sign of the new antipolitics of social activism was its abdication of basic notions of democratic responsibility toward the victims of terrorism inflicted by one's own government. The bloodiest war of the early 2000s, the war initiated by the Anglo-American invasion of Iraq in 2003, did not precipitate a social movement comparable to the movement that sought to end the Darfur conflict in Sudan.[5]

The events of 9/11 likewise spurred much criticism of Middle Eastern studies for its ostensible failure to predict those events and its failure to produce policy-relevant knowledge for the global war on terror. Nonetheless, the events of 9/11 reinvigorated the study of the Arab and Islamic worlds in ways that would have been unimaginable in the years prior. The tendency to view polities in North Africa and Southwest Asia as places of static politics came into crisis with the widespread protests of 2011—protests that led to the overthrow of three long-standing dictators and two bloody civil wars.[6] Related to these developments were trends in armed and unarmed conflicts that had gone unrecognized for many years until certain technologies of truth—statistical analysis and large comparative datasets—were applied to them. What these studies showed was a fact that had long been dismissed or ignored in the conflict sciences: strategic nonviolent action had become, over the course of the twentieth century, the most successful form of waging conflict.[7] Instead of reflecting on its inability to see these trends, the conflict sciences doubled down and began to incorporate them into preexisting structures.[8] Also related to the events of the 2011 Arab Spring was the global financial crisis of 2008, which should have constituted a crisis in the economic sciences as much as it was a crisis for economic management. Instead, the role of economics in both interpreting and governing societies only became more entrenched as politicians accepted economics' intellectual and managerial hegemony more and more. Along with that, the epistemological hegemony of economics' reductionistic and ultimately antipolitical approach to describing and explaining the world—an approach that had certainly contributed to the 2008 crisis in the first place—continued to colonize the social sciences voraciously.[9]

These trends speak to the problematic relationship between conflict science, conflict management, and crisis. They also elucidate the antipolitics that animates the relationship between these three elements. More than ever before, there exists a strong warrant to understand and confront this antipolitics given the confluence of two global challenges. One is the apparent decline in violence worldwide and the other is the emerging climate catastrophe. The worldwide, centuries-long decline in the number and intensity of wars and lesser armed conflicts is a good thing. But the most disturbing features of this trend—which could be the end of war and other forms of large-scale mass violence—are that explanations of the decline vary and, more important, today's unprecedented peace has come about despite any deliberate and coordinated global effort, apart from that of the United Nations.[10] Two major analyses of these trends have largely vindicated the antipolitics of our age, that is, the increasingly monochromatic vision of political life as it is currently organized under neoliberalism.[11] This political vision cannot be a good thing, however, when one considers its incapacity in the face of the global climate crisis. The world is more peaceful than ever before (but we do not know why) and yet the world is careening toward a multifaceted ecological crisis (and we do not have the will or imagination to avert it). So overwhelming is this confluence of forces and the ossification of global politics that a leading theorist of environmental conflict sees only hope in the opportunities afforded by global civilizational collapse.[12] It is difficult to imagine how such a collapse will not reinvigorate modalities of war long thought dormant: interstate, conventional, total, and maybe even nuclear. The science and management of conflict are incapable of doing anything about these trends, for reasons explicated throughout this book, but mainly because contemporary understandings of late warfare and efforts to manage it are embedded within a globalizing regime of antipolitical knowledge and power that neither the science nor management of mass violence is able to recognize, account for, or affect.

REFERENCE MATTER

ACKNOWLEDGMENTS

Abdullah Al-Mubarak Foundation Postgraduate Scholarship (British Society for Middle Eastern Studies), Kerry Adams, Saida Aich, American Institute for Maghrib Studies, Nathanael Andreini, Josef Ansorge, Zoubir Arous, Michael Barber, Thierry Becker, Omar Belhouchet, Elizabeth Bishop, Youcef Bouandel, Adnane Bouchaib, Nabil Boudraa, Reda Bouzinzin, David Campbell, James Carroll, Centre d'études diocésaines (Algiers), Centre d'études maghrébines en Algérie (Oran), Zine Cherfaoui, Hichem Chouadria, Peter Clasen, Colgate University (the dean of the faculty, the president, and the Research Council), Emmy Cottam, Martha Crenshaw, Brock Cutler, Geoffrey Dabelko, Hakim Darbouche, Abdelafid Dib, Tim Dunne, Daho Djerbal, Cherif Dris, John Entelis, Stefanie Fishel, Ricky Goldstein, Mohammed Hachemaoui, Roman Hagelstein, Connie Harsh, Clement Henry, Rachel Howes, the Institute of Arab and Islamic Studies at the University of Exeter, Jennifer Johnson, William Jordan, Jimmy Juarez, Jeremy Keenan, Theresa Kevorkian, Cherifa Kheddar, Moumen Khelil, Carrie Konold, Bill Lawrence, Azzedine Layachi, Miriam Lowi, William MacLean, Magnum Photos (Michale Shulman and Abbas), Mustapha Madi, Fayçal Métaoui, James McDougall, Adlène Meddi, Dan Monk, Jenny Morgan, Marie-Thérèse Mounier, Phillip Naylor, Bill Nelson, Ronald Neumann, Tim Niblock, Thierry Oberlé, Martin Oliver, James Onley, Arzo Osanloo, Bobby Parks, David Patel, William Quandt, Felix Rathje, Mariana Raykov, Phil Reese, Bruce Riedel, Nancy Ries, Hugh Roberts, Andrew Rotter, Blair Rubble, Theresa Ryan, Jeremy Simer, Scott Smiley, Nora Spiegel, Gareth Stansfield, Lise Storm, Anna Theofilopoulou, Martin Thomas, Susan Thomson, John Thorne, Ken Valente, Kate Wahl, Isabelle Werenfels, Zahia Yacoub, Fatima Yous, Yahia Zoubir, Stephen Zunes, and my family.

NOTES

PROLOGUE

1. "Terrible carnage près d'Alger: entre 98 et 300 civils égorges," Agence France-Presse, August 29, 1997.

2. See Hassane Zerrouky, "La barbarie intégriste s'abat sur le petit village de Raïs," *l'Humanité*, August 30, 1997.

3. "Algerian Islamic Leader Appeals for Truce in Wake of Massacres," Deutsche Presse-Agentur, August 30, 1997.

4. Boubker Belkadi, "Hundreds Feared Dead in Algerian Massacre," Agence France-Presse, August 29, 1997.

5. Rachid Khiari, "Three Hundred Killed in Algeria Massacre, Witnesses and Hospital Workers Say," Associated Press, August 29, 1997.

6. Jean Hatzfeld, "Près d'Alger, des villageois égorgés et brûlés," *Libération*, August 30, 1997.

7. Rachid Khiari, "Government Assures It's Boosting Security, but Exodus Continues," Associated Press, August 30, 1997. See also Amine Kadi, "Algérie. Moi, Messaoud qui étais à Raïs lors du massacre," *La Croix*, September 26, 1997, 24.

8. Elaine Ganley, "Algerian Survivor Rebuilds Life," Associated Press, November 27, 1997.

9. Barry Hugill, "Algeria Slides Deeper into Bloody Morass," *Observer*, August 31, 1997, 9.

10. Robert Fisk, "Algeria, This Autumn: A People in Agony," *Independent*, October 22, 1997, 1.

11. "Scores Await Burial as Survivors Describe Massacres in Algeria," *Houston Chronicle*, August 31, 1997, A32.

12. John Lancaster, "As Algeria's Savagery Grows, So Does Mystery Shrouding It," *Washington Post*, October 18, 1997, A1.

13. Anthony Loyd, "Algerian Terror Victims Plead for Death by Bullet," *Times*, October 23, 1997.

14. "Algeria's Agony," *New York Times*, September 3, 1997, A22.

15. Radio France Internationale, "Forty-Five Killed in Second Massacre in Two Days

in Béni Messous," BBC Summary of World Broadcasts, September 9, 1997; see also "Toll of 63 People Dead in Béni Messous Massacre," BBC Summary of World Broadcasts, September 8, 1997.

16. "Sixty-Three Civilians Massacred in Algeria," Agence France-Presse, September 6, 1997.

17. Rachid Khiari, "Algeria Massacre Kills at Least 87," Associated Press, September 6, 1997.

18. Rachid Khiari, "Algerians Barricade, Arm Themselves," Associated Press, September 7, 1997.

19. Agence France-Presse, "Nouveau massacre de civils après 15 jours de relative accalmie," September 21, 1997; see also "Deux semaines d'accalmie" in Le Figaro, September 22, 1997.

20. Boubker Belkadi, "Des dizaines de victimes enterrees pres de Bentalha," Agence France-Presse, September 23, 1997.

21. "Deux cent à 250 personnes massacrées à Bentalha, selon deux quotidiens," Agence France-Presse, September 24, 1997.

22. Lara Marlowe, "Families Hid and Listened to Dying Neighbours' Screams," Irish Times, October 21, 1997, 11.

23. David Hirst, "The Mystery of Algeria's Murder Squads: 'This Is Where They Shot My Wife,'" Guardian, October 20, 1997, 1; François d'Alançon, "Algérie. A trois jours des élections municipales, Bentalhâa continue de panser ses plaies," La Croix, October 21, 1997, 10.

24. Robert Fisk, "Stench of Death in Algeria's Perfumed Killing Fields," Independent, October 23, 1997, 16.

25. John Lancaster, "As Algeria's Savagery Grows, So Does Mystery Shrouding It," Washington Post, October 18, 1997, A1.

26. "L'escalade de l'horreur," Le Point, September 27, 1997.

27. Of the two- to four-dozen mass killing episodes recorded between September 28 (including Sidi Serhane, near Blida, forty-seven killed) and the December 23–24 Tiaret-Tissemsilt massacres, all reportedly claimed fewer than fifty casualties. See Aït-Larbi and others, "Anatomy of the Massacres." See also Sidhoum and Algeria Watch, Chronologie des massacres en Algérie.

28. "Seventy-Eight civils assassines dans l'ouest algérien," Agence France-Presse, December 31, 1997; Rachid Khiari, "Algerian Government Says 78 Massacred in Ramadan Attacks," Associated Press, December 31, 1997.

29. Rachid Khiari, "'Guerrillas' with Walkie-Talkies Herded Algerians to Slaughter," Observer, January 4, 1998, 4.

30. "New Bloodbath in Algeria: 412 Massacred," Agence France-Presse, January 3, 1998.

31. Alain Bommenel, "Les autorités et l'armée confrontées a l'escalade de la terreur," Agence France-Presse, January 3, 1998. See also "Report: Ramadan Massacres Killed More

Than 400 in Western Algeria," Associated Press, January 2, 1998; "Muslim Militants Hack 412 Villagers to Death in Algeria's Worst Massacre," Associated Press, January 3, 1998; "Survivors Relate Horror of Algerian Massacre," Reuters, January 4, 1998; "Twenty-Two More Slain in Algeria at Outset of Bloody Ramadan: Press," Agence France-Presse, January 5, 1998.

32. "Algerian Newspapers Report 172 Killed in Latest Massacres," Agence France-Presse, January 6, 1998. Although the Algerian government did not acknowledge these larger massacres, three smaller ones in the same area—Sidi Mammar, twenty-nine killed; Ouled Bounif, twelve killed; and Ihdjaidia, twenty-one killed (other spellings of these locations included Sidi Maamar or Oued Mâamar, Kalaat Ouled Bounif, and Hedjailia, respectively)—were officially disclosed as having occurred on the nights between January 5–7. See "More Massacres Hit Algeria as Pressure Mounts for Inquiry," Agence France-Presse, January 7, 1998; Reuters, "Massacres Claim 62 More Algerians: Pressure Grows for Outside Investigation," *Calgary Herald* (Alberta), January 8, 1998, A5.

33. "Algerian Massacre Victims Too Many to Bury," Reuters, January 10, 1998.

34. Associated Press, "Algerian Massacres Kill at Least 392—Including 200 in One Village," January 6, 1998.

35. "'The Dead Are the Lucky Ones,' Says Algerian Massacre Survivor," Agence France-Presse, January 7, 1998.

36. Reuters, "Massacres Claim 62 More Algerians: Pressure Grows for Outside Investigation," *Calgary Herald*, January 8, 1998, A5. See also "Algerians Flee Horror, Government Rejects Inquiry, West Seeks Solutions," Associated Press, January 6, 1998; "More Than 170 Slain in Latest Algerian Massacres: Papers," Agence France-Presse, January 7, 1998; Associated Press, "Government Rejects International Inquiry into Violence, Algerians Flee," January 7, 1998; "EU Grapples for Response to Algeria Blood-Letting," Agence France-Presse, January 8, 1998.

37. "'Dozens of Families Wiped Out in New Algerian Massacre," Agence France-Presse, January 12, 1998.

38. "Cent trois morts et 70 blesses a Sidi Hammed, selon un premier bilan officiel," Agence France-Presse, January 12, 1998.

39. "Algerian Government Denies Death Toll of 400," Agence France-Presse, January 13, 1998.

40. "Bloodbath at Sidi Hamed Brings New Horror in Algeria," Agence France-Presse, January 12, 1998.

41. "Graphic Accounts of Latest Algeria Massacre as EU to Send Team," Agence France-Presse, January 13, 1998.

INTRODUCTION

1. Documentary filmmaker Adam Curtis is perhaps today's most dedicated chronicler of managerialism and its dangers. His account of the rise of managerialism in mod-

ern politics and its articulation with neoliberal strategies of rule, elaborated in his films *Pandora's Box* (1992), *Century of the Self* (2002), *The Trap* (2007), and *All Watched Over by Machines of Loving Grace* (2011), was recently summarized in this interview: Rob Pollard, "Adam Curtis: 'We Don't Read Newspapers Because the Journalism Is So Boring,'" *New Statesman*, February 4, 2014, accessed February 2015, http://www.newstatesman.com /culture/2014/02/adam-curtis-interview.

2. A more far-reaching analysis of this dynamic is explored in Klein, *Shock Doctrine*.

3. Ferguson, *Anti-Politics Machine*.

4. Mitchell, "Work of Economics."

5. On problematizations, see Foucault and Rabinow, "Polemics, Politics and Problematizations."

6. Zulaika, *Terrorism*; Stampnitzky, *Disciplining Terror*.

7. Regan, *Sixteen Million One*.

8. A major study examining the impact of the international environment on civil wars ironically reaffirms the recent tendency to view them as innately domestic conflicts. Observing differences between the kinds of warfare practiced in civil wars before and those after the Cold War, the authors conclude that during the Cold War civil wars were affected by the bipolar international system. After the Cold War, civil wars changed owing to the end of proxy wars—Soviet and North Atlantic sponsorship of rebellion or repression in the Third World. The extent to which international forces affect civil wars since the Cold War is in the putative absence of such forces. See Kalyvas and Balcells, "International System and Technologies of Rebellion."

9. For example, Collier and Hoeffler, "Economic Causes of Civil War."

10. Fearon and Laitin, "Ethnicity, Insurgency, and Civil War."

11. Kalyvas, "'New' and 'Old' Civil Wars."

12. Mitchell, "Economists and the Economy"; Mitchell, "Middle East in the Past and Future of Social Science."

13. World Bank, *World Development Report 2011*. See also Human Security Research Group, *Human Security Report 2009–2010*, 37.

14. Ward, Greenhill, and Bakke, "Perils of Policy by P-Value," cited in Human Security Research Group, *Human Security Report 2009–2010*, 38.

15. Huntington, "Clash of Civilizations?"

16. Kaplan, "Coming Anarchy." See also Homer-Dixon, *Environment, Scarcity, and Violence*; Parenti, *Tropic of Chaos*.

17. Nordstrom, *Shadows of War*; Kaldor, *New and Old Wars*.

18. Merry and Coutin, "Technologies of Truth."

19. Collier and Sambanis, "Understanding Civil War."

20. For more thorough critiques of the new sciences of civil conflict, see Nathan, "Frightful Inadequacy"; Cramer, *Civil War Is Not a Stupid Thing*.

21. Goetze, "Statebuilding in a Vacuum."

22. See Zulaika, *Terrorism*; Stampnitzky, *Disciplining Terror*.

23. Kilcullen, *Accidental Guerrilla*.

24. As evidenced in the major textbooks and practitioner "handbooks" on the matter: Deutsch, Coleman, and Marcus, *Handbook of Conflict Resolution*; Bercovitch, Kremeniuk, and Zartman, *SAGE Handbook of Conflict Resolution*; Bercovitch and Jackson, *Conflict Resolution in the Twenty-First Century*; Ramsbotham, Woodhouse, and Miall, *Contemporary Conflict Resolution*; Kriesberg and Dayton, *Constructive Conflicts*; Wallensteen, *Understanding Conflict Resolution*.

25. The maximalist school of peace studies is the school of thought closely associated with the work of Johan Galtung, who is widely—though disputably—credited with being the founder of modern peace studies.

26. Gat, "Is War Declining—and Why?"

27. Goldstein, *Winning the War on War*.

28. Evans, "End of the Argument."

29. Weiss, "Sunset of Humanitarian Intervention?"

30. Krasner, *Sovereignty*.

31. Bass, *Freedom's Battle*.

32. Porch, *Counterinsurgency*.

33. De Waal, "Darfur and the Failure of the Responsibility to Protect"; Badescu and Bergholm, "The Responsibility to Protect and the Conflict in Darfur."

34. Bellamy and Williams, "New Politics of Protection."

35. Evans, "End of the Argument."

36. Weiss and Hubert, *Responsibility to Protect*; Knight and Egerton, *Routledge Handbook of the Responsibility to Protect*.

37. Perhaps most surprising of all (or not surprising at all) is Algeria's absence from the R2P project's intellectual labors given the presence of an esteemed Algerian diplomat, Mohamed Sahnoun, as cochair of the first iteration of the R2P project, the Canadian-supported International Commission on State Sovereignty and Intervention. See Evans and Sahnoun, "Responsibility to Protect."

38. Monk and Mundy, *The Post-Conflict Environment*.

39. Chapman and van der Merwe, *Truth and Reconciliation in South Africa*; Amnesty International, *Broken Promises*; Thomson, *Whispering Truth to Power*.

40. For background, see Headrick, *Tools of Empire*.

41. In the English translation of Luis Martinez's study, *imaginaire de la guerre* was translated as "war-oriented imaginaire." The translator suggested that *imaginaire* is similar to the English term *worldview* or the German *Weltanschauung*, though the option of "ideology" is not offered. See Martinez, *Algerian Civil War*, 1.

42. Roberts, "Algeria's Veiled Drama," 388–389; Werenfels, *Managing Instability in Algeria*, 128–129.

43. The precariousness of "postconflict" Algeria is described in Werenfels, *Manag-

ing Instability in Algeria; Roberts, *Demilitarizing Algeria*; Zoubir and Aghrout, "Algeria's Path to Reform."

44. Geopolitical in the sense described in Tuathail, *Critical Geopolitics*.

45. In using the idea of "meta-Algeria," I am borrowing David Campbell's approach to the study of the Bosnian conflict. See Campbell, *National Deconstruction*.

46. Scarry, *Body in Pain*.

47. Said, *Orientalism*, 54.

48. Anderson, *Imagined Communities*, 205.

49. From Nietzsche, *Genealogy of Morals*, quoted in Butler, *Gender Trouble*, 34.

50. For an account of the contemporary geopolitical moment, see Harvey, *Brief History of Neoliberalism*.

51. Hardt and Negri, *Empire*.

52. See Foucault, *"Society Must Be Defended,"* chapter 11.

53. Amar, *Security Archipelago*, 239.

CHAPTER 1

1. "Syria in Civil War, Says UN Official Herve Ladsous," BBC News, June 12, 2012, accessed August 21, 2014, http://www.bbc.co.uk/news/world-middle-east-18417952; Louis Charbonneau and Dominic Evans, "Syria in Civil War, U.N. Official Says," Reuters, June 12, 2012, accessed August 21, 2014, http://www.reuters.com/article/2012/06/12/us-syria-idUSBRE85B0DZ20120612.

2. "Is Syria in an 'Official' Civil War?" CBS News and Associated Press, June 13, 2012, accessed August 21, 2014, http://www.cbsnews.com/news/is-syria-in-an-official-civil-war. See also Juan Cole, "You Always Knew It, But Now . . . ," *Informed Comment*, June 13, 2012, accessed February 18, 2015, http://www.juancole.com/2012/06/you-always-knew-it-but-now.html.

3. "Syria Slides Towards Civil War: Qubeir," *Economist*, June 8, 2012, accessed August 21, 2014, http://www.economist.com/blogs/newsbook/2012/06/syria-slides-towards-civil-war; Louis Charbonneau and Andrew Quinn, "U.N. Says Syria Civil War 'Imminent,' West Urges Sanctions," Reuters, June 8, 2012, accessed August 21, 2014, http://uk.reuters.com/article/2012/06/08/uk-syria-crisis-un-idUKBRE8561EW20120608; Neil MacFarquhar, "U.N. Kept Out of a Town That Syria Says It 'Cleansed,'" *New York Times*, June 13, 2012, accessed August 21, 2014, http://www.nytimes.com/2012/06/14/world/middleeast/new-weapons-push-syrian-crisis-toward-civil-war.html.

4. Arnaud de Borchgrave, "Another War in 2012?" UPI, June 4, 2012, accessed August 21, 2014, http://www.upi.com/UPI-98761338806961.

5. Lara Setrakia, "It Is What It Is," *New York Times*, June 12, 2012, accessed August 21, 2014, http://latitude.blogs.nytimes.com/2012/06/12/call-the-syrian-conflict-a-civil-war.

6. Mamdani, "Politics of Naming."

7. Kalyvas, *Logic of Violence in Civil Wars*, 17.

8. Monk, *An Aesthetic Occupation*, 79.

9. Reuters and *Washington Post* report in "Chadli Pledges Political Reform," *Sydney Morning Herald*, October 12, 1988, 18. For background on the demonstrations, see Radio-Beur, *Octobre à Alger*.

10. "Moslem Fundamentalists Call for General Strike," Agence France-Presse, May 23, 1991.

11. John Hooper, "Militants Back Down to Avoid Civil War in Algeria," *Guardian*, June 8, 1991.

12. Jackie Rowland, "Algeria Cancels Elections, Upsets Opposition," *Morning Edition*, National Public Radio, January 14, 1992, transcript.

13. "Le pouvoir algérien cherche à mettre en place une direction collégiale," Agence France-Presse, January 14, 1992.

14. Robert Fisk, "The Battle for Algiers," *Independent*, January, 19 1992, 17.

15. Elaine Ganley, "Specter of Islamic State in Algeria Provokes Dreams, Nightmares," Associated Press, January 1, 1992.

16. "Rights Leader Predicts War in Algeria," *St. Petersburg Times*, January 15, 1992, 7A.

17. Eldad Beck, "Algeria's Prophet of Doom," *Jerusalem Report*, January 16, 1992, 32.

18. Quoted in David Hirst, "Between Plague and Cholera," *Guardian*, January 13, 1992, 19.

19. In the same interview, Boudiaf added, "If we want to destroy ourselves, we will descend into civil war." Quoted in "Algeria Interview with Boudiaf on His Role and That of Higher State Council," BBC Summary of World Broadcasts, February 6, 1992.

20. "Algeria: Former President Ben Bella Rules Out Possibility of Civil War," BBC Summary of World Broadcasts, September 11, 1992.

21. "Interior Minister: Present Crisis 'One of the Most Serious' Since Independence," BBC Summary of World Broadcasts, December 3, 1993.

22. Wolfgang Schweitzer, "'Il n'y a pas de guerre civile' en Algérie, déclare le Premier ministre," Agence France-Presse, October 10, 1994.

23. "PM Tells Transitional National Council Algeria Has Triumphed over Terrorism," BBC Summary of World Broadcasts, January 7, 1997.

24. "Algeria Gives Conditional Green Light to EU Mission," Agence France-Presse, January 8, 1998.

25. Benyamina, "Foreign Interference," 186. The "war against civilians" trope found purchase elsewhere. Feminist activist and future minister Khalida Toumi likewise deployed Glucksmann's turn of phrase to describe the violence in her country and to denounce the outlawed and armed opposition. See Messaoudi and Schemla, *Unbowed*, 144. An official with the rights monitoring group Freedom House echoed this sentiment before the US congress: "call it a civil war or more precisely a war against civilians." See Roger Kaplan, Prepared Statement, Hearings on Algeria, US Congress, House Committee on International Relations, Subcommittee on Africa, October 11, 1995. Omar Carlier

likewise showed preference for the phrase *war against civilians* over *civil war*. See Carlier, "D'une guerre à l'autre." See also Tahon, *Algérie*. Addressing accusations of government complicity in the violence, one journalist commented, "The label *civil war* fails to capture the random viciousness of the violence. It would be better to call it mutual terror." See Alan Sipress, "A Most Uncivil War," *Philadelphia Inquirer*, January 26, 1997, E04. Jacques Derrida noted the gendered aspect of the violence: "this *civil* war is also a *virile* war [. . .] a mute war against women." See Derrida, "Taking a Stand for Algeria," 121.

26. "Algeria: President Bouteflika Interviewed on Internal Situation, Ties with West, Mideast," BBC Monitoring, November 11, 1999.

27. Nora Boustany, "Muslim Right Presses Battle for Algeria," *Washington Post*, January 5, 1993, A10.

28. "RCD Leader Dismisses Dialogue with FIS 'Moderates,' Regime 'Discredited,'" BBC Summary of World Broadcasts, December 31, 1993. See also Tahi, "Algeria's Democratization Process," 206–207.

29. "Trade Union Leader Says Algeria Suffering 'Assassination' by Violence," BBC Summary of World Broadcasts, March 24, 1994.

30. Anonymous, "Veiled and Afraid in Besieged Algeria," *International Herald Tribune*, April 2, 1994.

31. "Le jour approche qui verra l'éclatement de l'armée. Et c'est à ce moment-là que la vraie guerre civile commencera. La vraie boucherie," quoted in Catherine Simon, "Algérie: l'introuvable 'troisième voie,'" *Le Monde*, October 22, 1994.

32. "Un islamiste modère candidat a la présidence, l'Algérie sous le choc," Agence France-Presse, September 3, 1995.

33. Julia Ficatier, "Algérie. 'On ne sait plus qui tue qui et pourquoi,' Louisa Hanoune," *La Croix*, October 9, 1996, 24.

34. Mark Dennis, "Algeria on the Brink," *Newsweek*, April 14, 1997, 60.

35. Quoted in Emmanuel Serot, "Les événements en Algérie dans la presse parisienne," Agence France-Presse, November 5, 1993.

36. "Algeria: Descent into the Abyss," *New York Times*, April 5, 1994, A20.

37. Craig R. Whitney, "History's Fetters Entangling France on Algeria," *New York Times*, October 21, 1995, I3.

38. "Vietnam on the Mediterranean," *Guardian*, January 23, 1997, 16.

39. Andrew J. Pierre and William B. Quandt, "The 'Contract' with Algeria," *Washington Post*, January 22, 1995, C1.

40. "Algeria's Ills," *Irish Times*, June 30, 1992, 11.

41. John Phillips, "SAS Veterans Benefit from Algeria Panic," *Times*, January 28, 1994; Mike Shuster, "United States Takes Wait and See Stance in Algeria," *All Things Considered*, National Public Radio, April 4, 1995, transcript; Andrew Gumbel, "Algeria on Verge of First Talks with FIS," *Guardian*, September 6, 1994, 8.

42. Howard LaFranchi, "Algeria's New Leader Calls On Islamists and Army to Negotiate," *Christian Science Monitor*, February 4, 1994, 6.

43. "Watching Algeria Explode," *International Herald Tribune*, February 8, 1995.

44. Susan Morgan, "The Terror That Is Preying on Algeria," *Independent*, February 20, 1994, 11.

45. "Algeria's Choice," *Washington Post*, November 24, 1995, A28.

46. Bob Edwards, "Violence in Algeria," *Morning Edition*, National Public Radio, January 2, 1998.

47. Stora, *Algeria, 1830–2000*, 216.

48. "Une guerre civile qui ne dit pas son nom," in Bruno Frappat, "Algérie. Le sang d'un peuple," *La Croix*, January 9, 1997, 1. "In Algeria, wars never say their name," Frappat claimed in a reference to one of the euphemisms given to the undeclared French-Algerian war of 1954–1962, "la guerre sans nom" (the war without a name).

49. Robert Fisk, "Assassination of Boudiaf a Strike at Secular Algeria," *Toronto Star*, June 30, 1992, A3.

50. Julian Nundy, "Priests Killed in Algeria After Hijack Rescue," *Independent*, December 28, 1994, 1.

51. Jean-Pierre Tuquoi, "Blow to Algeria as France Cuts Back Aid," *Guardian Weekly*, July 7, 1996, 19; Jean-Pierre Tuquoi, "L'Algérie entrouvre ses portes à une mission des Nations unies," *Le Monde*, July 23, 1998.

52. Frank Sesno, "Algeria Appears Poised for Islamic Revolution," CNN, March 1, 1994; Charles Bremner and Michael Binyon, "British Entry Will Be Barred to Key Algeria Militant," *Times*, September 1, 1994; Anna Husarska, "The Mean Streets of Algeria," *New Republic*, July 29, 1996, 19; "Algeria Condemned for 'Human Rights Disaster,'" *Guardian*, January 4, 1994, 9; "Twenty-Two More Slain in Algeria at Outset of Bloody Ramadan: Press," Agence France-Presse, January 5, 1998. See also International Crisis Group, *Algeria's Economy*, 1.

53. Martin Regg Cohn, "Priest Lives as Marked Man," *Toronto Star*, June 15, 1997, A12.

54. "*Meurtrière*" in "Algérie: l'armée au fond des urnes," *Le Point*, April 10, 1999.

55. "Algérie: le sang du ramadan," *Le Point*, February 1, 1997; Pierre de Boisdeffre, "L'Algérie de nos remords et de notre espérance," *Le Figaro*, February 14, 1997.

56. "Algeria's Brave Voters," *Times*, November 30, 1996; Christopher P. Winner, "Debate Erupts in France Over Media's Priorities," *USA Today*, September 8, 1997, 5A.

57. Roger Cohen, "Algeria's Main Rebel Faction Takes Risk and Calls Truce," *New York Times*, September 25, 1997, A8.

58. David Hirst, "Algeria Drowning in an Orgy of Bloodletting," *Guardian Weekly*, October 5, 1997, 12; David Hirst, "Fear as Algeria's Leader Quits," *Guardian Weekly*, September 20, 1998, 4.

59. "La guerre civile qui ravage l'Algérie," in "Algérie: 70 000 morts depuis 1992," *Le Figaro*, January 31, 1998; Alain Frachon, "Deux témoignages éprouvants sur l'itinéraire des membres du GIA en Algérie," *Le Monde*, March 8, 1999; "Ensanglante la terre algérienne," in "Algérie: la stratégie de la terreur," *Le Point*, April 26, 1997; "La

guerre civile qui déchire l'Algérie," in Michel Massenet, "L'engrenage algérien," *Le Figaro*, January 13, 1998.

60. Jacques Charmelot, "M. Leotard: 'la guerre civile en Algérie est un défi pour la communauté européenne,'" Agence France-Presse, December 15, 1993.

61. Roy Towers, "Europe Is Accused of Inaction as Algeria Teeters on Brink of Disaster," *Glasgow Herald*, January 10, 1994, 18.

62. "L'intervention télévisée du président de la République à l'occasion du 14 juillet, M. Mitterrand," *Le Monde*, July 16, 1994, cited in Roberts, "Algeria's Veiled Drama," 390.

63. Malley, *Call from Algeria*, 1, 11, 204–205.

64. Thomas W. Lippman, "U. S. Stakes Are High, Expectations Low, in Algeria's Impending Election," *Washington Post*, November 1, 1995, A26.

65. Fuller, *Algeria*, x, 64.

66. Peter W. Rodman, "The Time Bomb in Algeria," *Washington Post*, January 1, 1995, C1.

67. Quandt, *Between Ballots and Bullets*, 162.

68. For example, the term *civil war* was not used during US State Department daily press briefings, either by the spokesperson or by the journalists in attendance asking questions, throughout 1997 and 1998.

69. "Une situation de quasi-guerre civile," in Dominique Simonnet, "Bernard Miyet 'N'en demandons pas trop aux Casques bleus,'" *L'Express*, April 6, 1998.

70. Leveau, *L'Algérie dans la guerre*; Phillips, *Rising Threat*; Martinez, "Algérie: terrorismes et guerre civile"; Mortimer, "Islamists, Soldiers, and Democrats"; Callies de Salies, "Les luttes de clan exacerbent la guerre civile"; Brahimi, "Political Turmoil in Algeria"; Lazreg, "Islamism and the Recolonization of Algeria"; Rich, "Algerian Crisis"; Yacoubian and Deeb, *Algeria*; Wiktorowicz, "Centrifugal Tendencies"; Cavatorta, "Failed Liberalisation of Algeria"; Turshen, "Algerian Women"; Lloyd, *Multi-Causal Conflict in Algeria*; Takeyh, "Islamism in Algeria"; Volpi, *Islam and Democracy*; Hadj Moussa, "The Imaginary Concord and the Reality of Discord"; Henry, "Algeria's Agonies"; Heristchi, "The Islamist Discourse"; Tessler, Bonner, and Rief, "Islam, Democracy and the State in Algeria"; Le Sueur, *Uncivil War*; Lowi, "Anatomy of a Civil War"; Szmolka, "Algerian Presidential Elections of 2004"; Weinstein, *Inside Rebellion*; Werenfels, *Managing Instability in Algeria*; Ashour, *De-Radicalization of Jihadists*; Joffé, "National Reconciliation and General Amnesty in Algeria"; Tlemçani, *Algeria Under Bouteflika*. Scheele put *civil war* in quotes. See Scheele, "Algerian Graveyard Stories."

71. Martinez, *La guerre civile en Algérie*, 12–16. Martinez's argument for calling the Algerian conflict a civil war was not included in the English translation. There is no explanation from the author or the translator as to why this is the case. See Martinez, *Algerian Civil War*. Roberts's critique of Martinez is based on the French original. See Roberts, "Algeria's Veiled Drama."

72. The two most significant studies of the insurgency, which included fieldwork

and interviews with participants in the conflict and their victims, were largely confined to the Algiers region, the Mitidja, and adjacent areas. Martinez, *La guerre civile en Algérie*; Belaala, "Ethnicité, nationalisme et radicalisation islamiste violente." A notable exception, which examines the dynamics of violence in some western regions of Algeria, is Moussaoui, *De la violence en Algérie*.

73. Ruedy, *Modern Algeria*, 257.

74. Willis, *Islamist Challenge in Algeria*, 376; Quandt, *Between Ballots and Bullets*, 162.

75. In one account, the term *civil war* was used only to describe the fighting between the AIS and the GIA. See Evans and Phillips, *Algeria*, 221.

76. Roberts, "Algeria's Veiled Drama." See also Moussaoui, *De la violence en Algérie*, 436–437; Evans and Phillips, *Algeria*, 225; Darbouche and Zoubir, "The Algerian Crisis," 22. Moussaoui argues that the term *civil war* cannot be applied to the violence in Algeria because it was "localized" (his quotes) and so took on limited forms. See Moussaoui, *De la violence en Algérie*, 13.

77. Testas, "Algeria's Economic Decline," 83; Testas, "Roots of Algeria's Religious and Ethnic Violence," 178; Dillman, *State and Private Sector*, 213, 214.

78. Roberts, "Algeria's Veiled Drama," 391.

79. Lowi, "Anatomy of a Civil War"; Fearon and Laitin, "Algeria."

80. Sambanis, "What Is Civil War?," 835.

81. Bhatia, *Terrorism and the Politics of Naming*; Stampnitzky, *Disciplining Terror*.

82. That is, the Correlates of War (COW) project. See Sarkees and Wayman, *Resort to War*.

83. For a more thorough discussion, see Mundy, "Deconstructing Civil Wars."

84. Collier and Hoeffler, "Greed and Grievance in Civil War."

85. Sambanis, "What Is Civil War?," 818.

86. "Algeria: National Human Rights Monitoring Group: Over 600 Died from Violence in Last Year," BBC Monitoring, February 6, 1993; "Conflicts Which Have Been in Some Way Created or Exacerbated as a Result of the End of the Cold War," *Guardian*, December 31, 1992, 16; "Army Commander Faces Charges," Associated Press, February 6, 1993; Amnesty International, *Deteriorating Human Rights*, 1.

87. For example, the Associated Press claimed, on July 10, 1993, that twelve hundred Algerians had been killed in the fighting; several months later, on September 20, 1993, Agence France-Presse claimed a death toll of two thousand Algerians.

88. Stockholm International Peace Research Institute, *SIPRI Yearbook 1995*, 33.

89. A prominent study of civil wars cites 85,000 deaths in Algeria from 1992 to 2000, "a number about which there is little disagreement in the source literature." See Weinstein, *Inside Rebellion*, 316. Although this claim about the source literature is true, a lot of the source literature itself is flawed. For example, a major source of data on civil wars oddly claims eighty thousand *government* losses as of 1997; rebel losses are not indicated. See Sarkees, "Correlates of War Data on War." Another major source of data, the Stock-

holm International Peace Research Institute (SIPRI), provides a similar figure for the year 1997. See Stockholm International Peace Research Institute, *SIPRI Yearbook 1998*, 28. Figures maintained by the Uppsala Conflict Data Program at the Peace Research Institute Oslo (UCDP-PRIO) likewise rely on SIPRI's figures, augmenting them with data from, or related to, Project Ploughshares, a Canadian faith-based organization that monitors armed violence worldwide. The UCDP-PRIO yearly data were also arrived at by accepting the one hundred thousand figure and treating all of the deaths as battle related. They then trended yearly data—often arbitrarily doubling or tripling SIPRI figures—so as to give "preference to the estimate that totals nearly 90,000 battle deaths."

90. Sambanis provides a rate of twelve hundred deaths per month between 1994 and 1998. See Sambanis, "What Is Civil War?" He cites figures provided by the International Crisis Group. The Crisis Group actually applies this rate to the entire period of 1992 through 1998. See International Crisis Group, *Algerian Crisis*. Sambanis likely meant to cite Miriam Lowi, who claims fewer than twelve hundred deaths per month for 1992–1994, and twelve hundred deaths per month for 1994–1998. See Lowi, "Anatomy of a Civil War," 239.

91. Human Rights Watch, *World Report 1997*, 268.

92. Human Rights Watch, *World Report 1993*.

93. Amnesty International, *Deteriorating Human Rights*, 1.

94. Human Rights Watch, *World Report 1995*.

95. Amnesty International, *Repression and Violence Must End*, 1. See also Human Rights Watch, *World Report 1995*.

96. Human Rights Watch, *World Report 1997*; Human Rights Watch, *World Report 1999*.

97. U.S. Department of State, *Country Reports on Human Rights Practices 1998*.

98. See, for example, U.S. Department of State, *Country Reports on Human Rights Practices 2002*; Amnesty International, *Legacy of Impunity*, 6; Human Rights Watch, *World Report 2010*, 482.

99. For example, Amnesty International, *Truth and Justice Obscured*, 15–16.

100. "Official Death Toll Since February 1992 Reaches 10,000," BBC Summary of World Broadcasts, September 8, 1994.

101. "Two More FIS Leaders to Be Freed: Reports," Agence France-Presse, September 8, 1994.

102. According to a Radio France Internationale broadcast, the report detailed in *Le Parisien* indicated 38,500 civilian deaths (12,700 in Blida), 2,733 casualties among the security forces, and 7,297 losses among the "Islamists" between January and October 1994. See "Parisian Paper Publishes Secret Algerian Report on Death Toll," BBC Summary of World Broadcasts, December 30, 1994. The London *Times*, however, reported slightly different figures from the same source: "25,000 civilians, 7,000 alleged terrorists and 2,700 members of the security forces." See Adam Sage, "Algiers Admits Air Security

Lapses," *Times*, December 30, 1994. Reuters did so too: "35,000 people killed in fighting' during the first ten months of 1994." See Reuters, "Sixty-One Militants Killed, Algeria Says," *Globe and Mail*, December 30, 1994.

103. "More Than 5,000 Fundamentalists Killed in Year: Report," Agence France-Presse, June 12, 1996.

104. Amnesty International, *Fear and Silence*, 11–12.

105. "Bombes et faux barrage les jours de l'Aid," Agence France-Presse, January 31, 1998; "Algeria PM Defends Actions, Gives First Global Toll Since 1992," Agence France-Presse, January 22, 1998. Human Rights Watch (*World Report 1999*) and some media reports presented the 26,536 figure as encompassing all conflict-related deaths. See Clodfelter, *Warfare and Armed Conflicts*, 618.

106. Aït-Larbi and others, "Anatomy of the Massacres"; Sidhoum and Algeria Watch, *Chronologie des massacres en Algérie*.

107. "President on Peace, Referendum, Prisoners' Release, OPEC, France," BBC Summary of World Broadcasts, June 28, 1999.

108. Charles Trueheart, "Ignoring Army and His Own Iffy Election, Algerian Chases Peace," *Washington Post*, June 30, 1999, A25.

109. "Algerian President to Set Out Terms with Armed Foes," Agence France-Presse, June 4, 1999.

110. Rachid Khiari, "Amnesty Plan Moves Toward Parliament," Associated Press, June 28, 1999.

111. Francis David, "Les dimensions d'un génocide," *Sud Ouest*, December 16, 1996.

112. Florence Aubenas, "Plus de 9 000 morts cette année en Algérie," *Libération*, January 5, 2001, 12.

113. "Algeria: Army General Says There Are 650 Terrorists 'All Groups Included,'" BBC Summary of World Broadcasts, October 27, 2002; "Fewer than 650 Islamic Extremists Active in Algeria: General," Agence France-Presse, October 27, 2002. In October 2001, Algerian officials claimed that twenty thousand "terrorists" had been "neutralised" but did not indicate what percentage of these had been killed, captured, or amnestied. See Amnesty International, "Algeria" chapter in *Report 2002*, 29–31.

114. Quoted in Hugeux Vincent and Baya Gacemi Baya, "Algérie: les généraux sabre au clair," *L'Express*, November 7, 2002, 38.

115. "Algérie: entre 150.000 et 200.000 morts depuis 1992 dans les violences (Ksentini)," Agence France-Presse, March 18, 2006.

116. Salima Tlemçani, "Application de la charte pour la réconciliation nationale: 300 dossiers de terroristes ont été rejetés," *El Watan*, May 11, 2008, accessed September 30, 2010, http://www.elwatan.com/archives/article.php?id=93925.

117. Joffé, "National Reconciliation and General Amnesty," 217; Nezim Fethi, "National Reconciliation Moves Forward in Algeria," *Magharebia*, October 1, 2009, accessed August 21, 2014, http://magharebia.com/en_GB/articles/awi/features/2009/10/01/feature-01.

118. Human Rights Watch, *Time for Reckoning*, 15.

119. Adlène Meddi, "Gouvernement-familles des disparus: la rupture," *El Watan*, March 26, 2010, 3.

120. Nezim Fethi, "National Reconciliation Moves Forward in Algeria," *Magharebia*, October 1, 2009, accessed August 21, 2014, http://magharebia.com/en_GB/articles/awi/features/2009/10/01/feature-01.

121. Human Rights Watch, *Truth and Justice on Hold*, 11–12.

122. Collier, *Wars, Guns, and Votes*. Although Kaldor (*New and Old Wars*) conceptualizes "new" wars differently, her thoughts about how to remedy them function within the limits of neoliberal governmentality.

123. Collier and Hoeffler, *Greed and Grievance*; Fearon and Laitin, "Ethnicity, Insurgency, and Civil War."

124. Similar critiques have been raised by Nathan, "Frightful Inadequacy"; Cramer, *Civil War Is Not a Stupid Thing*.

CHAPTER 2

1. Robin, *Escadrons de la mort, l'ecole francaise*.

2. Porch, *Counterinsurgency*.

3. Amir Taheri, "Lessons from Algeria," *Jerusalem Post*, January 13, 2005, 15; Craig S. Smith, "Islam and Democracy: Algerians Try to Blaze a Trail," *New York Times*, April 14, 2004, A4; Dominique Moisi, "A Security Plan for the Mideast," *Financial Times*, October 8, 2003, 21; Harry Sterling, "Turkey's Unpopular Ban," *Montreal Gazette*, January 23, 1998, B3.

4. Roberts addresses these comparisons head on. See Roberts, "The Revolution That Wasn't."

5. Douglas Alexander, "The People, Not Generals," *Guardian*, August 22, 2013, 30; Roula Khalaf, "Egypt's Divisions Give Succour to Counter-Revolution," *Financial Times*, June 19, 2012, 13; *Al-Akhbar* (English), "Avoiding an 'Algerian Situation' in Post-Brotherhood Egypt," July 5, 2013.

6. Ian Black, "Egypt's Revolutionaries Should Heed Lessons from Algeria's Bloody Civil War," *Guardian*, July 4, 2013, http://www.theguardian.com/world/2013/jul/04/egypt-revolution-lessons-from-algeria; Hicham Yezza, "What Algeria 1992 Can, and Cannot, Teach Us About Egypt 2013," *Open Democracy*, July 23, 2013, http://www.opendemocracy.net/hicham-yezza/what-algeria-1992-can-and-cannot-teach-us-about-egypt-2013; William Lawrence, "Will Egypt Become the Next Algeria?" Washington Institute for Near East Affairs, July 17, 2013, http://www.washingtoninstitute.org/policy-analysis/view/will-egypt-become-the-next-algeria; Massoud Hayoun, "Will Egypt Repeat Algeria's 'Black Decade'?" *Aljazeera*, August 19, 2013, accessed February 2015, http://www.aljazeera.com/indepth/features/2013/08/201381810325176694.html; Yasmine Ryan, "Does the History of the Algerian Coup Offer Clues to What Egypt May Expect?" *Truthout*, January 10, 2014,

accessed February 2015, http://www.truth-out.org/news/item/21106-does -the-history-of -the-algerian-coup-of fer-clues-to-what-egypt-may-expect.

7. See Mirowski, *Machine Dreams*.

8. Roberts, "Algeria's Ruinous Impasse and the Honourable Way Out," 250–251; Quandt, *Between Ballots and Bullets*, 122.

9. "Chronology July 16, 1988–October 15, 1988," 87; "Chronology October 16, 1988—January 15, 1989," 263.

10. Roberts, "The Algerian State and the Challenge of Democracy," 434–436. See also Semiane, *Octobre*.

11. "Death Toll Put at 159 from Algeria Uprising," Associated Press, October 22, 1988.

12. See Rouadjia, *Les frères et la mosquée*; Al-Ahnaf, Botiveau, and Frégosi, *L'Algérie par ses islamistes*. Merrzak Allouache's acclaimed 1994 film *Bab El-Oued City* dramatizes the tensions and ambiguities of the years between October 1988 and January 1992. His novel expands on the film. See Allouache, *Bab El-Oued*.

13. "Chronology April 16, 1990–July 15, 1990," 683.

14. Georges Marion, "Algérie: le retour au calme," *Le Monde*, July 8, 1991. Madani reportedly said, in response to increased military deployments, "If the army does not return to its barracks, the FIS will have the right to call once again a Jihad, as in November 1954." See Rachid Khiari, "Military Deploys Around Capital, Bendjedid Resigns as Party Chief," Associated Press, June 28, 1991. One could certainly make the case that the analogy with November 1954 (that is, the implicit comparison of the Algerian government to the French colonial regime), rather than Madani's use of the term *jihad*, was the actual offense.

15. "Chronology October 16, 1991–January 15, 1992," 303.

16. See Kapil, "Portrait statistique."

17. "Chronology October 16, 1991–January 15, 1992," 303.

18. "Chronology October 16, 1991–January 15, 1992," 303.

19. This council was composed of Prime Minister Sid Ahmed Ghozali, Defense Minister General Khaled Nezzar, Chief of Staff Abdelmalek Guenaïzia, Interior Minister General Larbi Belkhir, Foreign Minister Lakhdar Brahimi, and Justice Minister Hamdani Benkhelil. Members of this group, particularly those in the military (Nezzar, Belkhir, and Guenaïzia), would become known as the *janvièristes*.

20. Also on the Council was Ali Kafi (secretary-general of the Organisation Nationale des Moudjahidine, the veterans of the 1954–1962 war), Ali Haroun (recent Human Rights Minister), and Tedjini Haddam (rector of the Paris Mosque).

21. "Cent trois morts, 414 blessés et 6. 786 détenus en Algérie depuis le début de l'année, selon un bilan officiel," Agence France-Presse, March 12, 1992.

22. "National Human Rights Monitoring Group: Over 600 Died from Violence in Last Year," BBC Summary of World Broadcasts, February 6, 1993; "Conflicts Which Have Been in Some Way Created or Exacerbated as a Result of the End of the Cold War," *Guardian*, December 31, 1992, 16.

23. For example, a former Egyptian ambassador to Algeria, Hussein Ahmed Amin, comparing each country's armed Islamist movements, claimed that the violence in Algeria was more intense because the political grievance was more substantial: "They were robbed of the fruits of their victory when the army cancelled the election. The Egyptian Islamists cannot make the same claim." See Lara Marlowe, "Why Once Similar Conflicts in Egypt and Algeria Now Differ," *Irish Times*, March 17, 1997, 13.

24. Willis, *Islamist Challenge in Algeria*, 206, 269. In 1982, under the leadership of Bouyali, a self-styled *amir* (leader), the MIA began carrying out sporadic attacks against Algerian security forces from bases in the mountains near Larbaâ (Blida province). The group allegedly planned to attack larger targets, both symbolic and human, but its insurgency was effectively ended in 1987 when Algerian security forces ambushed and killed Bouyali. See Burgat, *Islamic Movement in North Africa*, 265–268. Martinez claims that an Algerian Hizb Allah (Party of Allah) formed in early 1990, though it is not mentioned whether the objectives or intentions of this group were similar or not to those of the Lebanese Shi'ah political organization Hezbollah (in terms of armed militancy, Iranian inspiration, or actual Shi'ah devotion). Martinez, *Algerian Civil War*, 69. Willis claims that "Shi'ite Islamists," called Sunnah wa Shari'ah, attacked an Algerian courthouse in January 1990, but he provides no source. Willis, *Islamist Challenge in Algeria*, 143.

25. Georges Marion, "La traque des intégristes algériens," *Le Monde*, July 4, 1991.

26. Khelladi, *Le FIS à l'assaut du pouvoir*, 109–110.

27. See Souaïdia, Gèze, and Mellah, *Le procés de "La sale guerre"*; Samraoui, *Chronique des années de sang*.

28. On the role of counterfactuals in social science more generally, see Fearon, "Counterfactuals"; Levy and Goertz, *Explaining War and Peace*. In recognizing the insufficiency of all these accounts of the violence, Malley suggested that "in the end, the secret may well lie in the crass accidents of history [. . .]; or perhaps simply a wrong personality at the wrong place at the wrong time." See Malley, *Call from Algeria*, 248.

29. Even as late as 1995, Algeria's Islamic opposition was described as being somewhere between armed rebellion and political participation. See Labat, *Les islamistes algériens*.

30. Testas, "Algeria's Economic Decline," 102.

31. James Davies's seminal article on revolutions proposes that when long periods of economic improvement are suddenly met with a reversal, the risk of revolution increases. The problem is not poverty *per se* or wealth disparity, but a radical change that affects general perceptions of socioeconomic mobility. See Davies, "Toward a Theory of Revolution." Martinez rejects this account, along with other economic explanations, on the grounds that Algeria's socioeconomic crisis was already well in the making by the 1970s. See Martinez, *Algerian Civil War*, 2–3. Certainly no one has suggested that the 1986 oil price collapse is a sufficient starting point to understand the warfare of the 1990s. But

precisely which Algerian development policies, (nationalization, privatization, or both) and under what government (Boumedienne's, Bendjedid's, or both), exacerbated the crisis is a wide-ranging debate. For nuanced accounts, see Aissaoui, *Political Economy of Oil and Gas*; Lowi, *Oil Wealth*.

32. See Sereni, "L'Algérie, le FMI, et le FIS," cited in Quandt, *Between Ballots and Bullets*, 177.

33. Dillman, *State and Private Sector in Algeria*, 32–35. For general background on the role of oil in Algeria (pre- and post-independence), see Malti, *Histoire secrète du pétrole algérien*.

34. For an example of such research, see Evans, Rueschemeyer, and Skocpol, *Bringing the State Back In*.

35. For a general account of rentier theory, see Beblawi and Luciani, *Rentier State*. On rentier theory and on Algeria specifically, see Anderson, "Prospects for Liberalism"; Waterbury, "From Social Contracts to Extraction Contracts"; Zaimeche and Sutton, "Persistent Strong Population Growth"; Dillman, *State and Private Sector in Algeria*; Aïssaoui, *Algeria*; Werenfels, "Obstacles to Privatisation"; Henry, "Algeria's Agonies"; Hodd, "Economic Structure, Performance and Policy, 1950–2001"; Lowi, *Oil Wealth*.

36. Kouaouci, "Population Transitions," 36–37.

37. For a critique of this hypothesis, see Vreeland, "Effect of Political Regime on Civil War."

38. Testas, "Political Repression," 109–111.

39. In Algeria, *hogra* (*al-hagrah*) is understood as a sentiment of contempt expressed by those with more social, economic, and political power toward those with less. *Al-hagrah* or *al-hagra* comes from the root *haraqa*, which denotes scorn and disdain. In formal Arabic, a closer equivalent to the Algerian meaning of *hogra* is *zulm*: inequity, oppression, or tyranny expressed from a position of relative power. For examples in use, see Jean-Pierre Tuquoi, "Algérie: l'histoire est partie prenante dans la violence d'aujourd'hui," *Le Monde*, September 5, 1997; "Algeria: Just What the President Ordered," *Economist*, June 14, 1997, 48; Lara Marlowe, "The Double Life of Ali Habib," *Irish Times*, August 13, 1997, 13; "At Least 15 Dead in Northeastern Algeria Riots," Agence France-Presse, April 27, 2001; François d'Alançon, "Dans les banlieues d'Alger, les jeunes vivotent," *La Croix*, May 30, 1997, 5; Dominique Le Guilledoux, "Algérie, l'horreur et le doute," *Le Monde*, October 23, 1997; Nadjia Bouzeghrane, "Jours ordinaires à Annaba," *Le Monde diplomatique*, October 1997, 12–13. More extended analysis of Hogra can be found in Adjerid, *La Hogra*; Carlier, "D'une guerre à l'autre," 143; Evans and Phillips, *Algeria*, 297; McDougall, "Savage Wars?," 125; Quandt, "Algeria's Transition to What?," 86; Roberts, *Moral Economy or Moral Polity?*, 13; Tlemçani, *Algeria Under Bouteflika*, 1–2. Though often a term deployed by youth, it can also refer to specific oppression, such as that against women (see Lazreg, "Islamism and the Recolonization of Algeria," 43), Kabylies (see Bouandel, "Algeria: A Controversial Election," 99; Alilat and Hadid, *Vous*

ne pouvez pas nous tuer), Islamists (Martinez, *Algerian Civil War*, 67), and mothers of the "disappeared" (Collectif des familles de disparu(e)s en Algérie, *Les Disparitions Forcées en Algérie*, 51), and others.

40. Joffé, "Role of Violence," 38.

41. Testas, "Algeria's Economic Decline," 90–92.

42. Dillman, *State and Private Sector in Algeria*, 20, 29.

43. Kouaouci, "Population Transitions," 36–37.

44. Testas, "Economic Causes of Algeria's Political Violence," 136–137.

45. Swearingen, "Algeria's Food Security Crisis," 25. Insisting on the essentially political nature of discontent in Algeria as opposed to its apparent economic roots, other observers rejected comparisons between the October 1988 demonstrations and the "bread riots" endemic to many countries undergoing IMF structural adjustment programs in the 1980s. See Roberts, "Algerian State and the Challenge of Democracy," 435; Khelladi and Virolle, "Les démocrates algériens ou l'indisensable clarification," cited in Quandt, *Between Ballots and Bullets*, 39.

46. Fearon and Laitin, *Algeria*, 2, 17. See also Testas, "Economic Causes."

47. Fearon and Laitin, *Algeria*, 27–30. Concerns about the fundamental soundness of the Algerian military at the beginning of the conflict, regardless of whether was properly outfitted to fight conventional or irregular warfare, are not difficult to come by. Habib Souaïdia describes the disarray of the Algerian army in the early 1990s in his memoirs. See Souaïdia, *La sale guerre*, chapters 4 and 5.

48. Lowi, *Oil Wealth*, 114–115.

49. Dillman, *State and Private Sector in Algeria*, 127.

50. Kouaouci, "Population Transitions," 38–39.

51. See Zoubir, "Algeria's Multi-Dimensional Crisis."

52. Dillman, *State and Private Sector in Algeria*, 26.

53. Lowi, "War-Torn or Systemically Distorted?," 135.

54. Martinez, *Algerian Civil War*, 137–146.

55. Joffé, "Role of Violence."

56. Testas, "Roots of Algeria's Religious and Ethnic Violence," 164–165.

57. Collier and Sambanis, "Understanding Civil War," 4.

58. Collier, Hoeffler, and Rohner, "Beyond Greed and Grievance," 3.

59. Ibid., 3., citing Hirshleifer's "Machiavelli Theorem." See Hirshleifer, *Dark Side of the Force*, 10–11. Hirshleifer's view is actually more nuanced than Collier, Hoeffler, and Rohner suggest in "Beyond Greed and Grievance." "Machiavelli Theorem standing alone is only a partial truth," Hirshleifer explains. The other side of the coin is "[Ronald] Coase's Theorem," which is the claim that "people will never pass up an opportunity to cooperate by means of mutually advantageous exchange." Hirshleifer suggests that "our textbooks need to deal with both modes of economic activity."

60. See also the interview with Nezzar in Hamadouche, *Affaires d'état*, 38–39.

61. Lara Marlowe, "Algeria a Test Case for War on Terrorism," *Irish Times*, August 14, 2002, 14. In his testimony in 2002, Nezzar claimed that the FIS was pushing for the "Afghanization" of Algeria: "in one word, a Taliban State." See Raphael Hermano, "Un Algérien accable l'armée de son pays face à un ex-ministre de la Défense," Agence France-Presse, July 1, 2002. Nezzar likewise deployed the spectre of Afghanistan in his own account of 1990s Algeria. See Nezzar, *Algérie*.

62. "Former Algerian PM Defends Cancellation of Polls at Paris Trial," Agence France-Presse, July 2, 2002.

63. Samraoui, *Chronique des années de sang*, 162. Three million was roughly the number of Algerians who voted for the FIS in December 1991. In his testimony during the Souaïdia-Nezzar trial in 2002, Samraoui claimed that high officers within the security elite were already planning "total war" against the Islamists in the late 1980s and worked to create the conditions for the violent confrontation that followed. See Florence Beaugé et Jean-Pierre Tuquoi, "Un ancien du contre-espionnage algérien livre ses souvenirs," *Le Monde*, September 25, 2003.

64. Martinez, *Algerian Civil War*, 16.

65. Sidhoum and Algeria Watch, "Les milices," 8.

66. Sponsored by the Catholic Sant'Egidio Community in Rome, the January 1995 Rome Platform—signed by the major Algerian political parties, including the FLN and the FIS—outlined a path for an end to armed violence and a return to multiparty elections even though the victories of the FIS in 1990 and 1991 would not be restored. The Algerian regime, heavily dominated by the military in the 1990s, with the FLN delegitimized and marginalized, dismissed the Rome Platform as an affront to Algeria's sovereignty, as an unwanted and unnecessary foreign intervention into the conflict. For the regime, the Sant'Egidio initiative was unnecessary because a peace process was already under way inside Algeria. This process formally began with the Commission du Dialogue Nationale (Commission of National Dialogue), which took over the HCE's ostensible peacemaking role in October 1993. When Zéroual assumed the presidency in 1994, he launched a new dialogue with some political parties, and a secret dialogue with Abbassi and Benhadj. See Roberts, "Algeria's Ruinous Impasse," 256–263.

67. Roberts, "Dancing in the Dark," 111–112.

68. "Algeria: Country Report," *Economist Intelligence Unit*, February 7, 1997, 9.

69. "Algeria: Country Report," *Economist Intelligence Unit*, February 7, 1997, 8, 23–24.

70. Klein, *Shock Doctrine*.

CHAPTER 3

1. Huntington, "Clash of Civilizations?"

2. Lewis, "Roots of Muslim Rage."

3. Indeed, the explosion of economic research into the causes and dynamics of civil wars (the research examined and critiqued in Chapters 1 and 2) was often framed as a

data-driven response to, specifically, Huntington's theories and, more generally, the pervasive idea that emerged immediately after the Cold War that all armed conflicts were actually rooted in ethnicity, religion, and other identity-based antagonisms.

4. To borrow, crudely, from Jameson, "Postmodernism." An example of Jameson's methodology—an analysis that attempts to account for a regime of power, a regime that is otherwise unable to account for itself without also reproducing its self-image—applied to the Middle East can be found in Mitchell, *Rule of Experts*.

5. See Campbell, *National Deconstruction*.

6. Castells, *Power of Identity*.

7. Sen, *Identity and Violence*, xv; Hall, "Who Needs 'Identity'?," 2. See also Maalouf, *In the Name of Identity*, 30; Telhami and Barnett, "Introduction," 2.

8. Said, "Clash of Ignorance"; Mamdani, *Good Muslim, Bad Muslim*.

9. Roberts, *Demilitarizing Algeria*, 16.

10. Le Sueur, *Uncivil War*, 326.

11. Martinez, *La guerre civile en Algérie, 1990–1998*.

12. See Silverstein, "Excess of Truth."

13. Bensmaïa, "Phantom Mediators," 96. Speculation surrounding Boudiaf's murder began almost immediately. At his funeral, a woman held up the front page of the Algerian paper *La Nation*, which asked, "Who killed [*assassiné*] Boudiaf?" See Agence France-Presse, document reference no. APP2002052708167, July 1, 1992, last retrieved September 30, 2014, http://imageforum.afp.com.

14. See Burgat, *Face to Face*, 109–115.

15. José Garçon, "Quatre questions sur une tragédie," *Libération*, August 30, 1997.

16. Alain Bommenel, "Suspicion and Hatred Stalk the Streets of Massacre Village," Agence France-Presse, October 22, 1997; Lara Marlowe, "Families Hid and Listened to Dying Neighbours' Screams," *Irish Times*, October 21, 1997, 11; Christian Amanpour, "Massacre in Algeria," *60 Minutes*, CBS, January 18, 1998, transcript.

17. For example, Dominique Le Guilledoux, "Algérie, l'horreur et le doute," *Le Monde*, October 23, 1997.

18. See the quote from Said, *Orientalism*, 54, used in the Introduction.

19. Julia Ficatier, "Algérie. 'On ne sait plus qui tue qui et pourquoi' Louisa Hanoune," *La Croix*, October 9, 1996, 24.

20. Quoted in "Ex-president Decries 'Killing Machines' in Algeria," November 16, 1997.

21. John Lancaster, "As Algeria's Savagery Grows, So Does Mystery Shrouding It," *Washington Post*, October 18, 1997, A1.

22. Elaine Ganley, "Morale Drops, Tensions Climb as Violence Reigns in Algeria," Associated Press, December 8, 1993.

23. Roula Khalaf, "Algerian Violence Reaches New Crescendo," *Financial Times*, January 21, 1997, 4.

24. Mark Dennis, "Hurt, but Not Yet Beaten," *Newsweek*, June 30, 1997, 45.

25. Nidam Abdi, "'C'est devenu une guerre de tribus,'" *Libération*, September 24, 1997.

26. Robert Fisk, "Algeria's Terror: Witness from the Front Lline of a Police Force Bent on Brutality," *Independent*, October 30, 1997, 9.

27. Anthony Loyd, "Zeroual's Zombies Cast Vote," *Times* (London), October 24, 1997.

28. Amnesty International, *Fear and Silence*, 1.

29. Dominique Le Guilledoux, "Algérie, l'horreur et le doute," *Le Monde*, October 23, 1997.

30. Rachid Khiari, "Macabre Syndrome of Violence Gains Momentum Ahead of Referendum," Associated Press, November 17, 1996; John Phillips, "Army Link to Algeria Slaughter," *Sunday Times*, October 26, 1997; "Sixty-Three Civilians Massacred in Algeria," Agence France-Presse, September 6, 1997; Julia Ficatier and Amine Kadi, "Algérie. La nouvelle bataille d'Alger," *La Croix*, September 10, 1997, 3; Lara Marlowe, "Families Hid and Listened to Dying Neighbours' Screams," *Irish Times*, October 21, 1997, 11; Nadim Ladki, "Algerian Village Buries Massacre Victims," Reuters, January 13, 1998.

31. Harbi, Dhoquois-Cohen, and Ravenel, "Une Exigence," 169; Souaïdia, *La sale guerre*, 149–151. Criticisms of Souaïdia's account of a 1993 massacre perpetrated by special forces can be found in Nadjia Bouzeghrane, "Les fausses vérités de Souaïdia," *El Watan*, February 20, 2001; Blaise Robinson and Olivier Joulie, "La version des habitants de Zaâtria: 'Il n'y a jamais eu de massacre ici,'" *Le Nouvel Observateur*, no. 1899, March 29, 2001. In 2012, a new edition of *La sale guerre* was released. It included a new preface from Souaïdia, though he avoided mentioning any of the criticisms of the earlier editions. See Chapter 6 for a discussion of the fallout from Souaïdia's memoir between its release and the 2002 Souaïdia-Nezzar trial in Paris.

32. On August 19, 1996, *Al-Hayat* (London) reported the massacre on the basis of interviews with alleged witnesses. The identity of the attackers was not clear, only that they were armed and wore ragged clothing. Some of *Al-Hayat*'s "Algerian sources" even said that the objective of this attack was to "provoke insurrection between tribes." See no title, Agence France-Presse, August 19, 1996, on file with author; "'Al-Hayat' Cites Eyewitnesses on Bus Massacre of Batna Citizens," BBC Summary of World Broadcasts, August 21, 1996. The following day, the Algerian Brotherhood, an Islamist organization in France, "confirmed" the attack for *Al-Hayat* and blamed it on "the ideological (Franco-Berber) minorities' militias, backed by the intelligence service." See "'Neutral Sources in Algeria' Said to Have Confirmed Batna Massacre Report," BBC Summary of World Broadcasts, August 22, 1996. *Al-Hayat* initially reported that two buses on the Batna-M'Sila road were stopped and passengers were separated by place of residency; those from Batna were killed. The Algerian government strongly denied that the massacre had taken place, and Al-Hayat, which stood by its story, remained the only source; no Algerian papers confirmed or disproved it. According to one account, some of the local sources might simply have been confused about a recent and similar attack. Seventeen

male bus passengers had been killed in Sidi Ladjel, near Ain Oussera (Djelfa province), on August 15, an event that was reported in the Algerian daily *El Watan*. See "Algeria Says Extremists Didn't Massacre Civilians," *Africa News*, August 29, 1996; "Polémique sur un massacre," *Sud Ouest*, August 20, 1996; "Deux massacres, imputés aux islamistes, auraient fait 80 morts en Algérie," *Le Monde*, August 20, 1996. Two subsequent studies of the massacres nonetheless include the disputed Batna-M'Sila case in their datasets. See Aït-Larbi and others, "Anatomy of the Massacres"; Kalyvas, "Wanton and Senseless?"

33. Jean-Pierre Tuquoi, "Algeria's Horrific Settling of Scores," *Manchester Guardian Weekly*, September 14, 1997, 19.

34. Lara Marlowe, "Bloody Days, Savage Nights," *Time*, March 20, 1995, 48–51.

35. Craig R. Whitney, "Algeria Says Rebels Killed 93, Many Women, in Village Raid," *New York Times*, April 23, 1997, A13.

36. This relative lull coincided with parliamentary elections in June, the first since Bendjedid stepped down in 1992. That said, the Raïs massacre capped a summer of increasingly intense violence, with the Associated Press reporting some fifteen hundred deaths after the elections, half in August alone. Rachid Khiari, "Government Assures It's Boosting Security, but Exodus Continues," Associated Press, August 30, 1997.

37. "Terrible carnage près d'Alger: entre 98 et 300 civils égorges," Agence France-Presse, August 29, 1997; Jean-Pierre Tuquoi, "Algérie: les pires massacres en cinq ans de guerre civile," *Le Monde*, September 1, 1997.

38. Reuters, "Bloody Terror," *Sunday Tasmanian*, August 31, 1997.

39. Rachid Khiari, "Three hundred Killed in Algeria Massacre, Witnesses and Hospital Workers Say," Associated Press, August 29, 1997; "Ninety-Eight Slain in Algeria's Worst Massacre," Deutsche Presse-Agentur, August 29, 1997.

40. Boubker Belkadi, "Hundreds Feared Dead in Algerian Massacre," Agence France-Presse, August 29, 1997.

41. "At Least 80 People Said Slaughtered in Fresh Massacre in Algeria," Deutsche Presse-Agentur, September 6, 1997; Rachid Khiari, "Algerians Barricade, Arm Themselves," Associated Press, September 7, 1997; Jean-Pierre Tuquoi, "Un sentiment de panique et d'abandon gagne Alger," *Le Monde*, September 9, 1997, quoting the Algerian daily *El Watan*.

42. Roger Cohen, "Eighty-Five Slain in New Attack Near Algiers, Setting Off Panic," *New York Times*, September 24, 1997, A3.

43. Jean-Pierre Tuquoi, "Le bras arme du FIS ordonne un arrêt des combats," *Le Monde*, September 25, 1997.

44. "Former Algerian Official Claims Military Culpable for Massacres," Deutsche Presse-Agentur, September 29, 1997.

45. See Agence France-Presse's photo of Communiqué 51, dated September 27, 1997, and accompanying caption: Agence France-Presse document reference no. SAPA970927846740, available at http://www.imageforum-diffusion.afp.com, retrieved

September 30, 2014. See also Lara Marlowe, "Continuing Campaign of Violence Claims Lives of 11 Women Teachers," *Irish Times*, September 30, 1997, 9.

46. According to British intelligence services monitoring Kamel's phone, calls allegedly from the GIA were in fact coming from an Algerian army facility. See Patrick Forestier, "Derrière les tueries, de sordides intérêts immobiliers et fonciers?" *Paris-Match*, October 9, 1997, 93.

47. "Underground Algerian Newsletter Withdraws Support for GIA," Agence France-Presse, September 30, 1997.

48. "Islamic Salvation Army Calls for Ceasefire," Agence France-Presse, September 24, 1997. There was even some confusion as to the sequence of events. Both the *Washington Times* ("Algeria's Bloody Mess," September 27, 1997, C2) and Australia's *Courier Mail* ("Bloody Massacre Prompts Ceasefire Offer," September 26, 1997, 18) claimed that the Bentalha massacre had elicited the truce. See also Ben Macintyre, "Rebels in Algeria Urge Ceasefire to Expose 'Extremists,'" *Times*, September 25, 1997.

49. Elaine Ganley, "Mystery, Contradictions Plague Site of Largest Algerian Massacres," Associated Press, October 25, 1997.

50. Alain Bommenel, "Suspicion and Hatred Stalk the Streets of Massacre Village," Agence France-Presse, October 22, 1997; Jean Pierre Tuquoi, "Bentalha, ville martyre, ville fantôme d'Algérie," *Le Monde*, October 22, 1997. See also Jean Pierre Tuquoi, "Algérie, autopsie d'un massacre," *Le Monde*, November 11, 1997; David Hirst, "The Mystery of Algeria's Murder Squads: 'This Is Where They Shot My Wife,'" *Guardian*, October 20, 1997, 1; Robert Fisk, "Algeria, This Autumn: A People in Agony," *Independent*, October 22, 1997, 1.

51. Anthony Loyd, "Algerian Terror Victims Plead for Death by Bullet," *Times*, October 23, 1997; John Phillips, "Army Link to Algeria Slaughter," *Sunday Times*, October 26, 1997. See also Anthony Loyd, "Villagers Relive Terror of Night Massacres," *Times*, October 22, 1997.

52. Florence Aubenas, "Bentalha, le récit de dix heures de tuerie," *Libération*, October 23, 1997. There are strong echoes of Nesroulah Yous in Aubenas' article. See Yous and Mellah, *Qui a tué à Bentalha*.

53. Youssef Ibrahim, "Algeria Votes, Recalling Fateful Election of 1992," *New York Times*, October 24, 1997, A8; Youssef M. Ibrahim, "As Algerian Civil War Drags On, Atrocities Grow," *New York Times*, December 28, 1997, I1.

54. Salima Tlemcani, "Massacre de Bentalha: un plan minutieux préparé par Laâzraoui," *El Watan*, 2096, October 11, 1997. A study of the Algerian regime suggested that among the elite there was more general concern for what was said in *Le Monde* than for reports anywhere else in the media. See Werenfels, *Managing Instability in Algeria*, 149.

55. Lara Marlowe, "Algerians Tortured by Security Forces," *Irish Times*, October 30, 1997, 1; Lara Marlowe, "Ex-army Conscript Saw Colleagues Torturing and Murdering

Villagers," *Irish Times*, October 30, 1997, 9. See also Robert Fisk, "Conscript Tells of Algeria's Torture Chambers," *Independent*, November 3, 1997, 10; Saira Shah, "Triangle of Death," *Dispatches*, Channel 4, October 21, 1997; François Sergent, "Ils avaient de fausses barbes et du sang sur leur pantalons," *Libération*, October 23, 1997, reprinted as "Hands That Wield Algeria's Knives," *Observer*, October 26, 1997, 15; Robert Fisk, "Algeria's Horror," *Independent*, November 1, 1997, 17.

56. John Sweeney and Leonard Doyle, "'We Bombed Paris for Algeria,'" *Observer*, November 9, 1997, 9. The interviewee in this exposé, "Joseph," would later testify before a hearing of the British parliament's human rights committee as Captain Haroun. See also Jean Pierre Tuquoi, "Des fuites impliquent Alger dans les attentats de Paris," *Le Monde*, November 11, 1997; John Sweeney, "Atrocities in Algeria: We Were the Murderers Who Killed for the State," *Observer*, January 11, 1998, 14; Von Krusche, "Algerien: Mörderische Sippenhaft."

57. "Attackers Kill 59 People in Algeria, Government Says," Associated Press, December 24, 1997.

58. "Les massacres les plus meurtriers en Algérie depuis le début de l'année," Agence France-Presse, December 31, 1997.

59. "More Than 1,000 Killed During Ramadan in Algeria," Deutsche Presse-Agentur, January 28, 1998. A high-level official would later suggest that the government had downplayed the levels of violence experienced in western Algeria from late December through early January so as not to give the impression that they were losing the war. See Fayçal Metaoui, "Massacre de Ramka: 1000 morts!" *El Watan*, March 22, 2006, http://www.elwatan.com/Massacre-de-Ramka-1000-morts, no longer available, on file with author.

60. John Daniszewski, "Reports Put Number of Algerians Slain in Past Week Near 1,000," *Los Angeles Times*, January 7, 1998, 4; see also the reports in *La Tribune*, an Algerian paper, cited in "Algerian Newspapers Report 172 Killed in Latest Massacres," Agence France-Presse, January 6, 1998.

61. Rachid Khiari, "Algerian Killings Claim 78 Lives," Associated Press, December 31, 1997; "Survivors Relate Horror of Algerian Massacre," Reuters, January 4, 1998. The December 30–31 killing sites, according to secondhand reports via the Algerian francophone press (such as *l'Authentique*, *Liberté*, *El Watan*, *La Tribune*, *Le Matin d'Alger*), were reportedly clustered around the Oued Rhiou commune—specifically the villages of Ouled Kherarba (or Khourba), Ouled Sahnoun (or Sahnine), El-Abadel, and Ouled Taieb (or Tayeb).

62. Rachid Khiari, "Algerians Flee Horror, Government Rejects Inquiry, West Seeks Solutions," Associated Press, January 6, 1998.

63. "Algeria's Bloody Week: More Than 30 Murdered Each Day," Agence France-Presse, December 29, 1997.

64. Rachid Khiari, "Algerian Massacres Kill at Least 392—Including 200 in One Village," Associated Press, January 6, 1998.

65. "New Bloodbath in Algeria: 412 Massacred," Agence France-Presse, January 3, 1998. See also "More Than 410 People Killed in Worst Massacre in Algeria," Deutsche Presse-Agentur, January 3, 1998.

66. Alain Bommenel, "Carnages a répétition: la violence se déplace vers l'Ouest de l'Algérie," Agence France-Presse, January 1, 1998; Alain Bommenel, "Les autorités et l'armée confrontées a l'escalade de la terreur," Agence France-Presse, January 3, 1998; "New Bloodbath in Algeria: 412 Massacred," Agence France-Presse, January 3, 1998; no title, *El Watan*, no. 2183, January 21, 1998, on file with author; "Algeria: Recent Massacres Said to be Reprisal Against FIS Islamists," BBC Monitoring, January 9, 1998; Baki Mina and Baïla Karim, "Ce sont nos enfants qui nous égorgent," *L'Express*, January 22, 1998.

67. Rachid Khiari, "Government Under Fire After Insurgency's Worst Massacre," Associated Press, January 4, 1998.

68. Bob Edwards, "Violence in Algeria," *Morning Edition*, National Public Radio, January 2 1998, transcript.

69. Roger Cohen, "Algeria Killings: Brutal Ritual Defies Logic," *New York Times*, January 9, 1998, A1.

70. Lara Marlowe, "Amnesty Accused over Reporting on Algeria," *Irish Times*, November 27, 1996, 10; U.S. Congress, House Committee on International Relations, *Algeria's Turmoil*.

71. Khalida Messaoudi, "Le peuple sait qui tue," *Regards*, October 1, 1997, accessed August 20, 2009, http://www.regards.fr/article/?id=686. For more on Messaoudi's life and activism, see Messaoudi and Schemla, *Unbowed*. For an unflinching postcolonial critique of the Eurocentric, secular, and reactionary anti-Islamic feminist understandings of Algeria's violence, like that espoused by Messaoudi, see Lazreg, *Eloquence of Silence*.

72. José Garçon, "Une aubaine pour Alger," *Libération*, September 22, 2001, 15; Amer Ouali, "L'Algérie se sent confortée dans ses thèses," Agence France-Presse, September 13, 2001.

73. Kaplan, "Libel of Moral Equivalence," 22.

74. "La terreur islamiste," *Le Figaro*, February 16, 1998. That "one exception," though unnamed, was likely Abdennour Ali Yahia, head of Algeria's oldest independent human rights organization, the Ligue Algérienne de Défense des Droits de l'Homme.

75. See Martinez, *La guerre civile en Algérie, 1990–1998*; Moussaoui, *De la violence en Algérie*; Belaala, *Ethnicité, nationalisme et radicalisation islamiste violente*.

76. Hill, *Identity in Algerian Politics*; Evans and Phillips, *Algeria*; Le Sueur, *Between Democracy and Terror*.

77. For example, the Comité Algérien des Militants Libres de la Dignité Humaine et des Droits de l'Homme published a series of four reports, all under the title *Livre blanc sur la répression en Algérie*. Groups such as Algeria Watch, SOS Disparu(e)s (representing victims of state terror), and Djazairouna (representing victims of nonstate terror)

have published witness and survivor accounts as well. See also Reporters sans Frontières and others, *Algérie, Le Livre Noir*.

78. Committee to Protect Journalists, "Sixty Journalists Killed in Algeria Since 1992," accessed September 2010, http://cpj. org/killed/mideast/algeria; and "Allaoua Ait M'barak," accessed September 2010, http://cpj. org/killed/1996/allaoua-ait-mbarak. php.

79. Amnesty International, *Civilian Population Caught*.

80. Quoted in Lara Marlowe, "Government May Have Ordered Journalists' Murders, Says Report," *Irish Times*, March 19, 1997, 13.

81. Spelled "Zineddine Allian" in Ian Black, "Algerian Violence: Press Holed up in No Man's Land," *Guardian*, January 23, 1998, 13. See also Labter, *Journalistes Algériens*, 133.

82. Human Rights Watch, *Elections in the Shadow of Violence*, 26–33.

83. Ibid., 29.

84. Semiane, *Au refuge des balles perdues*, cited in Le Sueur, *Between Democracy and Terror*, 214, 222. See also Evans and Phillips, *Algeria*, 169.

85. For example, see "Rumours of de Charette Attack Were Disinformation: Algiers," Agence France-Presse, August 3, 1996; "Over 127 Islamists Killed by Algeria's Armed Forces: Press," Agence France-Presse, September 9, 1997; and note 32 above on the disputed 1996 roadside massacre between Batna and M'Sila.

86. Lara Marlowe, "'Madonna in Hell' Captures the Grief and Despair of War-Torn Algeria," *Irish Times*, October 20, 1997, 12; Doy, *Drapery*, 215–218; Delannoy, *La Pietà de Bentalha*.

87. Scott Peterson, "Algeria's Real War: Ending the Cycle of Violence," *Christian Science Monitor*, June 24, 1997, 1.

88. Robert Moore, "Hands That Wield Algeria's Knives," *Observer*, October 26, 1997.

89. Anthony Loyd, "Zeroual's Zombies Cast Vote," *Times* (London), October 24, 1997.

90. Steve Crawshaw, "Algeria Rejects UN Help as Stunned Survivors Tell of Massacre Horror," *Independent*, January 21, 1998, 7.

91. Human Rights Watch, *Elections in the Shadow of Violence*, 30.

92. Amnesty International, *Civilian Population Caught*, 29.

93. For example, "Terrible carnage près d'Alger: entre 98 et 300 civils égorges," Agence France-Presse, August 29, 1997.

94. "Radio Reports 'Massacre' of 98 South of Algiers," BBC Summary of World Broadcasts, September 1, 1997.

95. "Pope Condemns 'Barbaric Atrocities' in Algeria," Deutsche Presse-Agentur, August 31, 1997.

96. "Washington Condemns Massacre in Algeria," Agence France-Presse, April 23, 1997.

97. Kaplan, "Libel of Moral Equivalence," 22.

98. Quoted in José Garçon, "Terreur et psychose aux portes d'Alger," *Libération*, September 8, 1997.

99. The article below (see note 100) could be referencing the same sign in the photo

on page 78. Sidi Kebir and Oued Alleug are less than ten miles apart and precise massacre locations were often misidentified.

100. Rachid Khiari, "Macabre Syndrome of Violence Gains Momentum Ahead of Referendum," Associated Press, November 17, 1996.

101. Boubker Belkadi, "Cinquante et un morts a Larbaa," Agence France-Presse, July 29, 1997; Lara Marlowe, "Axemen Rule in Islam's Killing Fields," *Observer*, December 8, 1996, 18; Rachid Khiari, "School Massacre: Militants Kill 12 teachers; 19 Other Civilians Killed," Associated Press, September 29, 1997.

102. "Radical GIA Group Claims Algerian Massacres," Agence France-Presse, September 26, 1997.

103. Elaine Ganley, "Algerian Group Vows More Massacres," Associated Press, September 27, 1997.

104. The original report appeared in the staunchly anti-Islamist paper *Le Matin d'Alger*, August 27, 1997. In reports that picked up on this story, the group's name was translated as "fâchés contre Allah" (*La Croix*, September 10, 1997) and "Révoltés contre Dieu" (*Libération*, September 8, 1997). Whether or not the *Le Matin* article was based in fact, there is the possibility of a misunderstanding. In some dialects, the preposition 'ala can mean "alongside," and in some medieval texts it can mean "on the authority/ strength of." Indeed, the only precedent for something similar is in the Hadith, which speaks of the *ghadibun li-Allah*, those who are angry *for* God. One account contextualized stories about the al-Ghadibun 'ala Allah in terms of the rampant and unchecked production of wild rumors in Algeria during the most intense wave of massacres. See "Alger: la terreur au jour le jour," *Le Point*, October 4, 1997.

105. Reuters, "Blood Stains Village After 'Night of Hell,'" *Hamilton Spectator* (Ontario), August 28, 1997, C5. Literally, *Taghut* means false god, idol, tempter, or Satan, the negative connotations of which, within an Islamic context, are clear enough. In international press accounts and Algerian Islamist discourse, it was used to mean "tyrant." *Taghut* and *taghiya* (tyrant) have similar roots. Examples of this vocabulary in context can be found in Gacemi, *I, Nadia, Wife of a Terrorist*.

106. Lara Marlowe, "Left to Suffer and Die in Silence," *Irish Times*, August 30, 1997, 13; "Les habitants d'Alger continuent a s'armer, la psychose s'etend," Agence France-Presse, September 8, 1997. Marlowe defined *dhabbahin* ("Dhebbahine") as "égorgeurs: Literally, throat-slashers." See Lara Marlowe, "Understanding the Key Words of War," *Irish Times*, October 30, 1997, 9.

107. These reports were originally sourced to *Al-Ribat*, a FIS publication in Germany. See Le Monde, "La France est prête à apporter aide et coopération à l'Algérie affirme Jacques Chirac," January 9, 1998. The legend of "Al-Houal" has proven durable. See Craig Smith, "North Africa Feared as Staging Ground for Terror," *New York Times*, February 20, 2007, A3.

108. Attempting to put the 2004 beheading in Iraq of a US civilian contractor into

a historical Islamic context, *New York Post* columnist Amir Taheri presented the case of "Momo le nain" (Mohamed the dwarf), an apprentice butcher used by the GIA to behead 86 people during the Bentalha massacre. See Amir Taheri, "Chopping Heads," *New York Post,* May 14, 2004. Taheri not only misrepresents some basic elements of the Bentalha massacre, but a search of the Nexis news archive and the Algerian daily *El Watan* CD-ROM archive produces no corroborating accounts of his fantastic story. Taheri's tale has nonetheless been accepted as fact, as evidenced in any basic Google search of the term *momo le nain.*

109. Boutros Hani, "Les personnalités culturelles influentes et crédibles doivent se mobiliser," *Le Monde,* November 10, 1997. See also Boutros Hani, "Les kharidjites, précurseurs de la violence sectaire en terre d'islam," *Le Monde,* November 10, 1997. Such accusations were unrelated to the Berber-speaking *Ibadi* populations of Algeria's Mzab region in the north-central Sahara, groups that also have khawarij roots.

110. For example, see *Jane's Intelligence Review,* September 1, 1997, cited in Kazuhiko Fujiwara, "Algerian Radicals Change Killer Ideals," *Daily Yomiuri,* September 11, 1997, 6.

111. "Egypt's Top Cleric Condemns 'Barbaric Crimes' in Algeria," Deutsche Presse-Agentur, September 1, 1997.

112. "Bloody Ramadan" or *Ramadan sanglant* appears in dozens of articles on the conflict in Algeria well into the 2000s.

113. William C. Mann, "Bleak and Bloody Ramadan Comes to Violent End," Associated Press, March 12, 1994.

114. "Ramadan Perverted," *Jerusalem Post,* February 3, 1995, 6.

115. Boubker Belkadi, "Thirty-Eight Dead, 256 Wounded in Car-Bomb in Central Algiers," Agence France-Presse, January 30, 1995.

116. For an analysis of the possible cultural significance of heightened massacres during Ramadan, see Hannoum, *Violent Modernity,* chapter 5.

117. For example, Robert Fisk, "Algerian Rebels Mark Ramadan in Blood," *Independent,* January 18, 1996, 11; "A l'approche du Ramadan, les massacres se multiplient en Algérie," *La Croix,* December 26, 1997, 2; Arezki Ait-Larbi, "Plus de deux cents personnes ont été massacrées en une semaine," *Le Figaro,* December 26, 1997; Alain Bommenel, "Fasting and Bloodshed: Algeria Ushers in Ramadan," Agence France-Presse, December 30, 1997; *Le Monde,* "Le début du ramadan est marqué par de nouveaux massacres en Algérie," January 1, 1998.

118. "World in Brief," *Atlanta Journal-Constitution,* February 6, 1997, 6A.

119. Bob Edwards, "Violence in Algeria," *Morning Edition,* National Public Radio, January 2, 1998, transcript.

120. John Lancaster, "Hundreds of Algerians Reportedly Burned Alive in Holy Month Scourge," *Washington Post,* January 7, 1998, A14.

121. Roger Cohen, "Algeria Killings: Brutal Ritual Defies Logic," *New York Times,* January 9, 1998, A1.

122. Reuters, "Algerian Massacres Continue into Ramadan," *Seattle Post-Intelligencer*, January 1, 1998, A10.

123. Thomas Schiller, "Massacre at Rilizane: The Fanatical Craze to Murder During Ramadan," Deutsche Presse-Agentur, January 4, 1998. See also "Bloody Beginning to Algerian Ramadan," *Guardian*, January 1, 1998, 9; "Ramadan Massacre," *Independent*, January 1, 1998, 8.

124. David Hirst, "Algerian Slaughter Claims 1,000 Lives," *Guardian Weekly*, January 11, 1998, 1.

125. Moussaoui, *De la violence en Algérie*, 94; Ilkkaracan, "Women, Sexuality, and Social Change." See also Rachid Khiari, "Algerian Massacres Kill at Least 392—Including 200 in One Village," Associated Press, January 6, 1998. The international appetite for stories about the hundreds of women abducted, abused, and murdered by state, government-allied, or anti-Islamist agents was basically nonexistent. For background on state-authored violence against women, see Collectif des familles de disparu(e)s en Algérie, *Les disparitions forcées en Algérie*.

126. See Mahl, "Women on the Edge of Time," *New Internationalist*, no. 270, August 1995, 14–16. The GIA's use of "forced marriage" was allegedly one of the reasons behind the creation of Said Makhloufi's breakaway Mouvement pour un État Islamique (Movement for an Islamic State, or MEI) in 1994. See "Alternative Fundamentalist Government Hit by Withdrawal," Agence France-Presse, August 27, 1994. In Islam, *zaouadj el moutaa* (the usual French transcription in Algeria) is more commonly known as *nikah al-mut'ah*.

127. Reuters, "Blood Stains Village After 'Night of Hell,'" *Hamilton Spectator* (Ontario), August 28, 1997, C5.

128. Susan Stamberg, "Week in Review," *Weekend Saturday*, National Public Radio, August 30, 1997, transcript. See also Robert Fisk, "Hundreds Die in Algerian Slaughter," *Independent*, August 30, 1997, 9.

129. Alain Bommenel, "Fasting and Bloodshed: Algeria Ushers in Ramadan," Agence France-Presse, December 30, 1997. See also the firsthand accounts of abuses by the insurgency against women recounted in Sadou, "Martyrdom of Girls."

130. Stora, *La guerre invisible*, 90.

131. See Doy, *Drapery*, 215–218. The Madonna effect was not unique, however, to Hocine Zaourar's image from Bentalha. This pathology—constructing images of iconic Christian suffering amid humanitarian events—is traceable in recent living memory to at least the Ethiopian Famine of 1984. See van der Gaag and Nash, *Images of Africa*, 32; Campbell, "Salgado and the Sahel," 76. The winner of the 2012 World Press award, Samuel Aranda's photo of a veiled Yemeni woman cradling a wounded protestor, continues the Madonna tradition.

132. Salima Tlemcani, "Massacre de Bentalha: un plan minutieux préparé par Laâzraoui," *El Watan*, no. 2096, October 11, 1997, from the *El Watan* archive.

133. See Robert Fisk, "Brutal Killers Without Faces," *Independent*, October 26, 1997, 1.

134. Lara Marlowe, "Families Hid and Listened to Dying Neighbours' Screams," *Irish Times*, October 21, 1997, 11. See also "Troops Discover Mass Grave in Algerian Battle Zone," Agence France-Presse, October 9, 1997.

135. Reuters, "Sixty-Four Algerian Villagers Murdered in 'Night of Hell,'" *Guardian*, August 28, 1997, 11.

136. Ray Moseley, "Fanatics' War Grips Algeria as Death Toll Climbs into the Tens of Thousands," *Chicago Tribune*, October 12, 1997, 1; "Algérie: l'escalade de l'horreur," *Le Point*, September 27, 1997. Whether or not there was any program to flood and overwhelm the urban centers with rural populations, a commonly mentioned figure for the number of internally displaced population in Algeria during the 1990s is 1.5 million. See Joffé, "Algeria: Recovery or Stagnation."

137. "Twenty-Two More Slain in Algeria at Outset of Bloody Ramadan," Agence France-Presse, January 5, 1998; David Hirst, "Algerian Slaughter Claims 1,000 Lives," *Guardian Weekly*, January 11, 1998, 1.

138. "Algérie: 93 civils massacrés près d'Alger," *Le Figaro*, April 23, 1997; Associated Press, "Rebels Kill 93 in Village," *Houston Chronicle*, April 23, 1997, 17.

139. "New Bloodbath in Algeria: 412 Massacred," Agence France-Presse, January 3, 1998. This correlation was later explored and analyzed in Aït-Larbi and others, "Anatomy of the Massacres," 56–71.

140. Lara Marlowe, "Families Hid and Listened to Dying Neighbours' Screams," *Irish Times*, October 21, 1997, 11; Andrew Borowiec, "Carnage Without Logic Dominates Life in Algeria," *Washington Times*, September 14, 1997, A6.

141. Stathis Kalyvas, "Comprendre les massacres," *Le Monde*, February 4, 1998, 14. On the case of Bentalha specifically, see Jean-Pierre Tuquoi, "Algérie, autopsie d'un massacre," *Le Monde*, November 11, 1997.

142. Daniela Deane, "Algeria Strife Linked to Religious Rivalries," *USA Today*, September 25, 1997, 12A; Rachid Khiari, "93 Dead in Biggest Massacre of Five-Year Algeria Insurgency," Associated Press, April 22, 1997; Jean-Pierre Tuquoi, "Bentalha, ville martyre, ville fantôme d'Algérie," *Le Monde*, October 22, 1997; "New Bloodbath in Algeria: 412 Massacred," Agence France-Presse, January 3, 1998. See also Sidhoum and Algeria Watch, "Les Milices."

143. Since at least 1994, one of the GIA's alleged slogans had been "No truce, no dialog, no reconciliation." See "Le GIA, le 'djihad' jusqu'a la victoire," Agence France-Presse, March 4, 1995. See also no title, *El Watan*, no. 2083, September 25, 1997, on file with author.

144. "Algerian Upsurge Aimed at Stopping Dialogue: French FM," Agence France-Presse, September 11, 1997.

CHAPTER 4

1. Former Defense Minister Khaled Nezzar stated a week after 9/11, "It is in the interest of modern societies and those who wish to become modern societies, to join together

to combat this evil of the third millennium." "Algerian Aide Who Thwarted Islamic Party Decries Terrorism," Agence France-Presse, September 22, 2001. See also Amer Ouali, "L'Algérie se sent confortée dans ses thèses," Agence France-Presse, September 13, 2001.

2. Alexis Lacroix, "Terrorisme. Les conséquences du quadruple attentat aux Etats-Unis," *Le Figaro*, September 14, 2001.

3. "Le Bloc-Notes de Max Clos," *Le Figaro*, September 21, 2001.

4. James Haught, "What Causes 'True Believers' to Kill?" *Charleston Gazette*, September 12, 2001, P4A.

5. Quoted in Andrew Duffy, "New 'Superterrorism' May Produce Huge Casualties," *Ottawa Citizen*, September 14, 2001, C3.

6. U.S. Congress, House Committee on Government Reform, *Preparing for the War on Terrorism*, 112.

7. Marwan Bishara, "Bush Versus Bin Laden: An Arab Perspective," *International Herald Tribune*, September 21, 2001, 11. See also Marcus Gee, "The Hydra's 10 Biggest Heads," *Globe and Mail*, September 29, 2001, F8.

8. Giles Tremlett, "US Arms Algeria for Fight Against Islamic Terror," *Guardian*, December 10, 2002, 13. A few months earlier, Lara Marlowe offered a similar but more critical assessment, commenting, "For the past decade, Algeria has served as a horrific test tube for a 'war on terrorism.'" See Lara Marlowe, "Algeria a Test Case for War on Terrorism," *Irish Times*, August 14, 2002, 14. As the war on terror quickly expanded, US-Algerian cooperation seemingly did as well. See Zoubir, "Algeria and U.S. Interests."

9. For example, Ayoob, *Many Faces of Political Islam*, 36; Cook, *Understanding Jihad*, 140; Gerges, *Far Enemy*, 130; Kepel, *Jihad*, 256; Wiktorowicz, "Genealogy of Radical Islam," 94.

10. Ayoob, *Many Faces of Political Islam*, 18.

11. Gerges, *Far Enemy*, 101.

12. Wiktorowicz, "Genealogy of Radical Islam," 88.

13. Tibi, *Political Islam*, 51. See also Milton-Edwards, *Islam and Violence in the Modern Era*, 104.

14. Wiktorowicz, "Centrifugal Tendencies"; Hafez, "From Marginalization to Massacres"; Kepel, *Jihad*. For more careful analysis, see Roberts, "Logics of Jihadi Violence in North Africa"; Ashour, *De-Radicalization of Jihadists*.

15. Souaïdia, Gèze, and Mellah, *Le procès de "La sale guerre"*; Samraoui, *Chronique des années de sang*; Tigha and Lobjois, *Contre-espionnage Algérien*.

16. For example, Tilly, *Politics of Collective Violence*, 105–106; Weinstein, *Inside Rebellion*, 316–317; Fearon and Laitin, "Ethnicity, Insurgency, and Civil War," 80, citing. Kalyvas, "Wanton and Senseless?"

17. See National Consortium for the Study of Terrorism and Responses to Terrorism (START), Global Terrorism Database, data file, 2013, accessed September 29, 2014, http://www.start.umd.edu/gtd.

18. Human Rights Watch, Amnesty International, Reporters Without Borders, and the Fédération Internationale des ligues des Droits de l'Homme, "Algeria: A Call for Action to End a Human Rights Crisis," press release, October 15, 1997.

19. Amnesty International, *Civilian Population Caught*, 1, 9, 7–10; Human Rights Watch, *Elections in the Shadow of Violence*, 13–14.

20. See Amnesty International, *Legacy of Impunity*. The exception that proves the rule is the 2004 trial of Fouad Boulemia, who was already convicted of killing FIS leader Abdelkader Hachani in 1999. In 2004, he was sentenced to death for allegedly playing a role in the Bentalha massacre as well. See "Algerian Sentenced to Death for 1997 Massacre," Agence France-Presse, August 2, 2004. There are no other reports of anyone being held responsible for Bentalha or the other major massacres.

21. Mouffok, "Amnesia in Algeria"; Hadj Moussa, "Imaginary Concord and the Reality of Discord"; Goldstein, "L'Algérie entre amnistie et amnésie"; Moussaoui, "Entre espoirs et malentendus"; Joffé, "National Reconciliation and General Amnesty in Algeria."

22. See Chapter 5.

23. See Burgat, "Double Extradition," 16–17.

24. Simon Catherine, "Vertiges meurtriers en Algérie," *Le Monde*, September 14, 1995. Martinez later published an analysis of the massacres that explicitly refrained from addressing the *Qui tue?* question. He instead looked at the various enabling contexts of the massacres. Martinez, "Les massacres de civils dans la guerre." For more practical reasons of diplomacy, Roberts thought it best to avoid the who-killed-whom debate as well. See Roberts, "International Gallery," 210–211.

25. Laure Mandeville, "Bruno Etienne: 'Ce sont les généraux qui se déchirent,'" *Le Figaro*, August 30, 1997; Bob Edwards, "Violence in Algeria," *Morning Edition*, National Public Radio, January 2, 1998; Elaine Ganley, "In Bloodied Algeria, There's No Fathoming Who Is Killing, or Why," Associated Press, August 29, 1997; Mark Dennis and Carla Power, "Try, Try Again: Have 60,000 Deaths Taught Algeria's Leaders Anything About Compromise?" *Newsweek*, June 16, 1997, 12; Alan Sipress, "Aftermath of a Massacre: Algerian Killings Have Some Questioning the Official Story," *Philadelphia Inquirer*, January 8, 1998, A1.

26. Addi, "Algeria's Army, Algeria's Agony," 49; Emma Ross, "Algerian Exiles Say Authorities Are Responsible for Massacres," Associated Press, January 22, 1998; "Algeria's Agony," *Newshour*, Public Broadcasting System, January 20, 1998, transcript.

27. Jean-Christophe Ploquin, "Alger se protège mais ne protège pas la société," *La Croix*, September 2, 1997, 5; Michael Willis, "Atrocities in Algeria: Why Butcher Your Own People? *Observer*, January 11, 1998, 14; Alan Sipress, "Aftermath of a Massacre: Algerian Killings Have Some Questioning the Official Story," *Philadelphia Inquirer*, January 8, 1998, A1. See also Cooley, *Unholy Wars*, 173.

28. Smith, "Algeria: The Horror."

29. Evans and Phillips, *Algeria*; Cavatorta, *International Dimension of the Failed Al-*

gerian Transition; Hill, *Identity in Algerian Politics*; Lowi, *Oil Wealth*; Le Sueur, *Between Democracy and Terror.*

30. Cook, *Understanding Jihad*, 119–121.

31. Stampnitzky, *Disciplining Terror*; Zulaika, *Terrorism.*

32. Bedjaoui, Aroua, and Aït-Larbi, *Inquiry into the Algerian Massacres*; Kalyvas, "Wanton and Senseless?"; Hafez, "From Marginalization to Massacres"; Kepel, *Jihad.*

33. Kalyvas, "Wanton and Senseless?"; Hafez, "From Marginalization to Massacres"; Kepel, *Jihad.*

34. See the Algeria Watch website (http://www.algeria-watch.org) and Bedjaoui, Aroua, and Aït-Larbi, *Inquiry into the Algerian Massacres.*

35. A notable exception is journalist Abed Charef's investigation of a relatively small-scale massacre. See Charef, *Autopsie d'un massacre.*

36. Harbi, Dhoquois-Cohen, and Ravenel, "Une Exigence," 169.

37. The most significant allegation concerns a large-scale massacre of 173 persons in the region of Ténès (in the Chlef province) in May of 1994. However, Algeria Watch's list of massacres claims that 173 bodies were *found* there, suggesting a mass grave or body dump rather than a single mass killing episode. The two original sources for these claims can be found in two volumes published by the Comité Algérien des Militants Libres de la Dignité Humaine et des Droits de l'Homme, *Livre blanc sur la répression en Algérie (1991–1994)* and *Livre blanc sur la répression en Algérie (1991–1995).* The French Interior Ministry blocked the distribution of the first volume in France on the grounds that it contained hate speech and sought to affect government policy. See "Un 'Livre blanc sur la repression en Algerie' interdit en France," Agence France-Presse, September 13, 1995. Though out of print, these volumes are now available online at the website of the publisher, Hoggar (http://hoggar.org).

38. Souaïdia, *La sale guerre*, 149–151.

39. Nadjia Bouzeghrane, "Les fausses vérités de Souaïdia," *El Watan*, February 20, 2001.

40. Blaise Robinson and Olivier Joulie, "La version des habitants de Zaâtria: 'Il n'y a jamais eu de massacre ici,'" *Le Nouvel Observateur*, n. 1899, March 29, 2001.

41. See Human Rights Watch, *Six Months Later*; Amnesty International, *Killings in Serkadji Prison.*

42. Bedjaoui, Aroua, and Aït-Larbi, *Inquiry into the Algerian Massacres.*

43. Kalyvas, "Wanton and Senseless?"; Hafez, "From Marginalization to Massacres."

44. Ibid.

45. Bedjaoui, Aroua, and Aït-Larbi, *Inquiry into the Algerian Massacres.*

46. See also Sidhoum and Algeria Watch, *Chronologie des massacres en Algérie.*

47. Sidhoum and Algeria Watch, *Chronologie des massacres en Algérie.* Algeria Watch has also recorded massacres as late as 2003 and 2004.

48. Aït-Larbi and others, "Anatomy of the Massacres," 51–56.

49. For an analysis of the debate over the death toll of the entire Algerian conflict, see Chapter 1.

50. Andrew Borowiec, "Carnage Without Logic Dominates Life in Algeria," *Washington Times*, September 14, 1997, A6.

51. "Algeria: Bloodstained," *Economist*, September 25, 1997, 48. See also Rene Hardin quoted in Bernard D. Kaplan, "West Losing Faith in Algerian Regime," *Rocky Mountain News*, January 8, 1998, 41A.

52. A study conducted after the crisis of 1997–1998 largely confirmed a correlation between voting patterns in the early 1990s and the massacres in the second half of the decade. See Aït-Larbi and others, "Anatomy of the Massacres," 56–71, 121–125.

53. "Comment deux à trois cents tueurs peuvent-ils agir dans une zone normalement sous haute surveillance militaire et policière, en périphérie de la capitale [. . .]." See Jean Hatzfeld, "Près d'Alger, des villageois égorgés et brûlés," *Libération*, August 30, 1997.

54. Quoted in "Algeria's Agony Only Grows Worse: Uncertainty Over Who Is Behind Civil War's Brutal Slaughter," *San Francisco Chronicle*, October 23, 1997, C2.

55. "Algeria: Europe Continues to Back U. N. Investigation in Algeria," Inter Press Service, January 26, 1998.

56. Reuters, "Algerian Massacres Continue into Ramadan," *Seattle Post-Intelligencer*, January 1, 1998, A10; Deutsche Presse-Agentur, "More Than 1,000 Killed During Ramadan in Algeria," January 28, 1998.

57. Martinez, *La guerre civile en Algérie*; Kalyvas, "Wanton and Senseless?"

58. Roberts, "Algeria's Veiled Drama."

59. Scott Peterson, "Algeria's Real War: Ending the Cycle of Violence," *Christian Science Monitor*, June 24, 1997, 1.

60. "Aucune nouvelle des ambassadeurs," *Sud Ouest*, July 18, 1994.

61. "Suspected Islamists Kill More Algerian Security Officials," Agence France-Presse, October 10, 1994.

62. "Land Clashes?" *Newsweek*, July 7, 1997, 5.

63. Martin Regg Cohn, "Amid Carnage, Algerians Find Will to Vote," *Toronto Star*, June 1, 1997, A1.

64. France Info Radio report of August 5, 1997, in "Armed Groups Said Extending Scope of Attacks Across Whole Country," BBC Summary of World Broadcasts, August 6, 1997; "Perceived Change in FIS's Discourse and Zeroual's Approach May Bode Well for Algeria," *Mideast Mirror*, August 7, 1997; Reuters, "A Further 40 Die in Latest Spate of Killings," *Irish Times*, August 8, 1997, 9.

65. "Nouveau bilan du massacre de Larbaa," Agence France-Presse, July 29, 1997.

66. "Algeria: Mayhem," *Economist*, August 2, 1997, 28.

67. Alain Bommenel, "Les Algeriens elisent leur premiere Assemblee pluraliste," Agence France-Presse, June 5, 1997.

68. "Tuerie de Rais: une population traumatisée, le gouvernement au pied du mur," Agence France-Presse, August 30, 1997.

69. "Villagers Slaughtered in Algerian Attack," *Guardian*, July 30, 1997, 12.

70. "Legeroffensief Algerije lokt bloedige wraak uit," *de Volkskrant*, July 31, 1997, 20.

71. Reuters, "Guerrillas Slaughter Villagers," *Glasgow Herald*, July 30, 1997, 11.

72. "Algeria: Mayhem," *Economist*, August 2, 1997, 28. See also "La loi du sang: Massacres redoublés en Algérie," *Sud Ouest*, July 30, 1997.

73. "Une centaine de personnes massacrées, selon la presse," Agence France-Presse, August 2, 1997.

74. Amer Ouali, "Some 100 Killed in More Algeria Killings," Agence France-Presse, August 2, 1997.

75. Mourad Mansour, "Le témoignage d'un officier," *Le Monde*, September 16, 1994.

76. Quoted in John-Thor Dahlburg, "Terror on All Sides in Algeria," *Los Angeles Times*, June 24, 1996.

77. Robert Fisk, "Algeria's Terror," *Independent*, October 30, 1997, 9; Robert Fisk, "Algeria's Horror," *Independent*, November 1, 1997, 17.

78. Daniela Deane, "Algeria Strife Linked to Religious Rivalries," *USA Today*, September 25, 1997, 12A, ellipsis in original.

79. See the testimonies of Nezzar and Samraoui in Souaïdia, Gèze, and Mellah, *Le procés de "La sale guerre."*

80. Anthony Loyd, "Zeroual's Zombies Cast Vote," *Times*, October 24, 1997. See also Jack R. Payton, "While We Watched the Funeral, 500 Algerians Were Slain," *St. Petersburg Times*, September 9, 1997, 2A; John Lancaster, "As Algeria's Savagery Grows, So Does Mystery Shrouding It," *Washington Post*, October 18, 1997, A1; Charles Trueheart, "400 Killed in Algerian Massacres," *Washington Post*, January 4, 1998, A1.

81. Amine Kadi, "Algérie. Une armée suréquipée," *La Croix*, September 10, 1997, 4.

82. Al-Hayat report of September 8, 1997, translated and republished as "Army Said to Be on 'High Alert' After Béni Messous Killings," BBC Monitoring, September 10, 1997. See also "Over 127 Islamists Killed by Algeria's Armed Forces," Agence France-Presse, September 9, 1997.

83. Julia Ficatier and Amine Kadi, "Algérie. La nouvelle bataille d'Alger," *La Croix*, September 10, 1997, 3.

84. Boubker Belkadi, "Government Calls for Mobilisation in Wake of Brutal Massacre," Agence France-Presse, April 23, 1997; François d'Alançon, "Algérie. A trois jours des élections municipales, Bentalhâa continue de panser ses plaies," *La Croix*, October 21, 1997, 10; Robert Fisk, "Brutal Killers Without Faces," *Independent*, October 26, 1997, 1.

85. Lisa Ling, *World News Tonight*, ABC News, October 12, 1997, transcript.

86. "Algeria: A Change of French Tone?" *Economist*, October 11, 1997, 50; "Le chef de la 1ere région militaire remplace," Agence France-Presse, October 29, 1997.

87. Alain Bommenel, "Algerian Violence Shifting Location," Agence France-Presse, January 1, 1998.

88. U. S. Congress, *Algeria's Turmoil*, 33.

89. "Algérie. Une élection de plus pour Zéroual," *Le Point*, January 3, 1998.

90. Rachid Khiari, "Ninety-Three Dead in Biggest Massacre of 5-Year-Old Insurgency," Associated Press, April 22, 1997.

91. "At Least 80 People Said Slaughtered in Fresh Massacre in Algeria," Deutsche Presse-Agentur, September 6, 1997; Rachid Khiari, "Algerians Barricade, Arm Themselves," Associated Press, September 7, 1997.

92. Jean-Pierre Tuquoi, "Un sentiment de panique et d'abandon gagne Alger," *Le Monde*, September 9, 1997.

93. Alain Bommenel, "Bloodbath at Sidi Hamed Brings New Horror in Algeria," Agence France-Presse, January 12, 1998. See also "103 morts et 70 blesses a Sidi Hammed, selon un premier bilan offciel," Agence France-Presse, January 12, 1998; "Graphic Accounts of Latest Algeria Massacre as EU to Send Team," Agence France-Presse, January 13, 1998; "We Were Denied Guns, Algerian Survivors Tell British Ambassador," Agence France-Presse, January 15, 1998.

94. Amnesty International, *Civilian Population Caught*, 7–9.

95. Robert Moore, "Hands That Wield Algeria's Knives," *Observer*, October 26, 1997, 15.

96. Florence Aubenas, "Bentalha, le récit de dix heures de tuerie," *Libération*, October 23, 1997. A similar and more detailed account of the Bentalha massacre, as well as of the years leading up to it, can be found in Yous and Mellah, *Qui a tué à Bentalha*.

97. David Hirst, "The Mystery of Algeria's Murder Squads," *Guardian*, October 20, 1997, 1.

98. John Phillips, "Army Link to Algeria Slaughter," *Sunday Times*, October 26, 1997. A Bentalha survivor told Phillips, "There were about 35 or 40 of them [i.e., attackers]. Half of them were dressed in military tunics. The others wore civilian clothes. The ones in military tunics had automatic weapons. The others were carrying knives and axes. They shouted to us, 'Open up, we are the military.'"

99. Steve Crawshaw, "Algeria Rejects UN Help as Stunned Survivors Tell of Massacre Horror," *Independent*, January 21, 1998, 7.

100. Quoted in "Ex-president Decries 'Killing Machines' in Algeria," Agence France-Presse, November 16, 1997.

101. Jacques Duplouich, "Un transfuge accuse la police secrète d'Alger," *Le Figaro*, November 10, 1997; "Algerian President Calls for Massive Turnout in June Elections," Agence France-Presse, March 7, 1997.

102. "Ex-Diplomat Accuses Algeria Government," Associated Press, December 8, 1997.

103. Lara Marlowe, "Bloody Days, Savage Nights," *Time*, March 20, 1995, 48–51.

104. Charles Trueheart, "Killers Spread Fear Among Algeria's Poor," *Washington Post*, February 13, 1998, A30.

105. John Sweeney, "Surviving Algeria," *Observer*, June 29, 1997, 6.

106. Barry Hugill, "Algeria Slides Deeper into Bloody Morass," *Observer*, August 31, 1997, 9.

107. François Sergent, "Ils avaient de fausses barbes et du sang sur leur pantalons," *Libération*, October 23, 1997, reprinted as François Sergent, "Hands That Wield Algeria's Knives," *Observer*, October 23, 1997, 15; Saira Shah, "Triangle of Death," *Dispatches*, Channel Four, October 21, 1997; Lara Marlowe, "Algerians Tortured by Security Forces," *Irish Times*, October 30, 1997, 1; Lara Marlowe, "Ex-Army Conscript Saw Colleagues Torturing and Murdering Villagers," *Irish Times*, October 30, 1997, 9; Robert Fisk, "Conscript Tells of Algeria's Torture Chambers," *Independent*, November 3, 1997, 10; Robert Fisk, "Algeria's Horror: Nightmares of Torture Haunt Exiled Witness," *Independent*, November 1, 1997, 17.

108. John Sweeney, "Atrocities in Algeria: We Were the Murderers Who Killed for the State," *Observer*, January 11, 1998, 14.

109. Lutz Von Krusche, "Algerien: Mörderische Sippenhaft," *Der Spiegel* 3/1998, January 12, 1998, accessed September 29, 2014, http://www.spiegel.de/spiegel/print/d-7809924.html. Aggoun and Rivoire identify this officer as "Captain Ouguenoune." See Aggoun and Rivoire, *Françalgérie*, 373, 629.

110. Jean-Pierre Tuquoi, "Des fuites impliquent Alger dans les attentats de Paris," *Le Monde*, November 11, 1997; John Sweeney and Leonard Doyle, "'We Bombed Paris for Algeria," *Observer*, November 9, 1997, 9.

111. John Sweeney, "Surviving Algeria," *Observer*, June 29, 1997, 6.

112. "Trade Union Leader Says Algeria Suffering 'Assassination' by Violence," BBC Summary of World Broadcasts, March 24, 1994.

113. Barry Hugill, "Algeria Slides Deeper into Bloody Morass," *Observer*, August 31, 1997, 9.

114. Yassir Benmiloud, "It's the Generals, Stupid," *Newsweek*, January 19, 1998, 31. See also "Algerian Horrors," *Financial Times*, January 6, 1998, 15.

115. Mark Dennis, "Interview: Algeria on the Brink," *Newsweek*, April 14, 1997, 60; Lara Marlowe, "Slaughter Goes on as 173 Die in 10 Days," *Irish Times*, April 15, 1997, 11.

116. "Islamic Salvation Army Calls for Ceasefire," Agence France-Presse, September 24, 1997. See also Robert Fisk, "Algerian Rebel Group Claims Assassination," *Independent*, February 21, 1997, 9; "Un bulletin proche du FIS met en cause l'inaction de l'armée a Rais," Agence France-Presse, September 3, 1997; Ben Macintyre, "Rebels in Algeria Urge Ceasefire to Expose 'Extremists,'" *Times*, September 25, 1997; "Algerian Killings 'Crime Against Humanity': FIS," Agence France-Presse, January 4, 1998.

117. For example, see Jacques de Barrin, "L'Algérie silencieuse," *Le Monde*, June 26, 1992.

118. Mireille Duteil, "Algérie: Les tueurs sont-ils manipulés?" *Le Point*, September 13, 1997; Julia Ficatier, "Ces dix généraux qui gouvernent l'Algérie," *La Croix*, September 17, 1997, 3.

119. Jean-Pierre Tuquoi, "Les luttes de clans s'exacerbent au sein du pouvoir algérien," *Le Monde*, September 5, 1997.

120. José Garçon, "Quatre questions sur une tragédie. Censure, vengeances et conflits d'intérêts brouillent la vision du conflit," *Libération*, August 30, 1997. For background on the discourse of political clans in Algeria, see Labat, *Les islamistes algériens*; Roberts, "Algeria's Ruinous Impasse"; Zoubir, "Stalled Democratization"; Callies de Salies, "Les luttes de clan"; Vidal-Hall, "Killing Spree"; Charef, *Autopsie d'un massacre*.

121. Lisa Anderson, "Moderates on Both Sides of Algerian Conflict May Hold Key to Peace," *Boston Globe*, October 13, 1997, A15.

122. Laure Mandeville, "Bruno Étienne: 'Ce sont les généraux qui se déchirent,'" *Le Figaro*, August 30, 1997. See also Florence Aubenas and Jose Garçon, "Killers Close in on Algiers," *Guardian*, September 24, 1997, 16; Lahouari Addi, "L'armée algérienne confisque le pouvoir," *Le Monde diplomatique*, February 1998.

123. Jean-Christophe Ploquin, "'Alger se protège mais ne protège pas la société,'" *La Croix*, September 2, 1997, 5. See also Jean-Pierre Tuquoi, "Algérie: l'histoire est partie prenante dans la violence d'aujourd'hui," *Le Monde*, September 5, 1997.

124. Amnesty International, *Fear and Silence*, 21–22; Sidhoum and Algeria Watch, "Les Milices."

125. As another example, *Courrier International* claimed that a 1997 report on the Algerian army's internal security found that half of the country's *faux barrage* incidents—ritually blamed on insurgents—were actually the result of civilian militias operating such "false checkpoints." See "Algérie: Les négociations secrètes," *Courrier International*, n. 361, October 2, 1997, cited in Martinez, "Les massacres de civils dans la guerre," 56.

126. Quoted in Charles Trueheart, "Hundreds Die in Massacre Near Algiers," *Washington Post*, August 30, 1997, A21. See also M. D., "Algérie: l'escalade de l'horreur," *Le Point*, September 27, 1997.

127. José Garçon, "Pression internationale sur Alger: les demandes de commission d'enquête se multiplient," *Libération*, October 1, 1997.

128. José Garçon, "Quatre questions sur une tragédie," *Libération*, August 30, 1997.

129. Francis David, "Nouveau massacre en Algérie: 42 civils tués," *Sud Ouest*, April 25, 1997. The Associated Press, however, reported that "witnesses identified the attackers [at Omaria] as Muslim insurgents," suggesting either bad reporting (on the part of the AP or *Sud Ouest*), confused witnesses, or both. See Rachid Khiari, "Muslim Militants Reported to Kill 47 in New Massacres in Algeria," Associated Press, April 24, 1997.

130. José Garçon, "Algérie: 'Qui profite de cette situation?,'" *Libération*, May 7, 1997. See also Pierre Sané, "Algeria: When the State Fails," Amnesty International, AI Index MDE 28/047/1997, News Service 222/97, December 23, 1997.

131. Nidam Abdi, "'C'est devenu une guerre de tribus,'" *Libération*, September 24, 1997.

132. Alain Bommenel, "Suspicion and Hatred Stalk the Streets of Massacre Village," Agence France-Presse, October 22, 1997.

133. Rachid Khiari, "Government Under Fire After Insurgency's Worst Massacre," *Associated Press*, January 4, 1998.

134. Roula Khalaf, "Panic and Confusion over Algiers Killings," *Financial Times*, September 24, 1997, 4.

135. Dillman, *State and Private Sector in Algeria*, 126.

136. According to Robert Parks, a 1990 law (Algerian law number 90–25) began the process of restituting land to previous owners, those who had held it prior to Algeria's 1971 agrarian revolution. There were no provisions in the law, however, to address the claims or needs of those who had worked and otherwise occupied the farmlands from 1971 onward though a 1987 law had legitimized the post-1971 occupants. In the context of the governmental power vacuum of the 1990s, there were suspicions that some sectors of Algerian society were using violence to advance competing land claims that were otherwise contradictory under Algerian law. See Parks, *Local-National Relations and the Politics of Property Rights*, 222–224.

137. Marcus Gee, "World Treads Softly Around Algeria," *Globe and Mail* (Toronto), January 8, 1998, A12.

138. Michael Willis, "Atrocities in Algeria: Why Butcher Your Own People?" *Observer*, January 11, 1998, 14.

139. "Land Clashes?," *Newsweek*, July 7, 1997, 5; Christopher Dickey, "The Slaughter Goes On," *Newsweek*, September 8, 1997, 40.

140. "Maghreb. Un terrorisme mafieux lie aux privatisations sévit en Algérie," *La Tribune*, September 17, 1997, 8.

141. Words of journalist Charles Trueheart in "Killers Spread Fear Among Algeria's Poor," *Washington Post*, February 13, 1998, A30.

142. Alan Sipress paraphrasing John Entelis in "Aftermath of a Massacre: Algerian Killings Have Some Questioning the Official Story," *Philadelphia Inquirer*, January 8, 1998, A01.

143. "Un terrorisme mafieux lie aux privatisations sévit en Algérie," *La Tribune*, September 17, 1997, 8.

144. "Land Clashes?," *Newsweek*, July 7, 1997, 5.

145. Jean-Christophe Ploquin, "Alger se protège mais ne protège pas la société," *La Croix*, September 2, 1997, 5.

146. Linda Wertheimer, "Algeria," *All Things Considered*, National Public Radio, April 9, 1997, transcript.

147. José Garçon, "Quatre questions sur une tragédie," *Libération*, August 30, 1997. The idea that Harkis and their children were a significant constituency driving the Islamist insurgency in Algeria found its way into a wide variety of literatures, from scholarly accounts to fiction. See Chapter 6 for an examination of this idea.

148. Jean-Pierre Tuquoi, "Algerie: l'histoire est partie prenante dans la violence d'aujourd'hui," *Le Monde*, September 5, 1997; Nora Boustany, "A Massacre That Leaves a

World Frozen in Silence," *Washington Post*, October 8, 1997, A26; Sarah Chayes and Linda Wertheimer, "EU Mission to Algeria Frustrated," *All Things Considered*, National Public Radio, January 20, 1998, transcript.

149. Laure Mandeville, "Bruno Etienne: 'Ce sont les généraux qui se déchirent,'" *Le Figaro*, August 30, 1997.

150. Nidam Abdi, "'C'est devenu une guerre de tribus,'" *Libération*, September 24, 1997.

151. Anderson, *Imagined Communities*, 209.

152. Said, *Orientalism*, 54

153. Stampnitzky, *Disciplining Terror*; Zulaika, *Terrorism*.

CHAPTER 5

1. Niblock, *"Pariah States" and Sanctions in the Middle East*.

2. Evans, "End of the Argument"; Bellamy, "Libya and the Responsibility to Protect"; Weiss, "RtoP Alive and Well."

3. Roberts, "Who Said Gaddafi Had to Go?"

4. United Nations Human Rights Council, *Report of the International Commission of Inquiry on Libya*.

5. International Commission on Intervention and State Sovereignty, *Responsibility to Protect*; Weiss and Hubert, *Responsibility to Protect: Supplementary Volume*.

6. Power, *Problem From Hell*; Evans, *Responsibility to Protect*.

7. As Zoubir and Bouandel note, this was the default understanding of European and North American powers (i.e., to view the Algerian crisis as part of the global "rise of Islamism"). See Zoubir and Bouandel, "Islamism and the Algerian Political Crisis." Though this is certainly the case, this chapter and the previous two document how this default understanding began to break down in August and September 1997, reaching a true crisis of narrative and politics in January 1998.

8. Malmvig, *State Sovereignty and Intervention*.

9. One of the few efforts to locate the Algerian crisis in a geopolitical frame can be found in Zoubir, "Algerian Crisis in World Affairs."

10. Evans, "End of the Argument."

11. Spencer, "End of International Inquiries?," 126; Smith, "Algeria: The Horror."

12. For more background on the international response to the January 1992 "coup," see Cavatorta, *International Dimension of the Failed Algerian Transition*.

13. Robert Fisk, "Hundreds Die in Algerian Slaughter," *Independent*, August 30, 1997, 9; Robert Fisk, "The Agony of Algeria," *Sydney Morning Herald*, September 20, 1997, 39; Robert Fisk, "Algeria, This Autumn: A People in Agony," *Independent*, October 22, 1997, 1; John Lancaster, "As Algeria's Savagery Grows, So Does Mystery Shrouding It," *Washington Post*, October 18, 1997, A1; Ray Moseley, "Algerian Killing So Grisly the World Won't Look," *Star-Ledger* (Newark), October 12, 1997, 11B.

14. Christopher P. Winner, "In Algeria, 'Unspeakable' Horrors," *USA Today*, September 17, 1997.

15. Martin Woollacott, "Harsh Symphonies of Slaughter and Identity," *Guardian*, September 27, 1997: 21. See also "Algeria: But Why?" *Economist*, December 13, 1997.

16. "A Much-Needed Start: But the EU Needs Strong Words to Wake Algiers," *Guardian*, January 7, 1998, 14.

17. *Capital Gang*, CNN, January 3, 1998, transcript; see also the comments of William Schultz, director of the US branch of Amnesty International, on *Diplomatic License*, CNN, January 10, 1998, transcript.

18. Alain Bommenel (Agence France-Presse), "Four Hundred Slaughtered: Algeria Rings to Cries of Genocide," *Australian*, January 5, 1998: 7; "More Massacres Hit Algeria as Pressure Mounts for Inquiry," Agence France-Presse, January 7, 1998.

19. Agence France-Presse, "Algerian Terror Campaign Turns Holocaust as Massacre Toll Tops 400," *Australian*, January 14, 1998, 8.

20. For example, "The killing fields of Relizane," in Reuters, "Massacres Claim 62 More Algerians," *Calgary Herald* (Alberta), January 8, 1998, A5; "Villages into Killing-Fields," *Economist*, January 10, 1998, 36; Elie Chalala, "In Algeria's Killing Fields: A Hidden Governmental Role?" *Humanist*, March/April 1999, 5–6; *Worldview*, CNN, January 26, 1998, transcript; Robert Fisk, "Stench of Death in Algeria's Perfumed Killing Fields," *Independent*, October 23, 1997: 16.

21. "Algeria's Unholy War," *Boston Globe*, January 22, 1998, A20. The idea of an Islamic or "green" fascism (*fascisme vert*)—as opposed to the "brown" fascism of National Socialism or the "red" fascism of Communism—was often injected into the conversation on the Algerian massacres. See, for example, "Qui tue?," *La Tribune*, November 18, 1997, 28. Algerian-born philosopher and French media celebrity Bernard-Henri Lévy coined the phrase *Khmers verts* to describe the Islamist perpetrators of the massacres. See Bernard-Henri Lévy "Algérie: gare au syndrome Timisoara," *Le Monde*, February 12, 1998. Other writers also made facile comparisons between Algeria's rebels and the genocidal regime of Cambodia in the 1970s. As early as 1996, journalist Judith Miller had described the GIA as "Algeria's own Khmer Rouge." See Miller, *God Has Ninety-Nine Names*, 169. One US critic of political Islam, Daniel Pipes, who was Miller's co-guest on a US public television program in March 1995, likewise described Algeria's rebels as totalitarian Islamists bent on genocidal revolution. See "A Discussion of the Algerian Civil War," *Charlie Rose Show*, Public Broadcasting System, March 22, 1995.

22. Susan Stamberg, "Week in Review," *Weekend Edition Saturday*, National Public Radio, August 30, 1997.

23. Editorial, *Post and Courier* (Charleston, SC), September 4, 1997, A8.

24. Daniel Warner, "The Deadly Waiting Game: The West Has Said It Wants to Help End the Slaughter in Algeria but It Is Not That Simple," *Financial Times*, January 27, 1998, 20; Rupert Cornwell, "Savagery Strikes at Algeria's Heart," *Independent*, Septem-

ber 28, 1997, 11. See also Jack R. Payton, "While We Watched the Funeral, 500 Algerians Were Slain," *St. Petersburg Times* (Florida), September 9, 1997, 2A.

25. "Dialogue Is the Only Hope in Algeria's Darkest Hour," *Independent*, January 7, 1998, 18; Lee Michael Katz and Christopher P. Winner, "The World's Hands are Tied," *USA Today*, January 9, 1998, 9A. Fisk had already made a case for intervention on the grounds that the violence represented nothing short of the disintegration of Algeria. This claim drew on the state-collapse argument that had been prominent in international mobilization in former Yugoslavia. See Robert Fisk, "The Case for Intervention: No, Algeria, It's Not an 'Internal Affair,'" *Independent*, November 6, 1997, 23.

26. Bob Edwards, "Violence in Algeria," *Morning Edition*, National Public Radio, January 2, 1998.

27. Quoted in Susannah Herbert, "United States, EU Reaffirm Confidence in Algerian Rulers," *Calgary Herald*, January 14, 1998, D3.

28. Quoted in Rachid Khiari, "One Hundred Slaughtered in Algerian Attack," Associated Press, January 12, 1998. Pierre is also coauthor of two important policy-oriented works on Algeria. See Pierre and Quandt, "Algeria's War on Itself"; and Pierre and Quandt, *Algerian Crisis*.

29. Moïsi explicitly acknowledged that dispatching peacekeepers was impossible; all other forms of intervention, for him, would then be merely "symbolic." See Sarah Chayes and Linda Wertheimer, "EU Mission to Algeria Frustrated," *All Things Considered*, National Public Radio, January 20, 1998, transcript.

30. Lara Marlowe, "Jospin Breaks Official Silence on Algeria Despite Retaliation Fear," *Irish Times*, February 1, 1997, 12. At the same time, de Charette was not unaware of the increasing violence in Algeria; he admitted that, to the best of his understanding, some two hundred Algerians were being killed each week.

31. "Washington Condemns Massacre in Algeria," Agence France-Presse, April 23, 1997.

32. For example, *L'Express* ran a political cartoon in which a photographer claimed he had the latest photos from a massacre in Algeria, only to be rebuffed by an editor surrounded by images of Diana. See Christopher P. Winner, "Debate Erupts in France over Media's Priorities," *USA Today*, September 8, 1997, 5A. *Marianne* published an image from Algeria of severed children's heads in a bucket; underneath it ran this caption: "Here are photos of Algeria. Do you want to see them? Or do you prefer Diana?" Quoted in Lara Marlowe, "'Madonna in Hell' Captures the Grief and Despair of War-Torn Algeria," *Irish Times*, October 20, 1997, 12. On the extraordinary media impact of Diana's death, see Moeller, *Compassion Fatigue*, 33–34, 37.

33. "Annan Denounces Massacres in Algeria," Deutsche Presse-Agentur, August 29, 1997. The head of UNESCO, Fredreico Mayor Zaragoza, was likewise "horrified." See "GIA Commander and 46 Other Islamist Fighters Dead: Report," Agence France-Presse, August 31, 1997.

34. Quoted in Craig R. Whitney, "Ninety-Eight Die in One of Algerian Civil War's Worst Massacres," *New York Times*, August 30, 1997, 3.

35. "France Condemns Atrocities by Islamic Extremists," Xinhua, September 1, 1997.

36. U.S. Department of State, Daily Press Briefing, September 3, 1997.

37. "Pope Condemns 'Barbaric Atrocities' in Algeria," Deutsche Presse-Agentur, August 31, 1997.

38. Charles Trueheart, "U.N., Vatican Condemn Massacres in Algeria; Atrocities Intensify in Six-Year Civil War," *Washington Post*, September 9, 1997, A14.

39. "UN Leader Appeals for Dialogue in Algeria," Agence France-Presse, August 31, 1997; "UN Denies Annan Interfered on Algeria Violence," Agence France-Presse, September 2, 1997.

40. "UN Agency Warns Against Deporting Algerian Refugees," Agence France-Presse, September 18, 1997.

41. Christopher P. Winner, "In Algeria, 'Unspeakable' Horrors," *USA Today*, September 17, 1997. The accuracy of the comparison is debatable. The dominant impression of the Rwandan genocide is that it was largely carried out by machetes, not bullets.

42. "L'horreur et l'invraisemblance," *Le Monde*, September 1, 1997; "Algeria's Agony," *New York Times*, September 3, 1997, 22.

43. "Algeria's Ghastly Secret," *Economist*, September 6, 1997, 17.

44. "UNICEF Calls on World to Wake Up to 'Bloodbath in Algeria,'" Agence France-Presse, September 8, 1997.

45. Amnesty International, "Algeria: Amnesty International Condemns Massacres and Calls for Urgent Measures," press release, AI Index MDE 28/25/97, News Service 159/97, September 22, 1997.

46. Charles Trueheart, "U.N., Vatican Condemn Massacres in Algeria," *Washington Post*, September 9, 1997, A14.

47. Carol Landry, "US-Algeria," Agence France-Presse, September 14, 1997.

48. "EU Condemns Wave of Violence in Algeria," Algemeen Nederlands Persbureau, September 16, 1997.

49. "Euro MP Suggests Peace Dialogue with Algeria," Agence France-Presse, September 17, 1997.

50. Emmanuel Defouloy, "Algérie: 'l'Europe peut jouer les médiateurs,'" *La Croix*, September 22, 1997, 24.

51. "Euro MP Suggests Peace Dialogue with Algeria," Agence France-Presse, September 17, 1997.

52. Aileen McCabe, "Algeria's Secret War Leaves World Feeling Horrified, Powerless," *Vancouver Sun*, September 26, 1997, A12. See also "La France ressent avec 'abomination' la tuerie de Bentalha," Agence France-Presse, September 24, 1997. Former Foreign Minister de Charette took the opportunity to criticize France's policy of noninterference, even though he had recently defended it. See Herni Mamarbachi,

"La communauté internationale contrainte a la non ingérence," Agence France-Presse, September 24, 1997.

53. Richard Norton-Taylor, "The West Voices Shock but Little Else," *Guardian*, September 25, 1997, 13; Rupert Cornwell, "Algerian Rebels' Peace Call Shifts Blame for Slaughter," *Independent*, September 25, 1997, 14.

54. "Pressure Mounting on West to Intervene in Bloody Algeria," Agence France-Presse, September 25, 1997.

55. "Opposition Party Urges Bonn, Paris to Help Settle Algeria Conflict," Agence France-Presse, September 25, 1997. After the Bentalha massacre, the German opposition Green Party even called for an arms embargo on Algeria. See "Halt Military Exports, Loans to Algeria, German Greens Say," Deutsche Presse-Agentur, September 24, 1997.

56. "UN Human Rights Chief to Meet Algerian, UN Peace Role Denied," Agence France-Presse, September 26, 1997.

57. "U.N. Human Rights Chief Calls for Focus on Algeria's Killings," Deutsche Presse-Agentur, September 30, 1997.

58. "White House Condemns 'Savagery' of Massacre in Algeria," Agence France-Presse, September 24, 1997.

59. "UN Human Rights Chief to Meet Algerian, UN Peace Role Denied," Agence France-Presse, September 26, 1997. Alluding to Algeria's *Qui tue?* debate, Cohn-Bendit mocked Franco-American calls for Algiers to protect its civilians: "No one knows who is killing whom, no one knows who is protecting whom." Quoted in "Algeria: Europe Powerless in Face of Algerian Horror," Inter Press Service, September 26, 1997. An official from Human Rights Watch concurred that the basic facts of the massacre were unclear: "One of the problems is that we don't know." See "Former Algerian Official Claims Military Culpable for Massacres," Deutsche Presse-Agentur, September 29, 1997.

60. No title, Reuters, September 26, 1998, on file with author.

61. U.S. Department of State, Daily Press Briefing, October 6, 1997.

62. Ray Moseley, "Hidden War: Algeria Caught in Web of Terror," *Calgary Herald*, October 13, 1997, B4.

63. Jeffrey Ulbrich, "EU Sends Sympathy but Little Else to Algeria and the Middle East," Associated Press, October 26, 1997.

64. Ray Moseley, "Hidden War: Algeria Caught in Web of Terror," *Calgary Herald*, October 13, 1997, B4.

65. John Lancaster, "As Algeria's Savagery Grows, So Does Mystery Shrouding It," *Washington Post*, October 18, 1997, A01.

66. Amnesty International, International Federation of Human Rights, Human Rights Watch, and Reporters Sans Frontières, "Algeria: A Call for Action to End a Human Rights Crisis," press release, October 15, 1997.

67. "Algeria: A Change of French Tone?" *Economist*, October 11, 1997, 50.

68. For a summary of these concerns, see quotes from Pierre Sané (Amnesty In-

ternational) and Patrick Baudouin (Fédération Internationale des ligues des Droits de l'Homme) in, respectively, "Algeria: When the State Fails," Amnesty International, AI index MDE 28/047/1997, News Service 222/97, December 23, 1997; and "Algeria: Europe Continues to Back U.N. Investigation in Algeria," Inter Press Service, January 26, 1998.

69. See Chapters Three and Four.

70. "French Socialists Call for International Inquiry into Algeria," Agence France-Presse, November 12, 1997. Prime Minister Jospin was also responding to Algerian criticism of French government support for the November 10 "day of solidarity" with Algeria in Paris, organized by NGOs and featuring several celebrities, such as Gérard Depardieu, Isabelle Adjani, and Cheb Khaled.

71. "Arab League Opposes Outside Interference in Algeria," Agence France-Presse, November 16, 1997.

72. "Amnesty International Alleges 'Bullying' by Algerian Government," Agence France-Presse, November 18, 1997.

73. "Algerian Foreign Minister to Meet EU in Luxembourg," Agence France-Presse, November 25, 1997.

74. "UN Calls for Inspectors to Monitor Human Rights Abuses in Algeria," Agence France-Presse, December 18, 1997; "Algeria Protests UN Rights Envoy's Call for Monitors," Agence France-Presse, December 19, 1997.

75. Jean-Pierre Tuquoi, "Femme parmi d'autres," *Le Monde*, December 30, 1997.

76. See, for example, Ray Moseley, "World Community Prepares to Intervene in Algeria," *Seattle Times*, January 12, 1998; "Le pape condamne les massacres en Algérie et au Burundi," Agence France-Presse, January 4, 1998. Iran, which then supported the FIS and was also chairing the Organization of the Islamic Conference, criticized the "unjustifiable" "silence of international organisations" and the "indifference" of fellow Muslim nations. See "Iran Calls on Moslem World to End Indifference to Algeria Massacres," Agence France-Presse, January 3, 1998. The Iranian parliament even went as far as to accuse the Algerian government of being complicit in the January 12 massacres. See "Le Parlement iranien condamne les massacres en Algérie," *Les Echos*, January 13, 1998. The Arab League, however, continued to support the Algerian government's position and called on the international community to help Algeria confront terror, not to intervene in it. See "Arab League Condemns Killings, Calls for an End to Terrorism," Associated Press, January 4, 1998.

77. "Germany Demands Urgent EU Action on Algeria," Agence France-Presse, January 4, 1998.

78. "France Condemns Atrocities," *New York Times*, January 4, 1998, I7.

79. "Twenty-Two More Slain in Algeria at Outset of Bloody Ramadan: Press," Agence France-Presse, January 5, 1998.

80. "Britain Says Aid to Algerian Massacre Survivors a Possibility," Agence France-Presse, January 5, 1998.

81. Reuters, "Massacres Claim 62 More Algerians: Pressure Grows for Outside Investigation," *Calgary Herald*, January 8, 1998, A5. The envoy, Claude Laverdure, was in Algiers from January 12 to 13.

82. "The Secretary-General considers it particularly urgent and vital that the innocent civilian population, especially women and children, be protected from the forces of violence in Algeria." Quoted in "Annan Appeals for Protection of Algeria's Population," Agence France-Presse, January 12, 1998.

83. US Department of State, Daily Press Briefing, January 5, 1998.

84. "Algérie: l'attitude de Paris jugée 'inacceptable,'" *Le Figaro*, January 6, 1998.

85. Rachid Khiari, "Government Rejects International Inquiry into Violence, Algerians Flee," Associated Press, January 7, 1998.

86. US Department of State, Daily Press Briefing, January 5, 1998, emphasis added.

87. U.S. Department of State, Daily Press Briefing, January 6, 1998, emphasis added.

88. US Department of State, Daily Press Briefing, January 7, 1998.

89. US Department of State, Daily Press Briefing, January 9, 1997. On January 5, Rubin said, "We would like to see international inquiries get to the bottom of it." But a January 8 exchange between reporters and Rubin bordered on the facetious:

QUESTION: Jamie, what exactly does a "rapporteur" do? [. . .]

MR. RUBIN: He reports. That's what you do.

QUESTION: He doesn't investigate?

MR. RUBIN: Well, again, I don't want to get too deeply into the—I've been in New York, and I know what sweat and blood goes into the distinctions between different UN organizations and their mandates and what titles people get and all that goes with that. A UN special rapporteur, I can say with confidence, is a UN special rapporteur.

Two critics later compared this parsing to the US government's reaction to the unfolding genocide in Rwanda in 1994. See Waliken and Larioui, "The US and the Algerian Massacres." During the unfolding of the Rwandan atrocities, a reporter had asked the State Department, "How many acts of genocide does it take to make a genocide?" See Power, *A Problem from Hell*, 364.

90. Philip Waller, "International Investigators May Probe Algerian Human Rights," Associated Press, January 6, 1998.

91. Agence France-Presse, "Algeria Gives Conditional Green Light to EU Mission," January 8, 1998.

92. Craig R. Whitney, "Despite Carnage, Algeria Shuns Aid Offers," *New York Times*, January 7, 1998, A6.

93. Lee Michael Katz and Christopher P. Winner, "The World's Hands Are Tied," *USA Today*, January 9, 1998, 9A.

94. "Algeria Gives Conditional Green Light to EU Mission," Agence France-Presse, January 8, 1998.

95. "France Rejects International Force for Algeria," Reuters, January 12, 1998. Reuters quoted French Defense Minister Alain Richard.

96. One of Ambassador Hume's first meetings in Algiers was with the US business community, mainly energy companies. See Hume, *Mission to Algiers*. See also Roula Khalaf, "West Wonders What It Can Do in Algeria: But Algiers Wants No Outside Interference," *Financial Times*, January 8, 1998, 4; David Hirst, "Private View: Post-mortem Algeria Authorities Dread," *Guardian*, November 1, 1997, 17. See also Chapter Two.

97. "Country Report: Algeria," *Economist* Intelligence Unit, March 5, 1998, 7.

98. Nadim Ladki (Reuters), "Algeria Agrees to Visit by 3 European Envoys," *Philadelphia Inquirer*, January 16, 1998, A17; "Algeria's Unholy War," *Boston Globe*, January 22, 1998, A20.

99. "EU Grapples for Response to Algeria Blood-Letting," Agence France-Presse, January 8, 1998.

100. "Algeria Gives Conditional Green Light to EU Mission," Agence France-Presse, January 8, 1998.

101. "Britain Sees Chance for EU Ministers' Mission to Algeria," Agence France-Presse, January 14, 1998.

102. Alain Bommenel, "EU Delegation Arrives to Discuss Algeria Violence," Agence France-Presse, January 19, 1998.

103. Quoted in Elaine Ganley, "European Envoy Visits Algeria," Associated Press, January 19, 1998. See also "EU Mission Regrets Algerian Rejection of UN Rapporteur," Agence France-Presse, January 20, 1998.

104. United Kingdom Foreign and Commonwealth Office, "EU/Troika Mission to Algeria: Press Statement by Derek Fatchett," January 20, 1998.

105. In the weeks preceding the troika's visit, several other notable "interventions" had taken place. Widely reported in Algeria yet receiving scant attention internationally, the UK and US ambassadors in Algeria had visited, with the Algerian government's permission and supervision, the massacre site of Sidi Hamed on January 15 and 17 respectively. Hume went to "express sympathy," "speak out against terrorism," and "understand better." He arrived with the assumption that "Islamist terrorists" were behind the massacre and was willing to accept that "it was impossible for the government to protect all such rural sites in the country." See Hume, *Mission to Algiers*, 36.

106. Angus MacKinnon, "EU Demands Algeria Opens Doors to UN," Agence France-Presse, January 26, 1998.

107. Quoted in Hill and Smith, *European Foreign Policy*, 346–347.

108. Jeffrey Ulbrich, "EU Foreign Ministers Offer Sympathy but Little Help," Associated Press, January 26, 1998.

109. "Algeria: Europe Continues to Back U.N. Investigation in Algeria," Inter Press Service, January 26, 1998.

110. For example, "The European Union's second effort in a month to do something

about the horrific bloodletting in Algeria ended Thursday with no more success than the first." See Jeffrey Ulbrich, "Another EU Mission, Another Futile Effort," Associated Press, February 12, 1998.

111. Rachid Khiari, "EU Fact-Finding Mission Claims Nothing Being Left 'in Shadows,'" Associated Press, February 10, 1998.

112. Charles Trueheart, "Europeans Stymied in Algeria Mission," *Washington Post*, February 12, 1998, A27.

113. Stephane Barbier, "Aucun contact avec le FIS: les élus du PE donnent satisfaction au pouvoir," Agence France-Presse, February 11, 1998. One of the MEPs also attempted to hand over to the Algerian government a list of two thousand "disappeared" persons, but it was not accepted. Her Algerian counterparts apparently claimed that there were only thirty-one cases of people who had gone missing while under government supervision. See Marcus Mabry, "'We're Dead Already': Can a European Fact-Finding Visit Do Anything to Stop the Anonymous Massacres and Human-Rights Abuses?" *Newsweek*, February 23, 1998, 17.

114. "Algerian Parliament a Reality," European Parliament News Report, February 12, 1998; "Algeria: Dialogue with Algerian Parliament Must Be Pursued," European Parliament News Report, February 18 1998.

Hélène Carrère d'Encausse, one of the nine MEPs, echoed Soulier's words almost verbatim in the pages of *Le Figaro*. See Hélène Carrère d'Encausse, "La terreur islamiste," *Le Figaro*, February 16, 1998. As an indication of how pleased the Algerian government was with the MEPs intervention (and their assertion that foreigners were only encouraging the GIA with their accusations of government complicity), Ramtane Lamamra, then Algeria's ambassador to the United States, cited Carrère d'Encausse's article in a letter to *Newsweek*, which had recently summarized the five-day visit as "a symbol of the outside world's impotence." See Marcus Mabry, "'We're Dead Already': Can a European Fact-Finding Visit Do Anything to Stop the Anonymous Massacres and Human-Rights Abuses?" *Newsweek*, February 23, 1998, 17. Critics of the Algerian regime dismissed Soulier as a close ally of the FLN (Aggoun and Rivoire, *Françalgérie*, 546–47) or as a *godillot* (lackey or stooge) of the regime (Ali-Yahia, *La dignité humaine*, 116). Hugh Roberts noted that some MEPs criticized the mission because there was already a Maghrib relations group in the parliament. The fact that Algeria allowed a "human rights" delegation rather than a more neutral regional affairs group suggests Soulier's amenability with Algerian state interests at that time. See Roberts, "Dancing in the Dark," 121.

115. Rachid Khiari, "Three Bombs Rock Algiers as Peace Mission Draws to Close," Associated Press, February 12, 1998.

116. Emma Ross, "Algerian Exiles Say authorities Are Responsible for Massacres," Associated Press, January 22, 1998; Agence France-Presse, "Algerian Opposition in London Blames Algiers for Massacres," January 22, 1998; "Des exilés accusent," *Sud Ouest*,

January 23, 1998; Richard Norton-Taylor, "Algerian Violence: Security Service Linked to Killings," *Guardian*, January 23, 1998, 13.

117. See U. S. Congress, *Algeria's Turmoil*. The US hearings were prompted in part by a recent news exposé on the massacres, broadcast on the January 18, 1998, episode of *60 Minutes*, then one of the most widely viewed television programs in the United States. Featuring celebrity reporter Christiane Amanpour, who won an Emmy award for the segment, the report featured interviews with survivors who described the massacres; with former Algerian prime minister Abdelhamid Brahimi, who claimed that the government was behind the massacres; and with then prime minister Ahmed Ouyahia, who denounced calls for an international inquiry. See Christian Amanpour, "Massacre in Algeria," *60 Minutes*, January 18, 1998, transcript. The segment was referenced several times during the hearings.

118. "Algerian Media Hail US Envoy's Visit as Washington Turnaround," Agence France-Presse, March 14, 1998.

119. "US Policy Towards Libya and Other Countries of Africa's Maghreb Region," Federal News Service, Special State Department Background Briefing, March 19, 1998.

120. See the joint statement from Human Rights Watch, Amnesty International, International Federation for Human Rights, and Reporters Sans Frontières, "Algeria/UN: The Commission on Human Rights Must Act Now," April 7, 1998.

121. Farhan Haq, "Rights-Algeria: Activists Criticize Inaction over Massacres," Inter Press Service, April 22, 1998; "Kosovo Cannot Be Ignored US Diplomat Tells UN Human Rights Commission," Agence France-Presse, March 25, 1998; "UN Rights Chief Backs Algerian Human Rights Abuse Resolution," Agence France-Presse, March 31, 1998; "UN Human Rights Commission Takes Action on Right to Development, Children's Rights," M2 Presswire, April 27, 1998.

122. Amnesty International, "UN Commission on Human Rights: Political Horse-trading Triumphs over Rights Protection," News Service 71/98, April 24, 1998.

123. As the Commission's work came to an end, local officials and militia members in the region of Relizane, which had recently experienced the worst massacres of the conflict, were arrested for reportedly killing dozens of civilians, which likely did not help Algeria's case internationally. As an April 15, 1998, headline in *Le Figaro* read, "des 'patriotes' [i.e., pro-government militias] accusés de massacres." The original source of the accusations was surprising: the independent Algiers-based daily *Liberté*, known for its aggressive anti-Islamist agenda and alignment with the Kabylia-based RCD party. The matter was the subject of a book by an Algerian human rights activist from Relizane. See Smaïn, *Relizane dans la tourmente*. See also "Algérie: des patriotes faisaient régner la terreur," *Le Monde*, April 16, 1998. The same day that this news broke, fifty-seven winners of the Nobel Peace Prize (including Elie Wiesel, Desmond Tutu, and Jose Ramos-Horta) issued a statement from Algiers denouncing "the bloody acts of savagery committed by armed terrorist groups." See Amine Kadi, "Algérie: à Relizane, les 'patriotes' auraient massacré des civils," *La Croix*, April 16, 1998, 7.

124. United Nations, *Algeria: Report of Eminent Panel.*

125. Gustavo Capdevila, "Algeria: U.N. Investigates Human Rights Violations," Inter Press Service, July 21, 1998.

126. "Algeria: Guilty? Us?" *Economist*, July 25, 1998, 45; "U.N. Committee Laments Algeria's 'Unsatisfactory Responses,'" Associated Press, July 31, 1998.

127. Algerian authorities explained that Matoub's house was not "a source of information."

128. United Nations, *Algeria: Report of Eminent Panel.*

129. Amnesty International, *Algeria: UN Panel Report a Whitewash on Human Rights.*

130. Barry Hatton, "Head of U.N. Team to Algeria Laments President's Departure," Associated Press, September 26, 1998. The report's language is so close to Algerian government rhetoric that the entire document never mentions any insurgent group by name, whether the GIA or the AIS. Instead, it refers to "armed Islamic groups," but more often just to terrorists and to the phenomenon of terrorism.

131. Human Rights Watch, *Algeria's Human Rights Crisis*, 3. See also Spencer, "End of International Inquiries?," 129.

132. "U2's Lead Singer Keeps Promise to Sarajevo," ABC News, September 23, 1997.

133. In what seemed like an act of quick retaliation, the Algerian government removed the credentials of Agence France-Presse's reporter in Algiers for inflating the death figures from Bentalha. See Lara Marlowe, "Continuing Campaign of Violence Claims Lives of 11 Women Teachers," *Irish Times*, September 30, 1997, 9. Several months later, Algerian government radio and television claimed that Agence France-Presse had created a false image for profit and propaganda so as "to tarnish the image of Algeria." These reports cited local officials who claimed that the "Madonna" woman in Zaourar's photograph was not a resident of Bentalha and her true identity could not be established. "The fact is," one reporter claimed, "this lady was created by the European media for venomous propaganda campaigns against Algeria by diffusing false reports." See "Algerian Television Slams Anti-foreign Media Campaigns," BBC Monitoring, February 11, 1998. The woman in question, Oum Saad (or Um Saad Ghendouzi), eventually emerged and sued Agence France-Presse for defamation in 1998. She claimed that she had lost only her brother in the massacre and that she had come under threat from her neighbors as a possible insurgent sympathiser. As a Muslim, she also took offense at being called a Madonna. See Doy, *Drapery*, 215–218; Lara Marlowe, "Visitors to Chip Away at Fortress Algeria," *Irish Times*, July 29, 1998.

134. The *New York Times* decided to publish the photo on page 3. See Roger Cohen, "85 Slain in New Attack Near Algiers, Setting Off Panic," *New York Times*, September 24, 1997, A3.

135. "Le photographe de l'Agence France-Presse à Alger auteur de la meilleure photo 1997," Agence France-Presse, February 13, 1998.

136. John Henley, "Political Islam's Men of Violence," *Guardian*, September 26, 1997, 17.

137. Lara Marlowe, "'Madonna in Hell' Captures the Grief and Despair of War-Torn Algeria," *Irish Times*, October 20, 1997, 12. Historian Benjamin Stora would later boil it down to this: "100,000 dead and one image." See Stora, *La guerre invisible*.

138. "Un prix pour la photo de la 'madone' algerienne," Agence France-Presse, October 24, 1997.

139. "Le photographe de l'Agence France-Presse à Alger auteur de la meilleure photo 1997," Agence France-Presse, February 13, 1998.

140. Weiss and Hubert, *Responsibility to Protect: Supplementary Volume*.

141. Evans, "End of the Argument."

142. Bellamy and Williams, "New Politics of Protection."

CHAPTER 6

1. Thabo Mbeki and Mahmood Mamdani, "Courts Can't End Civil Wars," *New York Times*, February 6, 2014, accessed September 27, 2014, http://www.nytimes.com/2014/02/06/opinion/courts-cant-end-civil-wars.html.

2. For background, see Hayner, *Unspeakable Truths*.

3. Mamdani, *Saviors and Survivors*.

4. For example, see Judge Richard Goldstone's statement of faith in the TRC, which is prior to any evaluation of it, in Goldstone, *For Humanity*, 77.

5. See Freeman, *Truth Commissions*.

6. See Arad's argument in Yule, *After Auschwitz*.

7. The attention afforded to Souaïdia's memoir was reportedly of such concern that the head of Algeria's army, General Mohamed Lamari, considered it, in the words of French journalist José Garçon, "une affaire d'État." Garçon suggested that, unlike in previous internationalized media crises related to the violence in Algeria (e.g., the massacres of August 1997 to January 1998), the Algerian government was not able to find prominent French intellectuals to come to its aid, partially as a result of the book's "irreproachable" foreword, written by Italian prosecutor Ferdinando Imposimato, known for his work against mafias and terrorism. See José Garçon, "L'armée algérienne veut rassurer Paris," *Libération*, April 25, 2001, 11. The day after Souaïdia's book was published, a letter published in *Le Monde* argued that *La sale guerre* and *Qui a tué à Bentalha* provided the evidence to warrant a new push for international inquiry into Algeria's violence. Several intellectuals, including Pierre Bordieu and Pierre Vidal-Naquet, had signed the letter. See "M. Védrine et le bain de sang en Algérie," *Le Monde*, February 9, 2001. Algerian writers Yasmina Khadra and Rachid Boudjedra quickly attacked Souaïdia's claims; two hundred Algerian academics signed a letter denouncing *La sale guerre*. See "Algiers," *Times Higher Education Supplement*, April 6, 2001, 10.

8. Jean-Pierre Tuquoi, "Le témoignage d'un ancien officier algérien: on était devenus des sauvages," *Le Monde*, June 3, 2000; Lara Marlowe, "Europe Turns Blind Eye to Algeria's Dirty War," *Irish Times*, February 13, 2001, 14.

9. Amnesty International, "Algeria: Habib Souaidia's Trial Highlights Concerns over Failure to Conduct Investigations," press release, AI Index MDE 28/040/2002, News Service No. 107, June 28, 2002.

10. Yous and Mellah, *Qui a tué à Bentalha*. See also "Thinking the Unthinkable," *Economist*, November 11, 2000.

11. See Mohamed Ghoualmi (Algeria's ambassador to France), "A propos du livre *Qui a tué à Bentalha?*" *Le Monde*, November 21, 2000; Salima Tlemçani, "Massacre de Bentalha: un livre qui suscite des polémiques," *El Watan*, October 30, 2000. On November 11, 2000, the Algerian government organized a press conference where several residents of Bentalha countered Yous's narrative; a similar group was brought to France in January 2001 for the same purpose.

12. Roberts, "Truths About the Dirty War." As noted in Chapter 3, the claims about Douar Ez-Zaâtria proved controversial for several reasons. Souaïdia nevertheless stood by his account, underscoring that the massacre was in the "vicinity" of that locale. See Habib Souaïdia, "En Algérie, le roi est nu," *Le Monde*, April 17, 2001.

13. "Habib Souaidia prêt a témoigner devant une commission d'enquête," Agence France-Presse, February 13, 2001.

14. See "Les 'dérapages' de l'armée algérienne ont été sanctionnes," Agence France-Presse, April 21, 2001.

15. Patrick Saint-Paul, "Algérie: l'ancien ministre de la Défense est accusé de torture par des Algériens," *Le Figaro*, April 26, 2001. Nezzar eventually spoke with French police in April 2002. See Ceaux Pascal, "L'ancien ministre de la défense algérien est revenu s'expliquer devant la police à Paris," *Le Monde*, April 8, 2002. As the Nezzar-Souaïdia trial opened in July 2002, more torture charges were filed against Nezzar in a French court. See "Algerian General Target of New Torture Allegations in French Court," Agence France-Presse, July 1, 2002. Not one of these cases against Nezzar was successful.

16. See, for example, Catherine Tardrew and Henri Vernet, "La fuite du général algérien," *Le Parisien*, April 27, 2001; "World Briefing," *New York Times*, April 27, 2001, A8; Giles Tremlett, "Death and Dissent as Algeria Goes to Polls," *Guardian*, May 31, 2002, 15.

17. "Former Defence Minister Sues over 'Dirty War' Allegations," Agence France-Presse, August 23, 2001; Jon Henley, "Algerian Ex-general Sues over Army Massacres Claim: Author and French TV Station Accused of Libel," *Guardian*, August 24, 2001, 12.

18. In Algeria, *La sale guerre* earned Souaïdia an international arrest warrant and a twenty-year jail sentence following his trial there *in absentia*. See "Algerian Soldier Given 20–Year Jail Term over Critical Book," Agence France-Presse, April 30, 2002. Though they were widely attacked in the Algerian press, the accusations of Souaïdia, along with those of former DRS officer Mohammed Samraoui (author of an even more damning memoir, *Chronique des années de sang*) also helped provide cover for Algerians who had held suspicions about the informal role of private and state security interests in the violence. In December 2001, the Algerian papers *Le Jeune Indépendant* (December 4) and

Le Quotidien d'Oran (Abed Charef, "Escadrons de la mort: l'aveu de Zeroual," December 6) ran stories in which Louisa Hanoune, head of Algeria's Worker's Party, claimed that Zéroual had "confirmed" to her in 1998 the existence of "death squads" in Algeria. These were allegedly autonomous from the state security sector and run by opaque "interest groups." Zéroual, who has remained largely out of the public eye since leaving office in 1999, apparently never confirmed or denied Hanoune's claim. Rumors of private, paramilitary, or anti-Islamist death squads such as l'Organisation des Jeunes Algériens Libres (OJAL) emerged in the mid-1990s and have been an important feature in the *Qui tue?* debates. A possible context of Zéroual's purported claim could be the allegations of intense intraregime conflict in 1998 between Zéroual and his opponents in the military leadership. See Roberts *Demilitarizing Algeria*, 10–11. The April 1998 Fergane affair in Relizane (see note 75), for example, that included allegations of pro-government death squad-type activity (see Chapters 3 and 4) was often read as an effect of fighting between rival camps in the elite. Late 1998 allegations of death squad activity were likewise read as high-level interest groups attempting to undermine each other.

19. Notably, the accusations of Hichem Aboud, former chief of staff to General Mohamed Betchine. Betchine briefly headed the Sécurité Militaire (SM, or Military Security, that is, military intelligence, now the DRS) in the late 1980s. Like the other whistleblowers, Aboud became a political refugee in France. In June 2001, he gave a provocative interview to *Le Nouvel Observateur* about the 1987 assassination of opposition lawyer Ali Mecili. See Farid Aïchoune and Jean-Baptiste Naudet, "Hichem Aboud rompt la loi du silence," *Le Nouvel Observateur*, June 14, 2001. In March 2002, Aboud published his own polemical exposé. See Aboud, *La mafia des généraux*.

20. Souaïdia's statements can be found in Florence Aubenas, "Le général algérien Nezzar débouté à Paris," *Libération*, September 28, 2002, 11.

21. See Aussaresses, *Services Spéciaux Algérie 1955–1957*. After September 11, 2001, the book was quickly translated into English as Aussaresses, *The Battle of the Casbah: Terrorism and Counter-Terrorism in Algeria, 1955–1957*. A response of sorts came in the form of an English translation of *The Question*, by Henri Alleg, one of the people tortured by French troops in the 1954–1962 war. *The Question* was also released amid growing revelations regarding the use of torture in post-9/11 counterterrorism operations. Indeed, Algeria's history was a constant reference point following the 2003 Ango-American invasion of Iraq and the multidimensional insurgency it generated. There was also the release of a newly restored print of Gillo Pontecorvo's film *La battaglia di Algeri* and a new edition of Alistaire Horne's *A Savage War of Peace*, a history of the French-Algerian war.

22. See Ighilahriz and Nivat, *Algérienne*.

23. Raphaelle Bacque, "Jacques Chirac demande une journée nationale d'hommage aux harkis," *Le Monde*, February 8, 2001. See also Le Sueur, *Uncivil War*, 292–295, 318–319.

24. Sifaoui, apparently an early champion of Souaïdia, before *La sale guerre*, became one of the book's most prominent critics following its publication. He was originally

contracted as one of the coauthors but later claimed that 70 percent of the text was his writing. See Mohamed Sifaoui, "Une lettre de Mohamed Sifaoui," *Le Monde*, February 12, 2001. Even before the Nezzar-Souaïdia trial, Sifaoui had become a useful device in the Algerian government's efforts to discredit *La sale guerre*. For example, Sifaoui was cited in a letter to the editor from the Algerian embassy in Washington, DC: "Terrorists in Algeria," *Washington Post*, May 18, 2001, A30. In a lawsuit against Editions La Découverte, Sifaoui also alleged that Gèze had manipulated the text, downplaying Souaïdia's account of insurgent violence in order to highlight state abuses. See Hervé de Saint-Hilaire, "Polémique autour d'un ouvrage," *Le Figaro*, February 10, 2001. Gèze countersued Sifaoui and the magazine *Marianne*, which had carried an extended interview with Sifaoui. Gèze alleged that, as coauthor, Sifaoui was the one who had attempted to manipulate the memoir, adding accounts that Souaïdia had not experienced. The legal proceedings in September 2001, like those of the Nezzar-Souaïdia trial that followed the next summer, essentially became a "political trial" about the Algerian massacres. See José Garçon, "'La sale guerre' en procès à Paris," *Libération*, September 7, 2001, 9. And as with Nezzar's complaint against Souaïdia, the court dismissed the complaints by and against Gèze.

25. Hassane Zerrouky, "Pas de peine contre Habib Souaïdia," *L'Humanité*, July 7, 2002.

26. Harbi was so deeply affected by the historical ironies between Algeria of the late 1950s and Algeria of the late 1990s that he had to leave the proceedings at one point. See Simone Catherine, "La mémoire meurtrie de Mohammed Harbi," *Le Monde*, October 12, 2002.

27. Reportedly, Souaïdia had also hoped that a representative of the Mouvement Algérien des Officiers Libres (MAOL), a dissident officers group composed mainly of exiles, would testify in his favor. See "Les procès du général Nezzar embarrassent Paris," *Libération*, October 11, 2001, 21. This representative would likely have been Captain Hacine Ouguenoune (aka Captain Haroune), a political refugee in London who had formerly served in the SM/DRS. Pierre Vidal-Naquet was also slated to speak on Souaïdia's behalf but was unable to attend for reasons of personal health.

28. Elaine Ganley, "Former Defense Minister Confronts Best-Selling Author over Extremists," Associated Press, July 1, 2002.

29. Hassan Zerrouky, "Pas de peine contre Habib Souaïdia," *L'Humanité*, July 7, 2002.

30. "Algérie: le général Khaled Nezzar saisit la justice française contre l'auteur de La sale guerre," *Le Monde*, August 24, 2001.

31. Florence Aubenas, "'Le GIA est une création des services de sécurité': l'armee algérienne devant la justice française," *Libération*, July 4, 2002, 11.

32. See Souaïdia, Gèze, and Mellah, *Le procés de "La sale guerre,"* 229–246.

33. Ibid., 166.

34. Marie-Estelle Pech, "Fin, à Paris, du procès de Habib Souaïdia, qui avait dénoncé les 'massacres' des militaires," *Le Figaro*, July 6, 2002.

35. "French Court Dismisses Algerian Defamation Suit Against Author," Agence France-Presse, September 27, 2002.

36. "Algeria: Former General Khaled Nezzar Loses 'Defamation Case' Before French Court," BBC Summary of World Broadcasts, September 27, 2002.

37. "Nezzar renonce à faire appel," *Libération*, October 10, 2002, 9.

38. Samraoui, *Chronique des années de sang*.

39. "Dix ans de violence en Algérie," Agence France-Presse, January 9, 2002.

40. Lara Marlowe, "Algeria a Test Case for War on Terrorism," *Irish Times*, August 14, 2002, 14.

41. "1957: Arabs Slaughtered," *International Herald Tribune*, June 1, 2007, 2.

42. For background, see Stora, *Algeria, 1830–2000*, 59; Horne, *Savage War of Peace*, 221; Ruedy, *Modern Algeria*, 164. "Officials" quoted in Feraoun, *Journal, 1955–1962*, 211.

43. Claude Jacquemart, "Massacres en Algérie," *Le Figaro*, April 9, 1997.

44. Carlier, "D'une guerre à l'autre," 148.

45. Pierre Pasquini, "Des contraintes paralysent la France," *Le Figaro*, October 1, 1997.

46. François Géze and Pierre Vidal-Naquet, "L'Algérie et les intellectuels français," *Le Monde*, February 4, 1998.

47. For example, Catherine Simon, "Psychose de guerre en Algérie," *Le Monde*, July 25, 1994; Youssef Ibrahim, "As Toll Rises in Algeria's War, a Dearth of News," *New York Times*, December 28, 1994, A3; Fouad Ajami, "France's Poisoned Chalice," *US News and World Report*, January 9, 1995, 39; "Pourquoi les islamistes frappent en France," *Le Point*, August 26, 1995; Martin Evans, "Not Counter-insurgency but a Full-Scale War," *Independent*, June 25, 1999, 7; Provost, *La seconde guerre d'Algérie*.

48. For example, Henri Tinq, "La crise algérienne et ses répercussions," *Le Monde*, August 10, 1994; "La presse parisienne et la nouvelle guerre d'Algérie," Agence France-Presse, November 2, 1994; Jacques de Barrin, "La guerre d'Algérie franchit la Méditerranée," *Le Monde*, December 28, 1994; Jacques Duquesne, "Terrorisme: l'offensive des amateurs," *La Croix*, September 6, 1995, 20; "Chirac, la cote d'alerte," *Le Point*, October 28, 1995; Malti, *La nouvelle guerre d'Algérie*.

49. For example, Pierre Taillefer, "La nouvelle 'bataille d'Alger,'" Agence France-Presse, March 24, 1993; Sud Ouest, "La nouvelle bataille d'Alger," June 3, 1997; Julia Ficatier and Amine Kadi, "La nouvelle bataille d'Alger," *La Croix*, September 10, 1997, 3; Étienne, "La nouvelle bataille d'Alger."

50. Tilly, *Politics of Collective Violence*, chapter 2.

51. Robert Fisk, "Stench of Death in Algeria's Perfumed Killing Fields," *Independent*, October 23, 1997, 16.

52. See Albert Camus's "Lettre a un militant algérien" of October 1955 in *Actuelles III*.

53. Camus's prophecy was quoted in both Fouad Ajami, "France's Poisoned Chalice," *US News and World Report*, January 9, 1995, 39; and Miller, *God Has Ninety-Nine Names*,

168. For critique and context of Camus and the Algerian war of independence, see Haddour, *Colonial Myths: History and Narrative*, 79–80; Le Sueur, *Uncivil War*, 111–112.

54. Anthony Loyd, "Algerian Terror Victims Plead for Death by Bullet," *Times*, October 23, 1997.

55. Horne, *Savage War of Peace*, 537–538.

56. For example, "Fifty-Seven People Arrested in Laghouat Province for Helping 'Terrorist Group,'" BBC Summary of World Broadcasts, May 8, 1993, citing Republic of Algeria Radio report of May 6, 1993; "Seventeen 'Terrorists' Killed in Central and Eastern Algeria," BBC Summary of World Broadcasts, December 6, 1993, citing an Algerian state television report of December 4, 1993; "Seven 'Terrorists' Killed; Imam Shot Dead Outside Mosque," BBC Summary of World Broadcasts, March 19, 1994, citing an Algerian radio report of March 17, 1994; "Security Forces 'Eliminate 27 Terrorists,'" BBC Summary of World Broadcasts, March 23, 1994, citing Algerian state television report of March 21, 1994; "FLN Activist Assassinated in El Tarf," BBC Summary of World Broadcasts, September 27, 1994, citing an Algerian radio report of September 25, 1994.

57. Boukra, *La terreur sacrée*, 134–135.

58. Khadra, *Les agneaux du seigneur*.

59. Aileen McCabe, "Algeria's Secret War Leaves World Feeling Horrified, Powerless," *Vancouver Sun*, September 26, 1997, A12.

60. José Garçon, "Quatre questions sur une tragédie," *Libération*, August 30, 1997.

61. Jean-Pierre Tuquoi, "Algeria's Horrific Settling of Scores," *Guardian Weekly*, September 14, 1997, 19. Anthropologist Gilbert Grandguillaume, however, did not present this as a totalizing thesis. As noted in Chapter 4, he also considered other possible dimensions. The lasting effects of French rule and violent decolonization were only part of the story; another aspect was the fragmented (*éclaté*) nature of the Algerian nation from the time of the Ottoman Empire, a nation that could express itself only as the antithesis of French colonialism, which had furnished its condition of possibility. See Jean-Christophe Ploquin, "Alger se protège mais ne protège pas la société," *La Croix*, September 2, 1997, 5. The ultimate result was a society that, if not violent, was at least "hard" (*dure*), in his opinion. See Jean-Pierre Tuqoi, "Algérie: l'histoire est partie prenante dans la violence d'aujourd'hui," *Le Monde*, September 5, 1997.

62. Lisa Anderson, "Moderates on Both Sides of Algerian Conflict May Hold Key to Peace," *Boston Globe*, October 13, 1997, A15.

63. Stora, *Algeria, 1830–2000*, 232–233.

64. Joffé, "The Role of Violence Within the Algerian Economy," 29–30.

65. Lara Marlowe, "Ex-army Conscript Saw Colleagues Torturing and Murdering Villagers," *Irish Times*, October 30, 1997, 9.

66. Malley, *Call from Algeria*, 247.

67. Laure Mandeville, "Bruno Étienne: 'Ce sont les généraux qui se déchirent,'" *Le Figaro*, August 30, 1997.

68. Todorov, "In Search of Lost Crime"; Lara Marlowe, "Why Once Similar Conflicts in Egypt and Algeria Now Differ," *Irish Times*, March 17, 1997, 13.

69. Laure Mandeville, "Bruno Étienne: 'Ce sont les généraux qui se déchirent,'" *Le Figaro*, August 30 1997.

70. Martinez, *Algerian Civil War*.

71. Remaoun, "La question de l'histoire dans le débat sur la violence en Algérie," 41–42, quoted in McDougall, "Martyrdom and Destiny," 62. See also Soufi, "La fabrication d'une Mémoire"; Remaoun, "Pratiques historiographiques"; Carlier, "Civil War, Private Violence, and Cultural Socialization."

72. Ian Aitken, "I've Seen the Killing Game," *Guardian*, January 22, 1998, 19.

73. Sarah Chayes and Linda Wertheimer, "EU Mission to Algeria Frustrated," *All Things Considered*, US National Public Radio, January 20, 1998, transcript.

74. Quoted in Evans and Phillips, *Algeria*, 151.

75. An example is the January 1998 profile of militia leader Hadj Fergane. See "Algérie: Voyage au bout de l'horreur," *Le Point*, January 17, 1998. At the time, Fergane was the mayor of Relizane. He would face (and be acquitted of) serious charges of committing atrocities. The *Le Point* interview emphasized the fact that Fergane had not only survived the war of independence but had also put his knowledge to good use in his fight against the AIS and the GIA.

76. Human Rights Watch, *World Report 2000*.

77. See Lazreg, *Torture and the Twilight of Empire*.

78. Yacine, "Is a Genealogy of Violence Possible?" 24.

79. McDougall, *History and the Culture of Nationalism in Algeria*, 128; McDougall, "Martyrdom and Destiny," 62. See also McDougall, "Savage Wars?"

80. Quandt, *Between Ballots and Bullets*, 99.

81. Werenfels, *Managing Instability in Algeria*.

82. LaCapra, *History and Its Limits*, 122.

83. Roberts, *Demilitarizing Algeria*; Werenfels, *Managing Instability in Algeria*; Mesbah, *Problématique Algérie*.

84. Roberts, *Moral Economy or Moral Polity?*; International Crisis Group, *Algeria: Unrest and Impasse in Kabylia*; Parks, "Algeria and the Arab Uprisings."

85. Amnesty International, "Algeria: Truth and Justice Obscured"; Human Rights Watch, "Impunity in the Name of Reconciliation"; Amnesty International and others, "Algeria: Amnesty Law Risks Legalizing Impunity"; Amnesty International and others, "Algeria: New Amnesty Law."

86. Opgenhaffen and Freeman, "Transitional Justice in Morocco"; Hazan, *Morocco: Betting on a Truth and Reconciliation Commission*. For background and critique, see Slyomovics, *Performance of Human Rights in Morocco*.

87. Hayner, *Unspeakable Truths*.

88. Freeman, *Truth Commissions*, 227–228.

89. Klein, *Shock Doctrine*, 194–217.

90. Juan Carlos Sanz, "Abdelaziz Buteflika, presidente de Argelia: 'No soy un dictador,'" *El País*, July 28, 1999.

91. Quoted in Human Rights Watch, *World Report 2000*, 336.

92. Elaine Ganley, "Algerian Voters Overwhelmingly Back Plan to End Islamic Insurgency in Boost for President," Associated Press, September 30, 2005.

93. Goldstein, "Algeria's Amnesia Decree."

94. Goldstein, *Winning the War on War*.

95. Minow, *Between Vengeance and Forgiveness*.

96. Minow and Rosenblum, *Breaking the Cycles of Hatred*.

97. See Monk and Mundy, *The Post-Conflict Environment*.

98. I was shown this portfolio in the spring of 2008. Fisk reports being shown a similar folder close to its original creation date. See Robert Fisk, "Scenes from an Unholy War," *Independent*, April 16, 1995, 4.

99. Kaldor, *New and Old Wars*.

100. Many of these photos, along with some case details, are reproduced in Mara, *Devoir de mémoir*. For background, see also Collectif des familles de disparu(e)s en Algérie, *Les Disparitions Forcées en Algérie*.

101. Meddi, "Gouvernement-familles des disparus."

102. See International Center for Transitional Justice, *ICTJ Transitions*, October 2010, 4–7; International Center for Transitional Justice, *ICTJ Transitions*, November 2010, 4–6.

103. See McDougall, "Social Memories 'in the Flesh,'" 47.

CONCLUSION

1. The apparent ease with which Algerian insurgents, mainly the GSPC, began conducting operations in the Sahara (notably the 2003 capture of thirty-two European tourists in southern Algeria) has been the source of as much international security consternation as speculation. The most outspoken critic of the Algerian regime's alleged collusion with Saharan "terrorists" is British anthropologist Jeremy Keenan. See Keenan, *Dark Sahara* and *Dying Sahara*.

2. Bruce Ridel, "Algeria a Complex Ally in War Against al Qaeda," Brookings Institution, February 3, 2013, accessed September 27, 2014, http://www.brookings.edu/research/opinions/2013/02/03-algeria-riedel; Hugh Roberts, "Six Questions About Tigantourine," *London Review of Books*, January 20, 2013, accessed September 27, 2014, http://www.lrb .co.uk/blog/2013/01/20/hugh-roberts/six-questions-about-tigantourine; James McDougall, "Algeria's Terrorist Attacks Owe Little to Its 'Pathological' History," *Guardian*, January 22, 2013, accessed September 27, 2014, http://www.theguardian.com/commentisfree/2013/jan/22/algerian-terrorist-attacks-owe-little-pathological-history.

3. Gaddis, "International Relations Theory and the End of the Cold War"; Kratochwil, "Embarrassment of Changes."

4. Fukuyama, *End of History*; Huntington, "Clash of Civilizations?"

5. Mamdani, *Saviors and Survivors.*

6. Gause, "Why Middle East Studies Missed the Arab Spring."

7. Chenoweth and Stephan, *Why Civil Resistance Works.*

8. The Centre for the Study of Civil War at the Peace Research Institute in Oslo (PRIO) is a notorious example. Having contributed intensively to the study of a dying form of mass violence (civil war), it also contributed during its lifetime (2003–2012) to the obfuscation of the actual geopolitical trends in conflict, particularly the role played by nonviolent movements. In response to Chenoweth and Stephan's "revelations," PRIO simply began studying what had been obvious to the scholars of nonviolent action for decades.

9. Mirowski, *Never Let a Good Crisis Go to Waste.*

10. Goldstein, *Winning the War on War*; Gat, "Is War Declining—and Why?"

11. Pinker, *Better Angels of Our Nature*; Morris, *War!*

12. Homer-Dixon, *Upside of Down.*

BIBLIOGRAPHY

Aboud, Hichem. *La mafia des généraux*. Paris: Jean-Claude Lattès, 2002.

Addi, Lahouari. "Algeria's Army, Algeria's Agony." *Foreign Affairs* 77, no. 4 (1998): 44–53.

Adjerid, Abderrahmane. *La hogra, ou, l'humiliation du peuple algérien*. Paris: Editions Babylone, 1992.

Aggoun, Lounis, and Jean-Baptiste Rivoire. *Françalgérie: crimes et mensonges d'états*. Paris: Découverte, 2005.

Aissaoui, Ali. *Algeria: The Political Economy of Oil and Gas*. New York: Oxford University Press, 2001.

Aït-Larbi, Méziane, M. S. Ait-Belkacem, M. A. Belaid, M. A. Nait-Redjam, and Y. Soltani. "An Anatomy of the Massacres." In *An Inquiry into the Algerian Massacres*. Edited by Youcef Bedjaoui, Abbas Aroua, and Méziane Aït-Larbi, 13–195. Geneva: Hoggar, 1999.

Al-Ahnaf, Mustafa, Bernard Botiveau, and Frank Frégosi. *L'Algérie par ses islamistes*. Paris: Karthala, 1991.

Ali-Yahia, Abdennour. *La dignité humaine*. Algiers: INAS Éditions, 2007.

Alilat, Farid, and Shéhérazade Hadid. *Vous ne pouvez pas nous tuer, nous sommes déjà morts: l'Algérie embrasée*. Paris: Éditions 1, 2002.

Alleg, Henri. *The Question*. Translated by John Calder. Lincoln: University of Nebraska Press, 2006.

Allouache, Merzak. *Bab El-Oued*. Boulder, CO: Lynne Rienner, 1998.

Amar, Paul. *The Security Archipelago: Human-Security States, Sexuality Politics, and the End of Neoliberalism*. Durham, NC: Duke University Press, 2013.

Amnesty International. *Algeria: Deteriorating Human Rights Under the State of Emergency*. London: Amnesty International, 1993.

———. *Algeria: Repression and Violence Must End*. London: Amnesty International, 1994.

———. *Algeria: Killings in Serkadji Prison*. London: Amnesty International, 1996.

———. *Algeria: Fear and Silence: A Hidden Human Rights Crisis*. London: Amnesty International, 1996.

―――. *Algeria: Civilian Population Caught in a Spiral of Violence.* London: Amnesty International, 1997.

―――. *Algeria: UN Panel Report a Whitewash on Human Rights.* London: Amnesty International, 1998.

―――. *Algeria: Truth and Justice Obscured by the Shadow of Impunity.* London: Amnesty International, 2000.

―――. *Report 2002.* London: Amnesty International, 2002.

―――. *A Legacy of Impunity: A Threat to Algeria's Future.* London: Amnesty International, 2009.

―――. *Broken Promises: The Equity and Reconciliation Commission and Its Follow-Up.* London: Amnesty International, 2010.

Amnesty International, Human Rights Watch, International Center for Transitional Justice, and International Federation for Human Rights. *Algeria: New Amnesty Law Will Ensure That Atrocities Go Unpunished.* London, Paris, and New York: Amnesty International, Human Rights Watch, International Center for Transitional Justice and the International Federation for Human Rights, March 1, 2006.

Amnesty International, Human Rights Watch, International Commission of Jurists, International Federation for Human Rights, and International Center for Transitional Justice. *Algeria: Amnesty Law Risks Legalizing Impunity for Crimes Against Humanity.* New York: International Center for Transitional Justice, April 14, 2005.

Anderson, Benedict. *Imagined Communities: Reflections on the Origin and Spread of Nationalism.* Revised edition. New York: Verso, 1991.

Anderson, Lisa. "Prospects for Liberalism in North Africa: Identities and Interests in Preindustrial Welfare States." In *Islam, Democracy and the State in North Africa.* Edited by John P. Entelis, 127–140. Bloomington: Indiana University Press, 1997.

Ashour, Omar. *The De-Radicalization of Jihadists: Transforming Armed Islamist Movements.* New York: Routledge, 2009.

Aussaresses, Paul. *Services spéciaux Algérie 1955–1957: mon témoignage sur la torture.* Paris: Editions du Rocher, 2001.

―――. *The Battle of the Casbah: Terrorism and Counter-Terrorism in Algeria, 1955–1957.* Translated by Robert L. Miller. New York: Enigma Books, 2002.

Ayoob, Mohammed. *The Many Faces of Political Islam: Religion and Politics in the Muslim World.* Ann Arbor: University of Michigan Press, 2008.

Badescu, Cristina G., and Linnea Bergholm. "The Responsibility to Protect and the Conflict in Darfur: The Big Let-Down." *Security Dialogue* 40, no. 3 (2009): 287–309.

Bass, Gary Jonathan. *Freedom's Battle: The Origins of Humanitarian Intervention.* New York: Alfred A. Knopf, 2008.

Beblawi, Hazem, and Giacomo Luciani, eds. *The Rentier State.* London: Croom Helm, 1987.

Bedjaoui, Youcef, Abbas Aroua, and Méziane Aït-Larbi, eds. *An Inquiry into the Algerian Massacres.* Geneva: Hoggar, 1999.

Belaala, Salma. *Ethnicité, nationalisme et radicalisation islamiste violente. Etude culturelle du djihadisme en Algérie (1989–2007)*. PhD dissertation. Paris: Institut d'Études Politiques de Paris, 2008.

Bellamy, Alex J. "Libya and the Responsibility to Protect: The Exception and the Norm." *Ethics and International Affairs* 25, no. 3 (2011): 1–7.

Bellamy, Alex J., and Paul D. Williams. "The New Politics of Protection: Côte d'ivoire, Libya and the Responsibility to Protect." *International Affairs* 87, no. 4 (2011): 825–850.

Bensmaïa, Réda. "The Phantom Mediators: Reflections on the Nature of the Violence in Algeria." *Diacritics* 27, no. 2 (1997): 85–97.

Benyamina, Ahmed. "Foreign Interference in the Situation in Algeria: The Algerian Government's Position." *Cambridge Review of International Affairs* 11, no. 2 (1998): 184–196.

Bercovitch, Jacob, and Richard Jackson. *Conflict Resolution in the Twenty-First Century: Principles, Methods, and Approaches*. Ann Arbor: University of Michigan Press, 2009.

Bercovitch, Jacob, Viktor Aleksandrovich Kremeniuk, and I William Zartman, eds. *The SAGE Handbook of Conflict Resolution*. Thousand Oaks, CA: SAGE, 2008.

Bhatia, Michael Vinay, ed. *Terrorism and the Politics of Naming*. New York: Routledge, 2007.

Bouandel, Youcef. "Algeria: A Controversial Election." *Mediterranean Politics* 7, no. 2 (2002): 96–104.

Boukra, Liess. *Algérie: la terreur sacrée*. Lausanne: Favre, 2002.

Brahimi, Abdelhamid. "Political Turmoil in Algeria." *Cambridge Review of International Affairs* 12, no. 1 (1998): 247–262.

Burgat, François. *The Islamic Movement in North Africa*. Translated by William Dowell. Austin: Center for Middle Eastern Studies, University of Texas, 1997.

———. *Face to Face with Political Islam*. London: I.B. Tauris, 2003.

———. "Double Extradition: What Edward Said Has to Tell Us Thirty Years on from *Orientalism*." *Review of Middle East Studies* 43, no. 1 (2009): 11–17.

Butler, Judith. *Gender Trouble: Feminism and the Subversion of Identity*. Second edition. New York: Routledge, 2006.

Callies de Salies, Bruno. "Les luttes de clan exacerbent la guerre civile." *Le Monde diplomatique*, no. 523 (October 1997): 12–13.

Campbell, David. *National Deconstruction: Violence, Identity, and Justice in Bosnia*. Minneapolis: University of Minnesota Press, 1998.

———. "Salgado and the Sahel: Documentary Photography and the Imaging of Famine." In *Rituals of Mediation: International Politics and Social Meaning*. Edited by François Debrix and Cynthia Weber, 69–96. Minneapolis: University of Minnesota Press, 2003.

Camus, Albert. *Actuelles III: chroniques algériennes 1939–1958*. Paris: Gallimard, 1958.

Carlier, Omar. "D'une guerre à l'autre, le redéploiement de la violence entre soi." *Confluences Méditerranée*, no. 25 (1998): 123–137.

———. "Civil War, Private Violence, and Cultural Socialization: Political Violence in Algeria (1954–1988)." In *Algeria in Others' Languages*. Edited by Anne-Emmanuelle Berger, 81–106. Ithaca, NY: Cornell University Press, 2002.

Castells, Manuel. *The Power of Identity*. Malden, MA: Blackwell, 1997.

Cavatorta, Francesco. "The Failed Liberalisation of Algeria and the International Context: A Legacy of Stable Authoritarianism." *Journal of North African Studies* 7, no. 4 (2002): 23–43.

———. *The International Dimension of the Failed Algerian Transition: Democracy Betrayed?* Manchester, UK: Manchester University Press, 2009.

Chapman, Audrey R., and Hugo van der Merwe, eds. *Truth and Reconciliation in South Africa: Did the TRC Deliver?* Philadelphia: University of Pennsylvania Press, 2008.

Charef, Abed. *Algérie: autopsie d'un massacre*. La Tour d'Aigues: Aube, 1998.

Chenoweth, Erica, and Maria J. Stephan. *Why Civil Resistance Works: The Strategic Logic of Nonviolent Conflict*. New York: Columbia University Press, 2012.

"Chronology July 16, 1988–October 15, 1988." *Middle East Journal* 43, no. 1 (1989): 69–104.

"Chronology October 16, 1988–January 15, 1989." *Middle East Journal* 43, no. 2 (1989): 247–288.

"Chronology April 16, 1990–July 15, 1990." *Middle East Journal* 44, no. 4 (1990): 671–703.

"Chronology October 16, 1991–January 15, 1992." *Middle East Journal* 46, no. 2 (1992): 293–315.

Clodfelter, Micheal. *Warfare and Armed Conflicts: A Statistical Reference to Casualty and Other Figures, 1500–2000*. Second edition. Jefferson, NC: McFarland, 2002.

Collectif des familles de disparu(e)s en Algérie. *Les disparitions forcées en Algérie. Dossier No. 3*. Algiers: Collectif des familles de disparu(e)s en Algérie, May 2004.

Collier, Paul. *Wars, Guns, and Votes: Democracy in Dangerous Places*. New York: Harper, 2009.

Collier, Paul, and Anke Hoeffler. "On Economic Causes of Civil War." *Oxford Economic Papers* 50, no. 4 (1998): 563–573.

———. *Greed and Grievance in Civil War*. Washington, DC: World Bank Development Research Group, May 2000.

———. "Greed and Grievance in Civil War." *Oxford Economic Papers* 56, no. 4 (2004): 563–595.

Collier, Paul, and Nicholas Sambanis. "Understanding Civil War: A New Agenda." *Journal of Conflict Resolution* 46, no. 1 (2002): 3–12.

Collier, Paul, Anke Hoeffler, and Dominic Rohner. "Beyond Greed and Grievance: Feasibility and Civil War." *Oxford Economic Papers* 61, no. 1 (2009): 1–27.

Comité algérien des militants libres de la dignité humaine et des droits de l'Homme. *Livre blanc sur la répression en Algérie (1991–1994)*. Tome 1. Geneva: Hoggar, 1994.

———. *Livre blanc sur la répression en Algérie (1991–1995). Les vérités sur une guerre cachée*. Tome 2. Geneva: Hoggar, 1995.

Cook, David. *Understanding Jihad.* Berkeley: University of California Press, 2005.

Cooley, John K. *Unholy Wars: Afghanistan, America, and International Terrorism.* Third edition. London: Pluto Press, 2002.

Cramer, Christopher. *Civil War Is Not a Stupid Thing: Accounting for Violence in Developing Countries.* London: Hurst, 2006.

Darbouche, Hakim, and Yahia Zoubir. "The Algerian Crisis in European and US Foreign Policies: A Hindsight Analysis." *Journal of North African Studies* 14, no. 1 (2009): 33–55.

Davies, James C. "Toward a Theory of Revolution." *American Sociological Review* 27, no. 1 (1962): 5–19.

Delannoy, Pierre-Alban. *La pietà de Bentalha: Etude du processus interprétatif d'une photo de presse.* Paris: L'Harmattan, 2005.

Derrida, Jacques. "Taking a Stand for Algeria." *College Literature* 30, no. 1 (2003): 115–123.

Deutsch, Morton, Peter T. Coleman, and Eric C. Marcus, eds. *The Handbook of Conflict Resolution: Theory and Practice.* Second edition. San Francisco: Wiley, 2006.

Dillman, Bradford Louis. *State and Private Sector in Algeria: The Politics of Rent-Seeking and Failed Development.* Boulder, CO: Westview, 2000.

Doy, Gen. *Drapery: Classicism and Barbarism in Visual Culture.* London: I.B. Tauris, 2002.

Étienne, Bruno. "La nouvelle bataille d'Alger." *Revue des deux mondes,* no. 9 (1997): 104–119.

Evans, Gareth. *The Responsibility to Protect: Ending Mass Atrocity Crimes Once and for All.* Washington, DC: Brookings Institution Press, 2009.

———. "End of the Argument: How We Won the Debate Over Stopping Genocide." *Foreign Policy,* November 28, 2011, accessed September 27, 2014, http://www.foreign policy.com/articles/2011/11/28/gareth_evans_end_of_the_argument.

Evans, Gareth, and Mohamed Sahnoun. "The Responsibility to Protect." *Foreign Affairs* 81, no. 6 (2002): 99–110.

Evans, Martin, and John Phillips. *Algeria: Anger of the Dispossessed.* New Haven: Yale University Press, 2008.

Evans, Peter B., Dietrich Rueschemeyer, and Theda Skocpol. *Bringing the State Back In.* New York: Cambridge University Press, 1985.

Fearon, James. "Counterfactuals and Hypothesis Testing in Political Science." *World Politics* 43, no. 2 (1991): 169–195.

Fearon, James, and David Laitin. "Ethnicity, Insurgency, and Civil War." *American Political Science Review* 97, no. 1 (2003): 75–90.

———. "Algeria." Part of the Fearon and Laitin research project on Ethnicity, Insurgency, and Civil War. Stanford, CA: Stanford University, April 10, 2006, accessed September 17, 2014, http://www.stanford.edu/group/ethnic/Random%20Narratives/Algeria RN2.4.pdf.

Feraoun, Mouloud. *Journal, 1955–1962: Reflections on the French-Algerian War.* Edited by James D. Le Sueur. Translated by Mary Ellen Wolf and Claude Fouillade. Lincoln: University of Nebraska Press, 2000.

Ferguson, James. *The Anti-Politics Machine: "Development," Depoliticization, and Bureaucratic Power in Lesotho.* Minneapolis: University of Minnesota Press, 1994.

Foucault, Michel. *"Society Must Be Defended": Lectures at the Collège de France, 1975–76.* Translated by David Macey. New York: Picador, 2003.

Foucault, Michel, and Paul Rabinow. "Polemics, Politics and Problematizations." In *The Foucault Reader.* Edited by Paul Rabinow, 381–390. Translated by Lydia Davis. New York: Pantheon Books, 1984.

Freeman, Mark. *Truth Commissions and Procedural Fairness.* New York: Cambridge University Press, 2006.

Fukuyama, Francis. *The End of History and the Last Man.* New York: Simon and Schuster, 1992.

Fuller, Graham E. *Algeria: The Next Fundamentalist State?* Santa Monica, CA: RAND Corporation, 1996.

Gacemi, Baya. *I, Nadia, Wife of a Terrorist.* Translated by Paul Cote and Constantina Mitchell. Lincoln: University of Nebraska Press, 2006.

Gaddis, John Lewis. "International Relations Theory and the End of the Cold War." *International Security* 17, no. 3 (1993): 5–58.

Gat, Azar. "Is War Declining—and Why?" *Journal of Peace Research* 50, no. 2 (2013): 149–157.

Gause, F. Gregory. "Why Middle East Studies Missed the Arab Spring: The Myth of Authoritarian Stability." *Foreign Affairs* 90, no. 4 (2011): 81–90.

Gerges, Fawaz A. *The Far Enemy: Why Jihad Went Global.* New York: Cambridge University Press, 2005.

Goetze, Catherine. "Statebuilding in a Vacuum: Sierra Leone and the Missing International Political Economy of Civil Wars." In *The Post-Conflict Environment: Investigation and Critique.* Edited by Daniel B. Monk and Jacob Mundy, 25–67. Ann Arbor: University of Michigan Press, 2014.

Goldstein, Eric. "Algeria's Amnesia Decree." *Open Democracy,* April 10, 2006, accessed September 27, 2014, https://www.opendemocracy.net/globalization-institutions_govern \ment/algeria_3435.jsp.

———. "L'Algérie entre amnistie et amnésie." *Le Temps,* April 19, 2006, accessed September 27, 2014, http://www.hrw.org/fr/news/2006/04/18/lalg-rie-entre-amnistie-et-amn-sie.

Goldstein, Joshua S. *Winning the War on War: The Decline of Armed Conflict Worldwide.* New York: Dutton, 2011.

Goldstone, Richard J. *For Humanity: Reflections of a War Crimes Investigator.* New Heaven, CT: Yale University Press, 2000.

Haddour, Azzedine. *Colonial Myths: History and Narrative.* Manchester, UK: Manchester University Press, 2000.

Hadj Moussa, Ratiba. "The Imaginary Concord and the Reality of Discord: Dealing with the Algerian Civil War." *Arab World Geographer* 7, no. 3 (2004): 135–149.

Hafez, Mohammed M. "From Marginalization to Massacres: A Political Process Explanation of GIA Violence in Algeria." In *Islamic Activism: A Social Movement Theory Approach.* Edited by Quintan Wiktorowicz, 37–60. Bloomington: Indiana University Press, 2004.

Hall, Stuart. "Introduction: Who Needs 'Identity'?" In *Questions of Cultural Identity.* Edited by Stuart Hall and Paul Du Gay, 1–17. London: SAGE, 1996.

Hamadouche, Mehenna. *Affaires d'état: interviews.* Algiers: Chihab, 2004.

Hannoum, Abdelmajid. *Violent Modernity: France in Algeria.* Cambridge, MA: Harvard University Press, 2010.

Harbi, Mohammed, Régine Dhoquois-Cohen, and Bernard Ravenel. "Une exigence: la transparence." *Confluences Méditerranée,* no. 25 (1998): 167–173.

Hardt, Michael, and Antonio Negri. *Empire.* Cambridge, MA: Harvard University Press, 2001.

Harvey, David. *A Brief History of Neoliberalism.* New York: Oxford University Press, 2009.

Hayner, Priscilla B. *Unspeakable Truths: Facing the Challenge of Truth Commissions.* London: Routledge, 2002.

Hazan, Pierre. *Morocco: Betting on a Truth and Reconciliation Commission.* Washington, DC: U.S. Institute of Peace, 2006.

Headrick, Daniel R. *The Tools of Empire: Technology and European Imperialism in the Nineteenth Century.* New York: Oxford University Press, 1981.

Henry, Clement Moore. "Algeria's Agonies: Oil Rent Effects in a Bunker State." *Journal of North African Studies* 9, no. 2 (2004): 68–81.

Heristchi, Claire. "The Islamist Discourse of the FIS and the Democratic Experiment in Algeria." *Democratization* 11, no. 4 (2004): 111–132.

Hill, Christopher, and Karen Elizabeth Smith, eds. *European Foreign Policy: Key Documents.* London: Routledge, 2000.

Hill, Jonathan N. C. *Identity in Algerian Politics: The Legacy of Colonial Rule.* Boulder, CO: Lynne Rienner, 2009.

Hirshleifer, Jack. *The Dark Side of the Force: Economic Foundations of Conflict Theory.* New York: Cambridge University Press, 2001.

Hodd, Michael. "Algeria: Economic Structure, Performance and Policy, 1950–2001." In *Algeria in Transition: Reforms and Development Prospects.* Edited by Ahmed Aghrout and Redha Bougherira, 35–57. New York: RoutledgeCurzon, 2004.

Homer-Dixon, Thomas. *Environment, Scarcity, and Violence.* Princeton, NJ: Princeton University Press, 1999.

———. *The Upside of Down: Catastrophe, Creativity, and the Renewal of Civilization.* Washington, DC: Island Press, 2008.

Horne, Alistair. *A Savage War of Peace: Algeria, 1954–1962.* New York: New York Review Books, 2006.

Human Rights Watch. *World Report 1993.* New York: Human Rights Watch, 1992.

———. *World Report 1995.* New York: Human Rights Watch, 1994.

———. *Six Months Later, Cover-Up Continues in Prison Clash That Left 100 Inmates Dead.* New York: Human Rights Watch, August 1995.

———. *World Report 1997.* New York: Human Rights Watch, 1996.

———. *Algeria: Elections in the Shadow of Violence and Repression.* New York: Human Rights Watch, 1997.

———. *Algeria's Human Rights Crisis.* New York: Human Rights Watch, 1998.

———. *World Report 1999.* New York: Human Rights Watch, 1999.

———. *World Report 2000.* New York: Human Rights Watch, 2001.

———. *Time for Reckoning: Enforced Disappearances in Algeria.* New York: Human Rights Watch, 2003.

———. *Truth and Justice on Hold: The New State Commission on "Disappearances."* New York: Human Rights Watch, 2003.

———. *Impunity in the Name of Reconciliation: Algerian President's Peace Plan Faces National Vote September 29.* New York: Human Rights Watch, 2005.

———. *World Report 2010.* New York: Human Rights Watch, 2010.

Human Security Research Group. *Human Security Report 2009/2010.* Vancouver: Human Security Research Group, 2010.

Hume, Cameron R. *Mission to Algiers: Diplomacy by Engagement.* Lanham, MD: Lexington Books, 2006.

Huntington, Samuel P. "The Clash of Civilizations?" *Foreign Affairs* 72, no. 3 (1992): 22–49.

Ighilahriz, Louisette, and Anne Nivat. *Algérienne.* Paris: Fayard, 2001.

Ilkkaracan, Pinar. "Women, Sexuality, and Social Change in the Middle East and the Maghreb." *Social Research* 69, no. 3 (2002): 753–780.

International Commission on Intervention and State Sovereignty. *The Responsibility to Protect: Report of the International Commission on Intervention and State Sovereignty.* Ottawa: International Development Research Centre, December 2001.

International Crisis Group. *The Algerian Crisis: Not Over Yet.* Brussels: International Crisis Group, 2000.

———. *Algeria's Economy: The Vicious Circle of Oil and Violence.* Brussels: International Crisis Group, 2001.

———. *Algeria: Unrest and Impasse in Kabylia.* Brussels: International Crisis Group, 2003.

Jameson, Fredric. "Postmodernism, or the Cultural Logic of Late Capitalism." *New Left Review* 1, no. 146 (1984): 53–92.

Joffé, George E. "The Role of Violence Within the Algerian Economy." *Journal of North African Studies* 7, no. 1 (2002): 29–52.

———. "Algeria: Recovery or Stagnation." *Middle East International,* no. 752 (2005): 21–23.

———. "National Reconciliation and General Amnesty in Algeria." *Mediterranean Politics* 13, no. 2 (2008): 213–228.

Kaldor, Mary. *New and Old Wars: Organized Violence in a Global Era.* Second edition. Stanford, CA: Stanford University Press, 2007.

Kalyvas, Stathis. "Wanton and Senseless? The Logic of Massacres in Algeria." *Rationality and Society* 11, no. 3 (1999): 243–286.

———. "'New' and 'Old' Civil Wars: A Valid Distinction?" *World Politics* 54 (2001): 99–118.

———. *The Logic of Violence in Civil War.* New York: Cambridge University Press, 2006.

Kalyvas, Stathis, and Laia Balcells. "International System and Technologies of Rebellion: How the End of the Cold War Shaped Internal Conflict." *American Political Science Review* 104, no. 3 (2010): 415–429.

Kaplan, Robert D. "The Coming Anarchy: How Scarcity, Crime, Overpopulation, Tribalism, and Disease Are Rapidly Destroying the Social Fabric of Our Planet." *Atlantic Monthly*, February 1994.

Kapil, Arun. "Portrait statistique des elections du 12 juin 1990: chiffres-clés pour une analyse." *Les cahiers de l'Orient* 23 (1991): 41–63.

Kaplan, Roger. "The Libel of Moral Equivalence." *Atlantic Monthly* 282, no. 2 (August 1998): 18–28.

Keenan, Jeremy. *The Dark Sahara: America's War on Terror in Africa.* London: Pluto Press, 2009.

———. *The Dying Sahara: US Imperialism and Terror in Africa.* London: Pluto Press, 2012.

Kepel, Gilles. *Jihad: The Trail of Political Islam.* Fourth edition. Translated by Anthony F. Roberts. London: I.B. Tauris, 2006.

Khadra, Yasmina. *Les Agneaux Du Seigneur.* Paris: Julliard, 1998.

———. *In the Name of God.* London: Toby Press, 2000.

Khelladi, Aïssa. *Le FIS à l'assaut du pouvoir.* Algiers: Marsa, 2002.

Khelladi, Aïssa, and Marie Virolle. "Les démocrates algériens ou l'indispensable clarification." *Le Temps modernes,* no. 580 (1995): 177–195.

Kilcullen, David. *The Accidental Guerrilla: Fighting Small Wars in the Midst of a Big One.* New York: Oxford University Press, 2009.

Klein, Naomi. *The Shock Doctrine: The Rise of Disaster Capitalism.* New York: Metropolitan, 2007.

Knight, Andy W., and Frazer Egerton, eds. *The Routledge Handbook of the Responsibility to Protect.* New York: Routledge, 2012.

Kouaouci, Ali. "Population Transitions, Youth Unemployment, Postponement of Marriage and Violence in Algeria." *Journal of North African Studies* 9, no. 2 (2004): 28–45.

Krasner, Stephen D. *Sovereignty: Organized Hypocrisy*. Princeton, NJ: Princeton University Press, 1999.

Kratochwil, Friedrich. "The Embarrassment of Changes: Neo-Realism as the Science of Realpolitik Without Politics." *Review of International Studies* 19, no. 1 (1993): 63–80.

Kriesberg, Louis, and Bruce W. Dayton. *Constructive Conflicts: From Escalation to Resolution*. Fourth edition. Lanham, MD: Rowman & Littlefield, 2012.

Krusche, Lutz Von. "Algerien: Mörderische Sippenhaft." *Der Spiegel*, no. 3 (January 12, 1998), accessed September 30, 2014, http://www.spiegel.de/spiegel/print/d-7809924.html.

Labat, Séverine. *Les islamistes algériens entre les urnes et le maquis*. Paris: Seuil, 1995.

Labter, Lazhari. *Journalistes algériens 1988–1998: chronique des années d'espoir et de terreur*. Algiers: Chihab, 2005.

LaCapra, Dominick. *History and Its Limits: Human, Animal, Violence*. Ithaca, NY: Cornell University Press, 2009.

Lacina, Bethany, and Nils Petter Gleditsch. "Monitoring Trends in Global Combat: A New Dataset of Battle Deaths." *European Journal of Population* 21 (2005): 145–166.

Lazreg, Marnia. *The Eloquence of Silence: Algerian Women in Question*. New York: Routledge, 1994.

———. "Islamism and the Recolonization of Algeria." *Arab Studies Quarterly* 20, no. 2 (1998): 43–58.

———. *Torture and the Twilight of Empire: From Algiers to Baghdad*. Princeton, NJ: Princeton University Press, 2008.

Le Sueur, James D. *Uncivil War: Intellectuals and Identity Politics During the Decolonization of Algeria*. Second edition. Lincoln: University of Nebraska Press, 2005.

———. *Between Democracy and Terror: Algeria Since 1989*. New York: Zed, 2010.

Leveau, Rémy, ed. *L'Algérie dans la guerre*. Brussels: Editions Complexe, 1995.

Levy, Jack, and Gary Goertz, eds. *Explaining War and Peace: Case Studies and Necessary Condition Counterfactuals*. New York: Routledge, 2007.

Lewis, Bernard. "The Roots of Muslim Rage." *Atlantic Monthly*, 266, no. 3 (September 1990): 47–60.

Lloyd, Catherine. *Mutli-Causal Conflict in Algeria: National Identity, Inequality and Political Islam*. QEH Working Paper Series Working Paper no. 104. Oxford, UK: Queen Elizabeth House, April 2003.

Lowi, Miriam R. "Algeria, 1992–2002: Anatomy of a Civil War." In *Understanding Civil War: Evidence and Analysis*. Edited by Paul Collier and Nicholas Sambanis, 221–246. Washington, DC: World Bank, 2005.

———. "War-Torn or Systemically Distorted? Rebuilding the Algerian Economy." In *Rebuilding War-Torn Economies in the Middle East and North Africa*. Edited by Leonard Binder, 127–152. New York: Palgrave Macmillan, 2007.

———. *Oil Wealth and the Poverty of Politics: Algeria Compared.* New York: Cambridge University Press, 2009.

Maalouf, Amin. *In the Name of Identity: Violence and the Need to Belong.* New York: Penguin, 2003.

Malley, Robert. *The Call from Algeria: Third Worldism, Revolution, and the Turn to Islam.* Berkeley: University of California Press, 1996.

Malmvig, Helle. *State Sovereignty and Intervention: A Discourse Analysis of Interventionary and Non-Interventionary Practices in Kosovo and Algeria.* New York: Routledge, 2006.

Malti, Djallal. *La nouvelle guerre d'Algérie: dix clés pour comprendre.* Paris: Découverte, 1999.

Malti, Hocine. *Histoire secrète du pétrole algérien.* Paris: Découverte, 2010.

Mamdani, Mahmood. *Good Muslim, Bad Muslim: America, the Cold War, and the Roots of Terror.* New York: Pantheon Books, 2004.

———. "The Politics of Naming: Genocide, Civil War, Insurgency." *London Review of Books* 29, no. 5 (2007): 5–8.

———. *Saviors and Survivors: Darfur, Politics, and the War on Terror.* New York: Pantheon Books, 2009.

Mara, Tom O., ed. *Devoir de mémoir / A Biography of Disappearance: Algeria 1992–.* Photography by Omar D. London: Autograph ABP, 2007.

Martinez, Luis. "Algérie: terrorismes et guerre civile." *Confluences Méditerranée,* no. 20 (1996): 33–41.

———. *La guerre civile en Algérie, 1990–1998.* Paris: Karthala, 1998.

———. *The Algerian Civil War, 1990–1998.* Translated by Jonathan Derrick. New York: Columbia University Press, 2000.

———. "Algérie: les massacres de civils dans la guerre." *Revue Internationale de Politique Comparée* 8, no. 1 (2001): 43–58.

McDougall, James. "Savage Wars? Codes of Violence in Algeria, 1830s–1990s." *Third World Quarterly* 26, no. 1 (2005): 117–131.

———. *History and the Culture of Nationalism in Algeria.* New York: Cambridge University Press, 2006.

———. "Martyrdom and Destiny: The Inscription and Imagination of Algerian History." In *Memory and Violence in the Middle East and North Africa.* Edited by Ussama Makdisi and Paul A Silverstein, 50–72. Bloomington: Indiana University Press, 2006.

———. "Social Memories 'in the Flesh': War and Exile in Algerian Self-Writing." *Alif: Journal of Comparative Poetics,* no. 30 (2010): 34–56.

Meddi, Adlène. "Gouvernement-familles des disparus: la rupture." *El Watan,* March 26, 2010, accessed September 27, 2014, http://www.algeria-watch.de/fr/mrv/mrvdisp/gouvernement_familles_rupture.htm.

Merry, Sally Engle, and Susan Bibler Coutin. "Technologies of Truth in the Anthropology of Conflict." *American Ethnologist* 41, no. 1 (2014): 1–16.

Mesbah, Mohamed Chafik. *Problématique Algérie.* Algiers: Le Soir d'Algérie, 2011.

Messaoudi, Khalida, and Elisabeth Schemla. *Unbowed: An Algerian Woman Confronts Islamic Fundamentalism.* Translated by Anne Vila. Philadelphia: University of Pennsylvania Press, 1998.

Miller, Judith. *God Has Ninety-Nine Names: A Reporter's Journey Through a Militant Middle East.* New York: Simon & Schuster, 1996.

Milton-Edwards, Beverley. *Islam and Violence in the Modern Era.* New York: Palgrave Macmillan, 2006.

Minow, Martha. *Between Vengeance and Forgiveness: Facing History After Genocide and Mass Violence.* Boston: Beacon Press, 1998.

Minow, Martha, and Nancy L. Rosenblum, eds. *Breaking the Cycles of Hatred: Memory, Law, and Repair.* Princeton, NJ: Princeton University Press, 2003.

Mirowski, Philip. *Machine Dreams: Economics Becomes a Cyborg Science.* New York: Cambridge University Press, 2002.

———. *Never Let a Good Crisis Go to Waste: How Neoliberalism Survived the Financial Meltdown.* London: Verso Books, 2013.

Mitchell, Timothy. *Rule of Experts: Egypt, Technopolitics, Modernity.* Berkeley: University of California Press, 2002.

———. "The Middle East in the Past and Future of Social Science." In *The Politics of Knowledge: Area Studies and the Disciplines.* Edited by David L. Szanton, 74–118. Berkeley: University of California Press, 2004.

———. "Economists and the Economy in the Twentieth Century." In *The Politics of Method in the Human Sciences: Positivism and Its Epistemological Others.* Edited by George Steinmetz, 126–141. Durham, NC: Duke University Press, 2005.

———. "The Work of Economics: How a Discipline Makes Its World." *European Journal of Sociology* 46, no. 2 (2005): 297–320.

Moeller, Susan D. *Compassion Fatigue: How the Media Sell Disease, Famine, War, and Death.* New York: Routledge, 1999.

Monk, Daniel B. *An Aesthetic Occupation: The Immediacy of Architecture and the Palestine Conflict.* Durham, NC: Duke University Press, 2002.

Monk, Daniel B., and Jacob Mundy, eds. *The Post-Conflict Environment: Investigation and Critique.* Ann Arbor: University of Michigan Press, 2014.

Morris, Ian. *War! What Is It Good For? Conflict and the Progress of Civilization From Primates to Robots.* New York: Farrar, Straus and Giroux, 2014.

Mortimer, Robert A. "Islamists, Soldiers, and Democrats: The Second Algerian War." *Middle East Journal* 50, no. 1 (1996): 18–39.

Mouffok, Ghania. "Amnesia in Algeria." *Le Monde diplomatique,* English edition (2000): 8–9.

Moussaoui, Abderrahmane. *De la violence en Algérie: les lois du chaos*. Algiers: Barazakh, 2006.

———. "Algérie, la réconciliation entre espoirs et malentendus." *Politique Étrangère*, no. 2 (2007): 339–352.

Mundy, Jacob. "Deconstructing Civil Wars: Beyond the New Wars Debate." *Security Dialogue* 42, no. 3 (2011): 279–295.

Nathan, Laurie. *"The Frightful Inadequacy of Most of the Statistics"*: A Critique of Collier and Hoeffler on Causes of Civil War. London: Crisis States Programme, September, 2005.

Nezzar, Khaled. *Algérie: echec à une regression programmée*. Paris: Publisud, 2001.

Niblock, Tim. *"Pariah States" and Sanctions in the Middle East: Iraq, Libya, Sudan*. Boulder, CO: Lynne Rienner, 2002.

Nietzsche, Friedrich. *On the Genealogy of Morals and Ecce Homo*. Translated by Walter Kaufmann and R. J. Hollingdale. New York: Random House, 1967.

Nordstrom, Carolyn. *Shadows of War: Violence, Power, and International Profiteering in the Twenty-First Century*. Berkeley: University of California Press, 2004.

Opgenhaffen, Veerle, and Mark Freeman. "Transitional Justice in Morocco: A Progress Report." New York: International Center for Transitional Justice, November 2005.

Parenti, Christian. *Tropic of Chaos: Climate Change and the New Geography of Violence*. New York: Nation Books, 2012.

Parks, Robert. *Local-National Relations and the Politics of Property Rights in Algeria and Tunisia*. PhD dissertation. Austin: University of Texas at Austin, 2011.

———. "Algeria and the Arab Uprisings." In *The Arab Spring: Will It Lead to Democratic Transitions?* Edited by Clement Henry and Jang Ji-Hyang, 101–126. New York: Palgrave Macmillan, 2013.

Phillips, James. *The Rising Threat of Revolutionary Islam in Algeria*. Washington, DC: Heritage Foundation, November 9, 1995.

Pierre, Andrew, and William Quandt. "Algeria's War on Itself." *Foreign Policy*, no. 99 (Summer 1995): 131–148.

———. *The Algerian Crisis: Policy Options for the West*. Washington, DC: Carnegie Endowment for International Peace and the Brookings Institution, 1996.

Pinker, Steven. *The Better Angels of Our Nature: Why Violence Has Declined*. New York: Viking, 2011.

Porch, Douglas. *Counterinsurgency: Exposing the Myths of the New Way of War*. New York: Cambridge University Press, 2013.

Power, Samantha. *"A Problem from Hell"*: America and the Age of Genocide. New York: Perennial, 2003.

Provost, Lucile. *La seconde guerre d'Algérie: le quidproquo franco-algérien*. Paris: Flammarion, 1996.

Quandt, William. "Algeria's Transition to What?" *Journal of North African Studies* 9, no. 2 (2004): 82–92.

———. *Between Ballots and Bullets: Algeria's Transition from Authoritarianism.* Washington, DC: Brookings Institution Press, 1998.

Radio-Beur. *Octobre à Alger.* Paris: Seuil, 1988.

Ramsbotham, Oliver, Tom Woodhouse, and Hugh Miall. *Contemporary Conflict Resolution: The Prevention, Management and Transformation of Deadly Conflicts.* Third edition. Malden, MA: Polity, 2011.

Regan, Patrick M. *Sixteen Million One: Understanding Civil War.* Boulder, CO: Paradigm, 2009.

Remaoun, Hassan. "Pratiques historiographiques et mythes de fondation: le cas de la guerre de libération à travers les institutions algériennes d'éducation et de recherche." In *La guerre d'Algérie et les Algériens, 1954–1962: actes de la table ronde, Paris, 26–27 Mars 1996.* Edited by Charles-Robert Ageron, 305–322. Paris: Armand Colin, 1997.

———. "La question de l'histoire dans le débat sur la violence en Algérie." *Insaniyat,* no. 10 (2000): 31–43.

Reporters sans Frontières, Amnesty International, Fédération Internationale des ligues des Droits de l'Homme, and Human Rights Watch. *Algérie, Le Livre Noir.* Paris: Découverte, 1997.

Rich, Paul. "The Algerian Crisis and the Failure of International Mediation." *Cambridge Review of International Affairs* 11, no. 2 (1998): 134–151.

Riedel, Bruce. "Algeria a Complex Ally in War Against al Qaeda." In *Al-Monitor.* Washington, D.C.: Brookings Institution, February 3, 2013, accessed September 27, 2014, http://www.brookings.edu/research/opinions/2013/02/03-algeria-riedel.

Roberts, Hugh. "The Algerian State and the Challenge of Democracy." *Government and Opposition* 27, no. 4 (1992): 433–454.

———. "Algeria's Ruinous Impasse and the Honourable Way Out." *International Affairs* 71, no. 2 (1995): 247–267.

———. "The International Gallery and the Extravasation of Factional Conflict in Algeria." *Cambridge Review of International Affairs* 12, no. 1 (1998): 209–246.

———. "Algeria's Veiled Drama." *International Affairs* 75, no. 2 (1999): 383–392.

———. "Truths About the Dirty War." *Times Literary Supplement,* no. 5141 (October 12, 2001): 28–29.

———. "Dancing in the Dark: The European Union and the Algerian Drama." In *The European Union and Democracy Promotion: The Case of North Africa.* Edited by R. Gillespie and R. Youngs, 106–134. London: Frank Cass, 2002.

———. *Moral Economy or Moral Polity? The Political Anthropology of Algerian Riots.* London: Development Research Centre, London School of Economics, October 2002.

———. *Demilitarizing Algeria.* Washington, DC: Carnegie Endowment for International Peace, May 2007.

———. "Logics of Jihadi Violence in North Africa." In *Jihadi Terrorism and the Radicalisation Challenge in Europe*. Edited by Rik Coolsaet, 39–53. Aldershot: Ashgate, 2008.

———. "Who Said Gaddafi Had to Go?" *London Review of Books* 33, no. 22 (2011): 8–18.

———. "The Revolution That Wasn't." *London Review of Books* 35, no. 7 (2013): 3–9.

Robin, Marie-Monique. *Escadrons de la mort, l'ecole francaise*. Paris: Découverte, 2005.

Rouadjia, Ahmed. *Les frères et la mosquée: enquête sur le mouvement islamiste en Algérie*. Paris: Karthala, 1990.

Ruedy, John. *Modern Algeria: The Origins and Development of a Nation*. Second edition. Bloomington: Indiana University Press, 2005.

Sadou, Zazi. "Algeria: The Martyrdom of Girls Raped by the Islamic Armed Groups." In *Without Reservation: The Beijing Tribunal on Accountability for Women's Human Rights*. Edited by Niamh Reilly, 28–33. New Brunswick: Center for Women's Global Leadership at Rutgers University.

Said, Edward. *Orientalism*. New York: Vintage, 1978.

———. "The Clash of Ignorance." *Nation*, October 4, 2001, accessed September 27, 2014, http://www.thenation.com/article/clash-ignorance.

Sambanis, Nicholas. "What Is Civil War? Conceptual and Empirical Complexities of an Operational Definition." *Journal of Conflict Resolution* 48, no. 6 (2004): 814–858.

Samraoui, Mohammed. *Chronique des années de sang. Algérie: comment les services secrets ont manipulé les groupes islamistes*. Paris: Denoël, 2003.

Sarkees, Meredith Reid. "The Correlates of War Data on War: An Update to 1997." *Conflict Management and Peace Science* 18, no. 1 (2000): 123–144.

Sarkees, Meredith Reid, and Frank Wayman. *Resort to War: 1816–2007*. Thousand Oaks, CA: CQ Press, 2010.

Scarry, Elaine. *The Body in Pain: The Making and Unmaking of the World*. New York: Oxford University Press, 1985.

Scheele, Judith. "Algerian Graveyard Stories." *Journal of the Royal Anthropological Institute* 12, no. 4 (2006): 859–879.

Semiane, Sid Ahmed. *Octobre: ils parlent*. Algiers: Editions Le Matin, 1998.

———. *Au refuge des balles perdues: chroniques des deux Algérie*. Paris: Découverte, 2005.

Sen, Amartya. *Identity and Violence: The Illusion of Destiny*. New York: W. W. Norton, 2006.

Sereni, Jean-Pierre. "L'Algérie, le FMI, et le FIS." *Le Cahiers de l'Orient*, no. 25–26 (1992): 225–235.

Sidhoum, Salah-Eddine, and Algeria Watch. *Les milices dans la nouvelle guerre d'Algérie*. Berlin: Algeria Watch, December 2003.

———. *Chronologie des massacres en Algérie (1994–2004)*. Berlin: Algeria Watch, 2012, accessed September 27, 2014, http://www.algeria-watch.org/mrv/2002/bilan_massacres.htm.

Silverstein, Paul A. "An Excess of Truth: Violence, Conspiracy Theorizing and the Algerian Civil War." *Anthropological Quarterly* 75, no. 4 (2002): 643–674.

Slyomovics, Susan. *The Performance of Human Rights in Morocco.* Philadelphia: University of Pennsylvania Press, 2005.

Smaïn, Mohamed. *Relizane dans la tourmente: Silence! On tue.* St. Denis: Bouchène, 2004.

Smith, Barbara. "Algeria: The Horror." *New York Review of Books* 45, no. 7 (1998): 27–30.

Souaïdia, Habib. *La sale guerre: Le témoignage d'un ancien officier des forces spéciales de l'armée algérienne.* Paris: Découverte, 2012.

Souaïdia, Habib, François Gèze, and Salima Mellah. *Le procès de 'La sale guerre': Algérie, le général-major Khaled Nezzar contre le lieutenant Habib Souaïdia.* Paris: Découverte, 2002.

Soufi, Fouad. "La fabrication d'une mémoire: les médias algériens (1963–1995)." In *La Guerre d'Algérie et les algériens, 1954–1962. Actes de La Table Ronde, Paris, 26–27 Mars 1996.* Edited by Charles-Robert Ageron, 289–303. Paris: Armand Colin, 1997.

Spencer, Claire. "The End of International Inquiries? The UN Eminent Persons' Mission to Algeria July-August." *Mediterranean Politics* 3, no. 3 (1998): 126–33.

Stampnitzky, Lisa. *Disciplining Terror: How Experts Invented "Terrorism."* New York: Cambridge University Press, 2013.

Stockholm International Peace Research Institute. *SIPRI Yearbook 1995: Armaments, Disarmament and International Security.* New York: Oxford University Press and Stockholm International Peace Research Institute, 1995.

———. *SIPRI Yearbook 1998: Armaments, Disarmament and International Security.* New York: Oxford University Press, 1998.

Stora, Benjamin. *Algeria, 1830–2000: A Short History.* Ithaca, NY: Cornell University Press, 2001.

———. *La guerre invisible. Algérie, années 90.* Paris: Presses de Sciences-Po, 2001.

Swearingen, Will D. "Algeria's Food Security Crisis." *Middle East Report,* no. 166 (1990): 21–25.

Szmolka, Inmaculada. "The Algerian Presidential Elections of 2004: An Analysis of Power Relationships in the Political System." *Mediterranean Politics* 11, no. 1 (2006): 39–57.

Tahi, Mohand Salah. "Algeria's Democratization Process: A Frustrated Hope." *Third World Quarterly* 16, no. 2 (1995): 197–220.

Tahon, Marie-Blanche. *Algérie: la guerre contre les civils.* Québec: Editions Nota Bené, 1998.

Takeyh, Ray. "Islamism in Algeria: A Struggle Between Hope and Agony." *Middle East Policy* 10, no. 2 (2003): 62–75.

Telhami, Shibley, and Michael N. Barnett. "Introduction." In *Identity and Foreign Policy in the Middle East.* Edited by Shibley Telhami and Michael N Barnett, 1–25. Ithaca, NY: Cornell University Press, 2002.

Tessler, Mark, Michael Bonner, and Megan Rief, eds. "Islam, Democracy and the State in Algeria." *Journal of North African Studies,* Special Issue 9, no. 2 (2004): 1–230.

Testas, Abdelaziz. "The Economic Causes of Algeria's Political Violence." *Terrorism and Political Violence* 13, no. 3 (2001): 127–144.

———. "Algeria's Economic Decline, Civil Conflict and the Implications for European Security." *Contemporary Security Policy* 23, no. 3 (2002): 83–105.

———. "Political Repression, Democratization and Civil Conflict in Post-Independence Algeria." *Democratization* 9, no. 4 (2002): 106–121.

———. "The Roots of Algeria's Religious and Ethnic Violence." *Studies in Conflict and Terrorism* 25, no. 3 (2002): 161–183.

Thomson, Susan. *Whispering Truth to Power: Everyday Resistance to Reconciliation in Post-Genocide Rwanda.* Madison: Wisconsin University Press, 2013.

Tibi, Bassam. *Political Islam, World Politics and Europe: Democratic Peace and Euro-Islam Versus Global Jihad.* London: Routledge, 2008.

Tigha, Abdelkader, and Philippe Lobjois. *Contre-espionnage algérien: notre guerre contre les islamistes.* Paris: Nouveau monde, 2008.

Tilly, Charles. *The Politics of Collective Violence.* New York: Cambridge University Press, 2003.

Tlemçani, Rachid. *Algeria Under Bouteflika: Civil Strife and National Reconciliation.* Carnegie Papers No. 7. New York: Carnegie Endowment for International Peace, February 2008.

Todorov, Tzvetan "In Search of Lost Crime." *New Republic* 224, no. 5 (January 29, 2001): 29–36.

Tuathail, Gearóid Ó. *Critical Geopolitics: The Politics of Writing Global Space.* Minneapolis: University of Minnesota Press, 1996.

Turshen, Meredeth. "Algerian Women in the Liberation Struggle and the Civil War: From Active Participants to Passive Victims?" *Social Research* 69, no. 3 (2002): 889–911.

United Nations. *Algeria: Report of Eminent Panel, July-August 1998.* New York: UN Department of Public Information, September 10, 1998.

United Nations Human Rights Council. *Report of the International Commission of Inquiry on Libya.* New York: United Nations, March 2, 2012.

U.S. Congress, House Committee on Government Reform. *Preparing for the War on Terrorism.* Washington, DC: U.S. Government Publications Office, 2001.

U.S. Congress, House Committee on International Relations, Subcommittee on Africa. *Algeria's Turmoil: Hearing Before the Subcommittee on Africa of the Committee on International Relations.* One Hundred Fifth Congress: Second session. Washington, DC: U.S. Government Publications Office, February 1998.

U.S. Department of State. *Country Reports on Human Rights Practices 1998.* Washington, DC: U.S. Department of State Bureau of Democracy, Human Rights, and Labor, 1999.

———. *Country Reports on Human Rights Practices 2002.* Washington, DC: U.S. Department of State Bureau of Democracy, Human Rights, and Labor, 2003.

Van der Gaag, Nikki, and Cathy Nash. *Images of Africa: The UK Report.* Oxford: Oxfam, 1987.

Vidal-Hall, Judith. "The Killing Spree." *Index on Censorship* 26, no. 6 (1997): 17–19.

Volpi, Frederic. *Islam and Democracy: The Failure of Dialogue in Algeria.* London: Pluto Press, 2003.

Vreeland, James Raymond. "The Effect of Political Regime on Civil War: Unpacking Anocracy." *Journal of Conflict Resolution* 52, no. 3 (2008): 401–425.

Waal, Alex de. "Darfur and the Failure of the Responsibility to Protect." *International Affairs* 83, no. 6 (2007): 1039–1054.

Waliken, R., and A. Larioui. "The US and the Algerian Massacres." In *An Inquiry into the Algerian Massacres.* Edited by Youcef Bedjaoui, Abbas Aroua, and Méziane Aït-Larbi, 800–830. Geneva: Hoggar, 1999.

Wallensteen, Peter. *Understanding Conflict Resolution: War, Peace, and the Global System.* Third edition. Thousand Oaks, CA: SAGE, 2012.

Ward, Michael, Brian Greenhill, and Kristin Bakke. "The Perils of Policy by P-Value: Predicting Civil Conflicts." *Journal of Peace Research* 47, no. 4 (2010): 363–375.

Waterbury, John. "From Social Contracts to Extraction Contracts: The Political Economy of Authoritarianism and Democracy." In *Islam, Democracy, and the State in North Africa.* Edited by John P. Entelis, 141–176. Bloomington: Indiana University Press, 1997.

Weinstein, Jeremy M. *Inside Rebellion: The Politics of Insurgent Violence.* New York: Cambridge University Press, 2007.

Weiss, Thomas George. "The Sunset of Humanitarian Intervention? The Responsibility to Protect in a Unipolar Era." *Security Dialogue* 35, no. 2 (2004): 135–153.

———. "RtoP Alive and Well After Libya." *Ethics and International Affairs* 25, no. 3 (2011): 1–6.

Weiss, Thomas George, and Don Hubert. *The Responsibility to Protect: Supplementary Volume.* Ottawa: International Development Research Centre, 2001.

Werenfels, Isabelle. "Obstacles to Privatisation of State-Owned Industries in Algeria: The Political Economy of a Distributive Conflict." *Journal of North African Studies* 7, no. 1 (2002): 1–28.

———. *Managing Instability in Algeria: Elites and Political Change Since 1995.* New York: Routledge, 2007.

Wiktorowicz, Quintan. "Centrifugal Tendencies in the Algerian Civil War." *Arab Studies Quarterly* 23, no. 3 (2001): 65–82.

———. "A Genealogy of Radical Islam." *Studies in Conflict & Terrorism* 28, no. 2 (2005): 75–97.

Willis, Michael. *The Islamist Challenge in Algeria: A Political History.* New York: New York University Press, 1997.

World Bank. *World Development Report 2011: Conflict, Security, and Development.* Washington, DC: World Bank, 2011.

Yacine, Tassadit. "Is a Genealogy of Violence Possible?" *Research in African Literatures* 30, no. 3 (1999): 23–35.

Yacoubian, Mona, and Mary Jane Deeb. *Algeria: Facing Presidential Elections.* Washington, DC: Washington Institute for Near East Policy, April 1999.

Yous, Nesroulah, and Salima Mellah. *Qui a tué à Bentalha: chronique d'un massacre annoncé.* Paris: Découverte, 2000.

Yule, Paul. *After Auschwitz: The Battle for the Holocaust.* New York: Cinemaguild, 2001.

Zaimeche, Salah E., and Keith Sutton. "Persistent Strong Population Growth, Environmental Degradation, and Declining Food Self-Sufficiency in a Rentier Oil State: Algeria." *Journal of North African Studies* 3, no. 1 (1998): 57–73.

Zoubir, Yahia. "Algeria's Multi-Dimensional Crisis: The Story of a Failed State-Building Process." *Journal of Modern African Studies* (1994): 741–747.

———. "Stalled Democratization of an Authoritarian Regime: The Case of Algeria." *Democratization* 2, no. 2 (1995): 109–139.

———. "The Algerian Crisis in World Affairs." *Journal of North African Studies* 4, no. 3 (1999): 15–29.

———. "Algeria and U.S. Interests: Containing Radical Islam and Promoting Democracy." *Middle East Policy* 9, no. 1 (2002): 64–81.

Zoubir, Yahia, and Ahmed Aghrout. "Algeria's Path to Reform: Authentic Change?" *Middle East Policy* 19, no. 2 (2012): 66–83.

Zoubir, Yahia H, and Youcef Bouandel. "Islamism and the Algerian Political Crisis: International Responses." *Cambridge Review of International Affairs* 11, no. 2 (1998): 117–133.

Zulaika, Joseba. *Terrorism: The Self-Fulfilling Prophecy.* Chicago: University of Chicago Press, 2009.

INDEX

Note: page numbers followed by f, t, m, and n refer to figures, tables, maps, and endnotes, respectively.

al-Takfir wa al-Hijrah, 55

Taliban, 85

Ténès massacre (disputed) (May 1994), 205n37

terrorism and terrorism studies: Algerian violence as central to, 8, 86; antipolitics of, 10, 15–17, 91, 109, 110–11; antipolitics of conflict management and, 91–92; centrality of, 110–11; civil war framing vs., 91; Cold-War geopolitics and, 16; critical problematization of, 90–91; Global Terrorism Database, 87; *Harkis,* terrorists as children of, 148; inadequacy of other frameworks and, 109–10; irredeemable violence and, 17; power of violence and counterterrorism to create pasts, 110; September 11 and, 16, 85–86, 110; skepticism from area and country experts, 88; state complicity and, 88; state complicity counternarrative, 100–105; strangeness as organizing problem, 89–90; terrorism as war's "Other," 111; terrorization of Algerian violence, 86–87, 89; transnationalization and, 16. *See also* agents of Algerian violence, questions about; Islamic or *jihadi* violence

Tessier, Marc, 142

Tiaret-Tissemsilt massacres (Dec. 1997). *See* Ouarsenis massacres

Toumi, Khalida (Khalida Messaoudi), 179n25

transitional justice, 9–10, 137–39, 159–60. *See also* history and historiography; truth and reconciliation

transnational justice, 137–38, 140–45

"triangle of death" (*triangle de la mort*), 76, 99, 156

truth and reconciliation: Algerian ambiguity and, 24–25; amnesty and indemnity initiatives, 24, 62, 140, 151–52; arc of justice and prosecution in other postcolonial sites, 159; derision of Algeria's use of, 8–9; independent archives

and efforts, 155–59; international norms and antipolitics, 159–60; paradox in criticisms of, 26; performing national reconciliation, 150–55; silencing of victim's voices, 138, 139; South African model, 25, 138, 152–54; transparency, assumption of, 154; truth commission model, 25–26

Truth and Reconciliation Commission (TRC), South Africa, 25, 138, 152–54

Tunisia: accusations of Tunisian insurgents in Algeria, 81–82; Arab Spring and, 47; immunity to civil war, 58

Tuquoi, Jean-Pierre, 70, 125

UN Children's Fund, 120

UN Commission on Human Rights, 123, 130–31

UN High Commissioner for Human Rights, 122, 125

UN Human Rights Committee, 131–32

UN Security Council: democratization of, 19; Libya and sanctions, 113

UN special rapporteurs and, 126–27, 130–31

unemployment, 58

United Nations: call for investigation, 125; peacekeeping missions, 18–19, 123; proceduralization of military force for humanitarian intervention and, 20; Secretariat's *ad hoc* panel and report, 131–33; withdrawals from Rwanda and Bosnia, 20

United States: on Bentalha massacre, 122–23; Congressional hearings, 130, 221n117; humanitarian intervention and, 119–20, 121; on military intervention, 127

Uppsala Conflict Data Program at the Peace Research Institute Oslo (UCDP-PRIO), 184n89

Vatican, 120

Védrine, Hubert, 82, 119, 120, 122–23

Jonathan Marshall, *The Lebanese Connection: Corruption, Civil War, and the International Drug Traffic*
2012

Joshua Stacher, *Adaptable Autocrats: Regime Power in Egypt and Syria*
2012

Bassam Haddad, *Business Networks in Syria: The Political Economy of Authoritarian Resilience*
2011

Noah Coburn, *Bazaar Politics: Power and Pottery in an Afghan Market Town*
2011

Laura Bier, *Revolutionary Womanhood: Feminisms, Modernity, and the State in Nasser's Egypt*
2011

Samer Soliman, *The Autumn of Dictatorship: Fiscal Crisis and Political Change in Egypt under Mubarak*
2011

Rochelle A. Davis, *Palestinian Village Histories: Geographies of the Displaced*
2010

Haggai Ram, *Iranophobia: The Logic of an Israeli Obsession*
2009

John Chalcraft, *The Invisible Cage: Syrian Migrant Workers in Lebanon*
2008

Rhoda Kanaaneh, *Surrounded: Palestinian Soldiers in the Israeli Military*
2008

Asef Bayat, *Making Islam Democratic: Social Movements and the Post-Islamist Turn*
2007

Robert Vitalis, *America's Kingdom: Mythmaking on the Saudi Oil Frontier*
2006

Jessica Winegar, *Creative Reckonings: The Politics of Art and Culture in Contemporary Egypt*
2006

Joel Beinin and Rebecca L. Stein, editors, *The Struggle for Sovereignty: Palestine and Israel, 1993–2005*
2006